*Debt's Grip*

# Debt's Grip

RISK AND CONSUMER BANKRUPTCY

Pamela Foohey,
Robert M. Lawless,
and Deborah Thorne

UNIVERSITY OF CALIFORNIA PRESS

University of California Press
Oakland, California

© 2025 by Pamela Foohey, Robert M. Lawless, and Deborah Thorne

Cataloging-in-Publication data is on file at the Library of Congress.

ISBN 978-0-520-39414-8 (cloth : alk. paper)
ISBN 978-0-520-39415-5 (pbk. : alk. paper)
ISBN 978-0-520-39417-9 (ebook)

Manufactured in the United States of America

GPSR Authorized Representative: Easy Access System Europe,
Mustamäe tee 50, 10621 Tallinn, Estonia, gpsr.requests@easproject.com

34  33  32  31  30  29  28  27  26  25
10  9  8  7  6  5  4  3  2  1

To the people who bravely shared their bankruptcy journeys, without whom we could not have written this book.

# Contents

# Illustrations

## TABLES

# Acknowledgments

The genesis of this book was a conversation in Katie Porter's living room. Then a law professor at the University of Iowa, she had convened a conference of scholars who wrote the chapters for *Broke: How Debt Bankrupts the Middle Class*. That book used 2007 data from the Consumer Bankruptcy Project. As with any empirical project, writing up those data only raised new questions, and we were itching to get back in the field. A few of us gathered privately to talk about how to do new data collection. A plan was hatched. Eleven years of data collection later, we have a book.

We owe a huge debt to Katie. She left the project to serve three terms in the House of Representatives, which we decided was a decent excuse to leave us. The research design includes her intellectual contributions. In places, the book builds on papers we wrote with Katie, and we cite those articles where applicable. Her constituents and the nation will miss her as a voice in Congress to speak up for those run over by large financial institutions.

Terry Sullivan, Elizabeth Warren, and Jay Westbrook created the CBP. They taught us the importance of studying people who file bankruptcy and (literally) taught us how to do it. We are honored that they trusted us to continue the research. It is an academic cliché to say you stand on the shoulders of giants, and it is not enough here. This book came to be only because of their prior work.

A project like this needs a slew of support, and we appreciate how many people generously gave their time and resources. Financial support has come from the Program on Law, Behavior & Social Science and the Max L. Rowe professorship at the University of Illinois College of Law, the Samuel & Ronnie Heyman Center on Corporate Governance at the Benjamin N. Cardozo School of Law, and the College of Letters, the University of Georgia School of Law, Arts and Social Sciences at the University of Idaho. Sally Cook and Kelly Downs made sure our trains ran on time. We cannot thank them enough for making sure our surveys promptly got to the right people. Student research assistants have been integral to the data coding, and many of them are now practicing law in bankruptcy or related fields. We have had the great fortune to work with the following people during their time at the University of Illinois—Jake Andreasen, Daniel Applebaum, Katie Bethke, James Earl, Aaron Feld, Wenting Ge, Gloria Grand-Pierre, Luke Johnson, Alec Klimowicz, John Kroen, Nicole Langston, Ju-Hyung Lee, Justin Mahone, Alexis March, Israel Nery, Roman Perchyts, Diego Proietti, Jasmine Reed, Joseph Robinson, Alex Schnepf, Shivani Shah, Matthew Stuart, Daniel Vaknin, Jaleel Vazquez, and SY Yaw—and at Indiana University, Edward Kim and Lin Ye.

In working on the book, we have benefited from more conversations than we can count with generous friends and colleagues. The conversations have occurred formally at faculty workshops and symposia and informally in the hallway or faculty lounge. We also have learned from our conversations with judges and lawyers at various professional events. At the risk of making an omission, we would especially like to thank participants in workshops and symposia at the Association of American Law Schools, Brooklyn Law School, Carleton University, Duke University School of Law, Frank W. Koger Bankruptcy Symposium, Law and Society Association, Northeastern University School of Law, NW Bankruptcy Institute, Southeastern Association of Law Schools, University of Connecticut, University of Illinois, University of Minnesota Law School, University of North Carolina, Universidad Rey Juan Carlos, and Universidade NOVA de Lisboa Faculty of Law.

We thank Maura Roessner at the University of California Press for cornering us at a conference and telling us to think about writing a book. Her encouragement and enthusiasm for the project got it moving. Her editorial assistant, Sam Warren, and the team at the University of California Press have been outstanding in leading us through the technical details of the publication process. Thank you for your attentiveness in seeing this book to completion.

At our respective universities, our deans and department chairs gave us the support and space to get the project finished. Our families and friends put up with more than they should have had to as we labored to meet our deadlines. Thank you to all of them.

*Pamela Foohey*
*Athens, Georgia*

*Robert M. Lawless*
*Champaign, Illinois*

*Deborah Thorne*
*Moscow, Idaho*

# Introduction

Bankruptcy filing rates have gone up and down over the past thirty years, but on average, about one million individuals in the United States have filed every year during that time period. Roughly one of every eleven Americans files bankruptcy at some point during their lives.[1] Their bankruptcies are stories of personal struggle in the face of health battles, employment disruptions, and simply trying to keep up with daily expenses. Most consumer bankruptcies, however, are not stories of personal failure. They are stories of how society has failed its citizens.

The people who file bankruptcy in the United States, in aggregate, are a cross-section of households living on the financial edge. They are older, younger, single, married, divorced, and widowed. They live on isolated farms and in apartment buildings in large cities. Some have less than a high school education; others have professional and graduate degrees. They represent every race and ethnicity. They have young children, teenagers, grandchildren, and adult children living in their homes. They are recovering from health problems, from job loss, and from the death of loved ones. Some are young and will have decades to recover their financial footing, while others are in retirement with no idea of how they are going to finance their final years. They have dealt with repeated calls from debt collectors, lost their homes to foreclosure, and had their cars repossessed. They are our neighbors, our coworkers, the nurses who provide health care, the truck drivers who deliver goods to stores, and our children's teachers.

Bankrupt households show us the financial fault lines in our society. Two or three generations ago, the United States had a more robust social safety net that cushioned people from life's most powerful financial blows. Starting in the 1980s, we purposefully have ripped apart these protections. Without much support to deal with hardships, people file bankruptcy. This book tells their stories, describing what it means to teeter on the financial cliff and find that there is no net to catch your fall.

The most prevalent contributors to households' financial downfalls are health problems. People file bankruptcy in the wake of every type of health issue, from one-time health scares to chronic conditions. Health problems in turn lead to medical debt, missing work and a steady paycheck, outright job loss, or the inability to pay for future care or needed prescriptions. Sometimes the health crisis of a loved one creates financial issues. Sweeping reductions to federal health programs and legislative paralysis in enacting comprehensive health-care reforms have left people to fend for themselves and their loved ones during the scariest and most consequential moments of their lives.

The fastest growing group of bankruptcy filers is people in their elder years. They file when they realize that their meager retirement savings will not stretch far enough to cover their basic expenses, even if they are physically able to work into their seventies and eighties. Few employers now provide pensions, and Social Security benefits have lost purchasing power because of inflation and higher medical costs. Consequently, some senior Americans find themselves sitting in bankruptcy courts during their final years.

People also file bankruptcy in their younger years, as they begin to grow their families, only to find that their stagnant incomes cannot meet the essential expenses of starting a life. As college tuition increases, students must borrow more. Home prices have risen to the point that the cost of even a fixer-upper starter house is beyond many families. Employers barely increase employees' wages to match inflation, while executive compensation skyrockets. Gender and racial wage and wealth gaps persist. In their last-ditch attempts to make ends meet, families rack up credit card debt, take out expensive auto loans, and turn to fringe credit outfits, like payday lenders. For many families, bankruptcy is their last hope.

Dramatic changes in debt collection techniques may also push people into bankruptcy courts. Technology has made it possible for creditors to call, email, and text incessantly. Past-due debts are shuffled between debt collectors so frequently that it is difficult to know what debt is being called about, let alone whether to trust what the debt collector is claiming.[2] The costs of filing debt collection lawsuits are minimal, leading to a doubling of suits filed since the 1990s, with Black and Latine persons targeted for suit more often.[3] When faced with garnishment of their wages or bank accounts, foreclosure of their homes, and repossession of their cars, some people manage the immediate crisis by filing bankruptcy.

Beyond reflecting the weakening of the social safety net, a uniting theme of people's bankruptcy stories is their struggles in the years before their bankruptcies. Their struggles are a microcosm of household struggles. As they try to balance budgets and stay ahead of mounting debt, the people who ultimately file bankruptcy skip seeing the doctor and taking medications, go without food and utilities, look for extra work, move in with family, sell property, and try to negotiate with lenders.

The experiences of bankruptcy filers show how households collapse under the pressure of having to fend for themselves financially. Their bankruptcies collectively lay bare the structural reasons people continue to struggle. This book is the story of what happens to everyday people when risk remains privatized for decades while income inequality widens, told through the struggles of those who turned to the consumer bankruptcy system for help.

## PRECARITY AMID THE PRIVATIZATION OF RISK

Many households in the United States have lived on the financial edge for decades. Over the last forty years, how people survive has shifted substantially. They pay more for housing, utilities, health care, prescriptions, transportation, daycare for their kids, and education for themselves and their children. Pensions are largely a thing of the past, leaving most workers responsible for funding their retirement years. People are expected to know how to grow their retirement savings and insulate those savings from the whims of financial markets.

Most adults also earn less relative to their expenses than four decades ago. Incomes have not risen in step with even the basic costs of living, let alone necessary large expenditures. As of 2020, the gap between the rich and everyone else reached levels not seen since the Gilded Age, the era marked by the opulent lives of railroad tycoons and wealthy financiers. Combined with shouldering more of life's expenses, rising income disparity has contributed to widening wealth inequality and an inability to accumulate meaningful savings. People have fallen behind financially, with Black persons and female-led households bearing the brunt of wage stagnation and the rising costs of living.

The privatization of risk accomplished by transferring major expenses away from the public and employer-sponsored programs and onto individuals has been termed by Jacob Hacker "the great risk shift."[4] When people must cover the full range of life's expenses, financial risk shifts onto individuals and families. Monthly expenses rise. People know that they should be planning far ahead for significant expenditures, such as purchasing homes and cars and financing their retirement, but they find it nearly impossible to do so. They also know that they should not trust that the government or their employers will support them in their educational goals or provide much meaningful assistance in times of unexpected need, such as if they or a family member falls ill or if the world faces a global pandemic.

The "great risk shift" is a product of neoliberalism's insistence that systemic risks, once deemed public and to be shared, must be dealt with privately. Neoliberalism relies on simplified notions about how free markets and trickle-down economics operate. A version of neoliberalism is Reaganomics, so called because of President Ronald Reagan's policies that emphasized individualism over the social safety net constructed during the Great Depression and in the aftermath of World War II.[5]

Privatization of risk manifests as *precarity*, a term used in sociology, anthropology, and philosophy to characterize how particular populations are denied stable lives because of failing social and economic networks.[6]

In the United States, many people now exist in a constant state of economic insecurity.[7] The privatization of risk that has created this precarity has occurred across almost every major household expense.

Housing costs more compared to twenty or thirty years ago. Home values have outpaced inflation, and rents have risen more than income in nearly every state.[8] The cost of insurance and health care has skyrocketed. The average household now spends $5,000 per year on health-care expenses, more than half of which goes to paying for insurance. According to government data, adjusted for inflation, this is nearly double what households spent per year on health care in the 1980s. Employed parents also must budget about a thousand dollars a month for their kids' daycare. For decades, the cost of attending a four-year college rose at twice the rate of inflation, although it has leveled off more recently.[9] Because defined-benefit pensions are so rare, most people must independently save and invest to have an adequate income for their retirement years.

All of this requires money. Sometimes lots of money. For instance, one financial services firm advised clients who retired in 2023 to anticipate spending another $315,000 in health-care costs during their retirement years.[10] Absent health-care reform, these costs will only increase in the coming years.

Conventional wisdom teaches that higher education is the gateway to financial stability and growth. But many students find that the conventional wisdom does not match reality. The government has retreated from supporting public education, especially smaller public universities that emphasize their educational mission over research and that used to be the mainstay for providing a higher education for the middle class. The idea that higher education is a public good that benefits all has become a quaint anachronism. To pay for their education and the education of their loved ones, people borrow.

Until 2006, student loan debt was such a small part of overall consumer debt that the Federal Reserve did not separately track it. Today, the Federal Reserve reports that households have more student loan debt than they owe on credit cards and as much as they owe on car loans. After borrowing tens of thousands of dollars in student loans, people work decades to repay their education debt, putting off buying homes, getting married, and starting families in the process.[11]

Black students and women students are even less likely to reap the benefits of higher education. Increased college attendance was supposed to chip away at the racial wealth gap. Instead, getting an education has put the median Black student even further behind their white counterpart. Black college graduates owe more on student loans and have not seen their incomes grow. Women tend to take on more education debt than men. Through a combination of lower earnings after graduation and childcare and eldercare responsibilities, women overall take longer to pay back student loans. Black women take on the most debt and struggle the most to pay off that debt.[12]

This shifting of risk onto individuals forces many people to spend their lives perpetually and single-handedly confronting financial instability and uncertainty. Households are expected to take care of their every need, yet they have few options when planning for their futures or when facing money troubles. The precarity people experience stems from their reliance on savings and wealth as their sole source of safety, while they are simultaneously living in an economy set up to prevent most people's accumulation of those savings and wealth.

To stay afloat, people take on debt for almost every expense, large or small. They purchase their homes with less money down and with higher interest payments. They finance their cars with seven-year auto loans. They put medical expenses on credit cards. They balance the cost of childcare by paying for necessities, like food, with credit cards. When conventional credit sources dry up, they turn to companies offering short-term, high-cost loans, such as payday lenders and auto title loan outfits. They take out student loans but often default on these loans because, quite simply, they have no more money.

Crucially, it has been this way in the United States for decades now. The roots of the economic policies that have plunged many households into precarity trace back to the early 1980s. Governmental inaction over the following forty years in the face of a changing economic and social context has further loaded risk onto individuals.

How people handle their financial precarity also has evolved over the past forty years. With the ubiquity of the internet, companies offer home loans and auto loans via cell phones and tablets. Many workers make a portion of their income in the "gig economy," a phrase that was meaningless to most a mere ten years ago. Side hustles include starting YouTube channels and live streaming shopping events as part of retailing for multilevel-marketing companies.[13] Setting up a GoFundMe campaign is an accepted and expected way to pay for life's emergencies. These examples illustrate how, for many people, a constant jumble of differing income sources has replaced a steady paycheck. Not surprisingly, debt collection has burgeoned into an industry with an annual revenue of about $13.4 billion.[14]

Of course, a family falling on financial hard times is nothing new. But the individualization of the financial risk and the associated struggles have been the norm for more than four decades, and they now seem routine and may go unnoticed. When people cannot manage financially, they draw accusations of overspending, irresponsibility, and lack of self-awareness. For example, Dave Ramsey, a self-proclaimed personal finance expert, tells millions on his popular radio shows that the answer to financial problems is "learning how to control yourself and your behavior with money." Financial problems are a "behavior issue."[15]

In reality, people cannot "personal finance" themselves out of skyrocketing rent, medical costs, and wage stagnation. Despite what they may hear about budgeting, many people are one illness, one job loss, or one unexpected pregnancy away from a financial tailspin. That financial tailspin, almost necessarily, will lead some people to file bankruptcy, and the bankruptcy files will tell us the story of that tailspin.

## BANKRUPTCY AND THE CONSEQUENCES OF PRECARITY

The people who file bankruptcy reflect the financial precarity of households across the United States. Not everyone who experiences a large financial shock or the slow accumulation of debt will turn to bankruptcy for relief. Some may recover. Others may slip so far into debt and lose so much that filing bankruptcy will do virtually nothing to help them. Still others may worry about what their families and friends will think of them if they declare bankruptcy and will decide against it, even though they may benefit from filing.

Not everyone may file bankruptcy, but bankruptcy is a story of America.

The people who file bankruptcy bring with them accounts of the reality of decades of loading risk onto households. Their struggles prior to filing and what they hope to achieve through bankruptcy link with the structural barriers people face in their quests for financial stability. *Debt's Grip* tells how the landscape of households' finances has changed since the initial push of economic policies in the 1980s toward individualism that has led people to experience precarity. How people take out loans, the types of expenses for which they must incur debt, how their creditors and debt collectors deal with them in and out of court, and how those interactions push people into bankruptcy have shifted. Filers' journeys to and through bankruptcy illustrate how the core of Americans survive today in a society that has failed many.

In this book, we draw on data from the Consumer Bankruptcy Project, a long-term study of people who file bankruptcy. The roots of the CBP trace to 1981, when Teresa Sullivan, Elizabeth Warren, and Jay Lawrence Westbrook set out to describe bankruptcy filers. As they detailed in *As We Forgive Our Debtors*, the people who landed in bankruptcy courts were a cross-section of the American middle class.[16] They were not, as so many assumed, profligates—cheats and overspenders who filed bankruptcy to escape debts that they definitely could pay, if only they wanted to. They also were not those from the lowest rung of the socioeconomic ladder, who might be thought to be most in need of debt relief. *As We Forgive Our Debtors* established who uses the consumer bankruptcy system. It also was a study of a bankruptcy system in flux. A congressional overhaul of the federal bankruptcy law had taken effect in 1979, only two years before Sullivan, Warren, and Westbrook gathered their data.

Their updated research in 1991 studied a bankruptcy system that had fully adjusted to the significant revamping of the bankruptcy law. Between the early 1980s and the late 1990s, consumer bankruptcy filings per capita more than doubled.[17] Little had changed about the bankruptcy filers themselves. They remained a cross-section of the middle class, often having moved downward in financial and social class. In *The Fragile Middle Class*, Sullivan, Warren, and Westbrook combined questionnaires and case file data from bankruptcy filers to identify the main ways in which households were being financially squeezed so that more of them turned to the bankruptcy system for protection. They identified five stressors: volatility in income and jobs, the rising cost of consumer credit, divorce and solo parenting, substantial rises in health-care costs, and increases in the cost of housing. These stressors reflected the early effects of the great risk shift on households' ability to survive financially. *The Fragile Middle Class* hinted at the connection between the privatization of risk and consumer bankruptcy filings.

In this book, readers will find similar details about the people who file bankruptcy. Since the 1990s, the number of consumer bankruptcy filings per year has remained rather steady and predictable. Except for a spike during the years surrounding the passage of 2005 legislation that changed bankruptcy law considerably, over a million households filed bankruptcy every year through the early 2010s. As the economy recovered from the Great Recession of 2007–2009, filings declined to around 750,000 per year for the remainder of the last decade; most recently they fell again during the COVID-19 pandemic that began in 2020.[18]

During those thirty years, bankruptcy filers also have remained a cross-section of the middle class. They continue to come to bankruptcy courts with many of the same problems that stressed households in prior decades but also with new problems such as student loans and supercharged debt collection.[19] Our main focus in this book is what happens to individuals and families when risk remains privatized for decades. In drawing on stories of people's financial collapse, we necessarily discuss the place of bankruptcy law for people facing the consequences of shifting risk and explore the who or why of consumer bankruptcy. But at its core, *Debt's Grip* focuses on the structural reasons that households struggle financially in today's economy and society.

## THE CURRENT CONSUMER BANKRUPTCY PROJECT

Over the past forty years, the CBP has functioned in iterations. The first took place in the 1980s and drew data from consumer bankruptcy cases filed in 1981. Ten years later, the second iteration drew data from people's bankruptcy filings in 1991.[20] The third and fourth iterations were based on data from bankruptcy filings in 2001 and 2007, respectively, both supplemented by surveys of and interviews with the people who filed.[21] Where relevant, we refer to these previous studies by their year of data collection (e.g., "the 2007 CBP").

In 2013 we launched the fifth and current iteration of the CBP.[22] We switched from episodic collection of large samples to continuous data collection of samples that individually are smaller but aggregate to larger datasets than in the previous iterations. We refer to this iteration as the "current CBP." We collect our data from two sources.

First, we gather data from documents in bankruptcy cases. Bankruptcy court files are public records and electronically available. Every three months, we draw a random sample of two hundred consumer bankruptcy cases from all the consumer bankruptcy cases filed across the United States. The households in our study come from every state and are found in rural, suburban, and urban settings. The data we draw from in this book come from court records for eighty-eight hundred households that filed bankruptcy in the eleven-year period between the beginning of 2013 and the end of 2023.

From those cases, we collect financial information, such as assets, debts, income, expenses, and employment history. We also track the cases' outcomes: whether debtors receive discharges of their debts as provided by bankruptcy law or have their cases dismissed, leaving them to again face all the debts they owed when they filed.

Second, we mail each household in our sample a survey that asks about their circumstances before and after their bankruptcy filings, their money management techniques before bankruptcy, their reasons for filing, their interactions with their attorney, some basic health information, and their demographics. At several points in the survey, we provide space for people to write about their struggles and decisions to file bankruptcy. In total, of the 8,800 households in our sample, 2,314 (26 percent) returned the survey to us.

The survey responses provide key information about age, education, race, and cohabitation and marital status that bankruptcy court records do not contain. People's responses also add texture about their struggles to the financial information that debtors are required to submit to bankruptcy courts. In this book, we provide excerpts of what people wrote on the surveys. Some state that the experiences that led them to file bankruptcy are still too raw for them to write anything. Others write long, complex stories of the travails that led them to turn to bankruptcy for help. When we draw from what people write, we disguise their names and other identifying information to protect their privacy. When people include dollar figures in what they write, we generally inflate those figures for consistency with other dollar figures used in this book; we indicate when we have done so by putting inflated figures in brackets. Other than these edits, we include what people wrote, exactly as they wrote it. The debtors in this book are not composites. They are actual individuals and families who have lived through the consequences of the systematic gutting of the social safety net.

Between the court records and surveys, the current CBP includes tens of thousands of pieces of data. The current CBP also is the first study of consumer bankruptcy that collects data on a rolling basis. We use our entire database, drawing on data from eleven years. This allows us to look for changes over time in the characteristics and financial problems of the people who turn to bankruptcy for help.

The nitty-gritty details about our methodology are included in the appendix. In it, we provide more history about the CBP, our data collection process, and tests for response bias. Of note, the data we collect from court records are self-reported. However, almost all bankruptcy filers enlist the help of an attorney or bankruptcy petition preparer. The Bankruptcy Code requires attorneys and bankruptcy petition preparers to collect supporting documents to corroborate the debtor's financial information. Debtors sign the bankruptcy petition under penalty of perjury, swearing that the information provided is true and accurate to the best of their ability. Attorneys must certify they have "no knowledge after an inquiry" that anything in the case file is incorrect. The bankruptcy trustee assigned to the case will review everything that is submitted and then question the debtors, under oath, about their finances. People risk losing the bankruptcy discharge and being subject to other penalties if they misrepresent or omit the required information. In extreme cases, the penalties can include criminal convictions for fraudulently concealing information in their bankruptcy forms. These legal safeguards do not guarantee 100 percent accuracy, but they do mean the court-record data are not wild guesses about asset values, debts owed, and income levels.

Obviously, people respond to our surveys without these legal consequences in the background. Money troubles and filing bankruptcy are stigmatizing and shameful.[23] In general, discussing one's salary and finances, even with one's own family, is often frowned upon.[24] People who return the survey show courage in being willing to answer questions about their lives and share stories about some of their most difficult moments. Some write notes expressing their hope that by providing their information they can help others in a similar situation. We can corroborate some survey information from the court records. Nonetheless, our survey data rely on the respondents' self-reported information, as is the case for most surveys. We offer the survey data for what they are: valuable firsthand accounts of the lived experience of financial precarity, including people's stories in the words with which they wrote them.

Personal finance and bankruptcy filings are sensitive subjects laden with value judgments. Everyone has attitudes about how they and others spend money, including us. In the chapters that follow, we examine the circumstances of the people who file bankruptcy to highlight the reality of living on a financial cliff. We organized this book around findings based on current CBP data using unsupervised statistical techniques. These techniques are "unsupervised" because they draw inferences from the data without mediation by researchers, meaning that the results of the analysis around which we have organized this book were not driven by our preconceptions of bankruptcy filers.[25]

## FINANCIAL COLLAPSE AND BANKRUPTCY AMID PRECARITY

This is a book about how people's bankruptcies reflect a failure of the United States to provide for its citizens. Financial insecurity is pervasive. In 2019 more than half of Americans said they were struggling with some aspect of their financial lives, and almost one-fifth said they were struggling with all or nearly all parts of their financial lives.[26] A few months into the COVID pandemic, the depth of the financial precarity of households was on full display. Fifty-four percent of households with incomes under $100,000 reported serious financial problems, with Black and Latine households hit the hardest.[27] How bankruptcy sometimes remedies financial problems aligns with what we know about the barriers to financial stability that many households now face.

### The Road to Bankruptcy

In chapter 1 of the book, we explain the consumer bankruptcy system in a way that presupposes the reader has no prior knowledge of its workings. The book's institutional setting is bankruptcy law. Although the law is not in the book's foreground, one must understand this institutional setting to understand its findings.

People's financial problems begin long before they formally file bankruptcy. The years leading up to their bankruptcies are filled with worry about how to make ends meet; tough decisions about whether to sell homes and where to move; trying to find more work to make a few extra bucks; and skimping on food, utilities, and medications. These coping mechanisms exacerbate health problems and cause tension with spouses and partners, children, family, and friends. Their struggles also deplete assets and resources, making it less and less likely that they will recover financially. Under the weight of mounting debts and diminishing options to deal with those debts, some people will turn to bankruptcy for help.

Although the people who file bankruptcy are a cross-section of the middle class, there are patterns in their bankruptcy cases. These patterns describe the consequences of decades of offloading risk onto households. The patterns also allow us to tease apart and explore the structural reasons that so many individuals and families are struggling now.

### Seeking a Financial Reset

Filing bankruptcy is a declaration that one cannot pay all their debts. Being able to pay one's debts requires enough income to meet what is owed when it becomes due. That financial formula may seem tautological. But the details about how public policies have affected its two sides—income and expenses—are the main reasons bankruptcy filers are seeking a financial reset.

Some people who file bankruptcy are concerned about specific debts that have grown out of control. Mortgages and car loans are secured debts, meaning they are secured by collateral. When people fall behind on them, their continued ownership of a house or car is threatened. Mortgage and car loans are pervasive. US policies have prioritized homeownership. Most Americans own their homes rather than renting. Moving is complicated. Approval for rental housing is uncertain, particularly for those with fair or poor credit scores. Bankruptcy offers people a way to hold onto their homes while dealing with mortgage delinquencies. Similarly, surviving without a car in most parts of the United States is difficult. Eighty-five percent of households own at least one car. People file bankruptcy hoping to hold onto their cars and deal with car loans.

Debt incurred because of medical problems has stood out in bankruptcy filings for decades. Two-thirds of filers now cite a medical contributor to their bankruptcies, either expenses from a health problem or illness-related work loss. Health-related financial issues show up in credit card debt from the medical expenses themselves or from the buildup of small expenditures during health crises, including the time that people must take off from work to care for themselves or sick loved ones. The continued frequency of medical bankruptcies is an indictment of the health-care system.

People also file bankruptcy to deal with unsecured debts separate from medical expenses. Primarily, these are student loans and debt incurred to deal with the vagaries of employment. Public policies have individualized the funding of higher education. People also rack up balances on credit cards and take out other unsecured debts because they cannot make enough money to stay afloat. This includes students who have attended college, some of whom are trying to pay hefty education loans, and people who start their own small businesses as an alternative to traditional employment. Workers without college degrees often are left even further behind as job opportunities have become more limited.[28]

## Surviving in a Rigged Society

The finances of bankrupt households demonstrate an economy that squeezes individuals and families by foisting on them the bulk of the expenses of every facet of life, from finding a place to live, to financing the education that will get them a job, to paying for every aspect of a health crisis. Many are crushed, but some are bulldozed. American society is not equal. Some groups live in social contexts that make surviving financially more precarious. This precarity shows up in bankruptcy courts through skewed demographics of the people who file.

Three demographic groups take center stage. First, Black persons are significantly overrepresented in bankruptcy. Black households make up 27 percent of the households that file bankruptcy, which is more than double the proportion of the population that is Black. The reasons Black households turn to bankruptcy reflect systemic disparities and discrimination in the economy and society, from paying more for homes, cars, mortgages, car loans, and education, to being less likely to find stable employment and being paid less in the jobs they find.

Second, women are more likely to file bankruptcy than their share of the population. Fifty-seven percent of bankruptcy filers are women. Single women appear to be more vulnerable to bankruptcy than single men. There are more than twice as many single women in bankruptcy (37 percent) as single men (16 percent). The remaining filers are married, which matches the marriage rate across the United States. Bankruptcy continues to be a women's issue.[29]

As with Black households, why single women, in particular, may turn to bankruptcy more often reflects disparities and discrimination inherent in the economy and society. Many single women, but fewer single men, who file are responsible for children. Women pay more for education and face employment problems because they tend to be their families' first responders for childcare and health-care emergencies. When we searched for patterns in bankruptcy cases, the intersection of Black and women-led households comprised a distinct group of filers. Black single women deal with the same disparities and discrimination, but the effects on their lives are magnified as compared to other women, a reality apparent in their bankruptcy cases.

Third, bankruptcy filers are older than the general population. The rate at which older Americans (sixty-five and over) file bankruptcy has increased markedly over the last few decades; it is fair to characterize older Americans as the fastest growing demographic of bankruptcy filers. Those over sixty-five now make up 18 percent of people who use the bankruptcy system. In 1991 that figure was 2 percent. The magnitude of growth of the elderly filing bankruptcy is so large that the broader trend of an aging US population can explain only a small portion of the effect.

Why older individuals turn to bankruptcy reflects failures in public policies that provide for people as they age. Older persons file when they can no longer work and earn enough money to survive, when their retirement savings run out, and when they face daunting and unending end-of-life medical bills. As with Black households and single women, the increasing prevalence of older Americans filing bankruptcy shows the effects of decades of privatizing risk.

### Dealing with Legal Woes

Prior to filing bankruptcy, people may feel as though their debts are haunting them. Part of this haunting comes from creditors' and debt collectors' attempts to extract payment for past due debts. Many people simply cannot pay, no matter how many times collectors call them or how many lawsuits collectors file against them in state courts. More than three-quarters of the people who file cite debt collection as a contributor to their bankruptcy. Half of filers come to bankruptcy court in the wake of a lawsuit, such as home foreclosure, car repossession, or wage garnishment. Debt collection attempts exacerbate the misery of the prebankruptcy experience, with persons in debt collection reporting more privations than those who were not contacted by collectors.

Not everyone with financial problems waits for years to file bankruptcy or files following lawsuits. We searched for *resourced filers*, people who might reasonably be described as "can pay" debtors looking to escape from obligations they could otherwise afford to repay. Because the concept of "can pay" is subjective, we think about the concept in several different ways, but we find almost no filers who fit the definition. For filers whose financial circumstances facially suggest some ability to repay, a more careful review of the bankruptcy file shows they were only exercising their legal rights to solve a problem they had. Most often, these are attempts to save a home. Rather than "can pay" debtors, *savvy* is the more apt term.

This book ends with the bankruptcy system itself. To a degree, bankruptcy has become the legal proceeding that certain groups of people who suffer from discrimination and inequities turn to for help. Bankruptcy law can exacerbate these socioeconomic disparities. In identifying how and when it does, our data offer pathways for reforms to make bankruptcy work better for the people who use it—while we wait for the United States to confront the structural reasons that people struggle in today's economy and society.

*Debt's Grip* is about people who file bankruptcy. It also is a book about the consequences of decades of risk privatization. Most people come to bankruptcy after seriously struggling to pay their debts for years. After we describe the consumer bankruptcy system in the next chapter, we turn to their stories of living with financial precarity.

# 1 Filing Bankruptcy and the Bankruptcy System

> I am totally broke and then when you go to talk to the
> attorney you find that even though you are broke they need
> $4,000 to file bankruptcy. So it's just a circle of hell. But I'm
> 69½ and I don't want to leave my family to have to pay my
> debts if and when I die.
>
> —Retired, divorced white woman who filed chapter 13

This book is not about the bankruptcy system as such. Rather, it looks to the people who file bankruptcy to illuminate what it means to live in financial precarity. Nonetheless, everyone in the book decided to file bankruptcy, a choice that brought legal and economic consequences even if sociological and psychological factors also played an important role in the decision. To put the data in context, this chapter explains those consequences.

Bankruptcy experts might cavil at the broad legal outline that follows. It is not a treatise on bankruptcy law. It is meant to provide the necessary background for nonexperts. That background includes data about how the system works in practice. Those who are experts in the field will learn from these data. We begin with how people find their bankruptcy attorneys. Throughout, we include details about the system, such as filing rates for different types of bankruptcy, pro se filing rates, and outcomes.

The US Constitution empowers Congress to pass "uniform Laws on the subject of Bankruptcies."[1] Bankruptcy is thus federal law. Generally speaking, however, state law will determine what rights the filer brings to bankruptcy. For example, if the debtor owns land, state law will determine the debtor's rights in that land. Similarly, if the debtor claims to have a defense to a debt, such as breach of warranty or fraud, state law will determine the validity of that defense. Bankruptcy law distributes whatever the debtor might have to creditors using these state law outcomes.

A specialized set of federal courts hears bankruptcy cases. Not surprisingly, these are called US Bankruptcy Courts. Every federal judicial district has a US Bankruptcy Court. This book uses data from the ninety-one judicial districts in the fifty states and the District of Columbia. Within almost every judicial district, there are several locations in which the court sits and hears cases.

Bankruptcy courts hear the chapter 11 reorganization cases of the country's largest corporations and the much smaller cases of households in financial distress. Each year there are more bankruptcy cases than federal civil and criminal cases combined, meaning the bankruptcy court is the part of the federal court system that an everyday person is most likely to encounter. Debtors and creditors can appeal rulings of the bankruptcy court through the federal court system, all the way to the US Supreme Court, which typically hears a few bankruptcy cases each year.

To explain the bankruptcy system, this chapter uses a running example of a married couple, Chris and Jessica. This example illustrates some important features of consumer bankruptcy law. It is important to keep in mind, however, that Chris and Jessica are also an atypical example. First, only 46 percent of all bankruptcy filers are married or have a domestic partner. Although married couples (and only married couples) can file bankruptcy together, in 42 percent of cases with a married couple, one spouse files independently. Second, the median bankruptcy filer does not have any dependents. Women, and particularly Black women, are more likely to file by themselves and more likely to have dependents when they file. Chapter 7 of this book explores the intersection of gender and race.

## GETTING TO THE LAWYER

To be considering bankruptcy, Chris and Jessica will need to owe debt. That may seem an obvious point, but it is an important one. Bankruptcy does not generate income. It only eliminates past debts. If they are like most people who file bankruptcy, Chris and Jessica struggled to pay those debts for years before filing bankruptcy, possibly going without necessities, and trying various tactics to cope with their debts, as examined in the next chapter. This book documents financial precarity, but every person in the book at one time had the income and resources to incur debt. As desperate as many of the stories are, they omit an even more deeply distressed group of persons: those who have never had the financial resources and sufficient income to participate in the economic system as consumer borrowers.

For Chris and Jessica to be thinking about bankruptcy, they also will need to have concluded that the legal system can address their financial struggles. Everyone has problems: family problems, health problems, workplace problems. Chris and Jessica will have to put their financial struggles into a mental bucket called "legal problems." Even as it oversimplifies, the classic framework for when people bring their problems to the legal system is known as "naming, blaming, and claiming."[2] An essential part of that process is for the person to identify their debt issue as a legal one.[3] The same mental process applies to the decision to file bankruptcy. Chris and Jessica need to conceptualize their problem as one the legal system can help with, as opposed to, for example, a financial one that could be solved by getting a second job. The pathways to bankruptcy are not well understood. Some filers are "brought to law" by creditors' collection attempts or legal actions.[4] Others may have talked to a friend, a family member, or a clergy member who suggested bankruptcy. A television advertisement or billboard could have planted the idea of using the law to deal with mounting debts.

We pick up Chris and Jessica's story after they have made the decision to file bankruptcy. In our data, 7 percent of people file bankruptcy themselves, without any help whatsoever. Another 3 percent do so with the assistance of a bankruptcy petition preparer, a nonlawyer who will complete the forms based on information provided by Chris and Jessica but will not give any legal advice or represent them in court. About half of cases filed without a lawyer are dismissed, compared to about one in five cases filed by an attorney. If the court dismisses a bankruptcy case, it is as if the case was never even filed, and creditors can continue to

*Table 1.1.*   Methods Used to Find a Lawyer

| Method | Percent |
| --- | --- |
| Searched for lawyer on Google or Yelp | 44 |
| Lawyer's office was near home or work | 31 |
| Lawyer recommended by friend or relative | 31 |
| Saw an ad for lawyer on television, internet, or billboard | 29 |
| Did not shop around for a lawyer | 28 |
| Compared how much different lawyers charged | 23 |
| Met with more than one lawyer | 15 |
| Had used or worked with lawyer in the past | 14 |
| Lawyer was someone filer knew | 9 |
| Lawyer was provided by legal aid | 3 |

NOTE: Respondents (n = 711) could choose more than one method of finding a lawyer.

pursue the person for the debts owed. The dismissal can create consequences if a person attempts to refile, and it can even prevent refiling for some time.

Dismissal rates are also highly correlated with the bankruptcy chapter filed. In chapter 7, very few (2.3%) attorney-filed cases end in dismissal, compared to about one in four pro se cases. In chapter 13, 54 percent of attorney-filed cases are dismissed, which sounds high until one compares that to the 88 percent dismissal rate for pro se cases.

Like 90 percent of filers, Chris and Jessica decide to use a lawyer. In 2020 we began asking people to identify all the ways they found their attorneys; the results are detailed in table 1.1. Most people take some actions that suggest some effort toward hiring an attorney, such as asking for recommendations, meeting with more than one lawyer, and searching on the internet.

There is a fair chance that Chris and Jessica may not have devoted a lot of attention to the decision about whom to hire. Serendipity may have played a surprising role despite the importance of the lawyer in shaping the result Chris and Jessica will get from bankruptcy. Almost a third of filers reported using a lawyer who happened to have an office near their home or work, and more than a quarter reported that an advertisement played a role in their choice. Twenty-eight percent admitted to not shopping around for a lawyer.

Once they settle on a lawyer, Chris and Jessica will have an intake session. Depending on the size of the law firm and how many bankruptcies it processes, a paralegal may perform the intake. The intake likely will involve completing a lengthy questionnaire about themselves, their employment, and their finances. The paralegal or attorney also will ask Chris and Jessica to provide six months of pay stubs and last year's tax return. Local practice may require providing even more pay stubs and tax returns. Chris and Jessica will need to produce other financial information, such as mortgage statements, car loan statements, and bank account statements. A nonfinancial cost of filing bankruptcy is the time and hassle of gathering all this information. Unless they are exceptionally well organized, Chris and Jessica will call and email back and forth with their attorney's office to put together the necessary information.

## CHAPTER CHOICE

An important decision for Chris and Jessica will be which bankruptcy chapter to file. Most consumers have two choices: chapter 7 and chapter 13. For now, it is only important to understand their differences broadly. Chapter 7 is a liquidation in which the filer's assets are sold and the proceeds are paid to creditors, although only 5 percent of chapter 7 filers have any assets of value. Chapter 13 requires filers to make monthly payments to their creditors under a three- to five-year plan.

In theory, Chris and Jessica could file chapter 11, more famously known for large corporate reorganizations such as Enron, Chrysler, and more recently Purdue Pharma and FTX. A chapter 11 is quite expensive, and it does not make sense for individuals to file this type of bankruptcy if they can file under another chapter. From 2013 to 2022, according to data from the US courts, only 0.2 percent of all chapter 11s were filed by natural persons, mainly by persons with large business or investment debts. Chapter 12 is available for family farmers, but Chris and Jessica are not family farmers. Less than 0.1 percent of bankruptcies are chapter 12s.[5]

Although the phrase "chapter choice" is used frequently, it is a misnomer. The most significant determinant for which chapter Chris and Jessica will "choose" is likely to be where they live. From 2013 to 2023, 36 percent of all people across the country filed chapter 13, but there is substantial variation in filing rates across the country, as illustrated in figure 1.1. In the Great Plains states, only 10 to 15 percent of filings are chapter 13s. In contrast, in most parts of the Deep South consumers file chapter 13 more than half of the time, with some locales reporting more than 70 percent of their cases as chapter 13s.

Scholars have noted the disparity in bankruptcy chapter "choice" for decades, attributing it to "local legal culture."[6] That local norms develop within a professional community is to be expected. But it is not well understood what creates these norms, particularly in a way that causes them to diverge so dramatically across the country. Differences in state law contribute to the discrepancies. There is substantial variation within states in chapter choice, however, and these in-state differences suggest that more than differences in formal state law must be at work. Regardless, the complexity of bankruptcy law means that Chris and Jessica's lawyer will have a considerable influence on which chapter they use. The local norms of where Chris and Jessica live will have shaped their lawyer's advice.

Another factor that will contribute to their chapter choice decision is Chris's and Jessica's races. All things being equal, Black households are twice as likely to file chapter 13 as other households. Chapter 6 of this book expands on the racial disparities in bankruptcy filings generally and chapter choice specifically.

The bankruptcy chapter Chris and Jessica choose also will determine how they pay for their lawyer, who will charge more for a chapter 13 because its greater complexity places more demands on the lawyer's time. Across the country, the median attorney's fee is $1,456 for a chapter 7 and $4,483 for a chapter 13.

Although chapter 7 will cost Chris and Jessica less, there is a wrinkle. If they do not pay for the bankruptcy in advance, any money Chris and Jessica owe their lawyer will be treated like any other debt owing before the chapter 7 case is filed and therefore will be wiped out by bankruptcy's debt discharge. Although a few bankruptcy courts have adopted procedures allowing chapter 7 lawyers to defer their fees, those procedures are

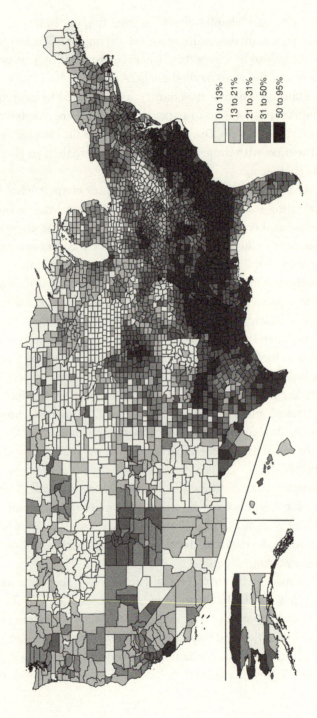

*Figure 1.1.* Percentage of bankruptcy filers in each county who filed chapter 13, 2013–23

Legend:
- 0 to 13%
- 13 to 21%
- 21 to 31%
- 31 to 50%
- 50 to 95%

not widespread, and they face legal challenges. Therefore, Chris and Jessica's lawyer will ask for payment upfront before filing the chapter 7 case.

Many people who want to file chapter 7 need to save up to afford bankruptcy. Almost two-thirds of our survey respondents reported that they waited to file bankruptcy until they had saved money to pay for a lawyer. Filers often tap an income tax refund to pay for a lawyer, which is why bankruptcy filings spike in March and April every year.[7] From 2013 to 2023, March filings averaged over 25 percent higher than filings in February. Chris and Jessica can avoid these up-front costs by filing chapter 13, because they can pay their lawyer over time through the repayment plan, essentially using chapter 13 to finance their bankruptcy case. Many chapter 13s are complete "no money down" cases, in which the filer pays the entire attorney's fee through the case. Even after controlling for financial variables that capture ability to pay, the main determinants of whether someone will file chapter 13 with no money down are whether the filer is Black and the judicial district where the filer lives. The same factors determine whether someone files chapter 13 with "near no money down."[8] The finding suggests that local tolerance for whether people can use the bankruptcy process to pay for a chapter 13 helps to drive the differences in how often filers, and particularly Black persons, end up in chapter 13.

Thus, there are three extralegal factors that strongly influence chapter choice: location, race, and ability to pay. That is not to suggest that the legal outcomes do not matter. If Chris and Jessica have been well counseled, these legal outcomes will determine whether to file bankruptcy and which chapter to use. The best way to understand those outcomes is to start with chapter 7 as a baseline and then consider how chapter 13 alters that baseline.

## CHAPTER 7

Before Chris and Jessica get to the bankruptcy court, the law requires them to complete prebankruptcy credit counseling. The "credit counseling" will not be a serious attempt to help Chris and Jessica avoid bankruptcy or even to help them understand the basics of financial literacy. The session, which will be done online, perhaps in their lawyer's office, costs about $25 and lasts about an hour. In court opinions, judges have described the counseling as "perfunctory," "inane," and "absurd." Nonetheless, it is a legal requirement. The credit counseling is Chris and Jessica's ticket into bankruptcy, and if they fail to do it, the court has no choice but to dismiss their case.[9]

Chris and Jessica will begin their case by filing a bankruptcy petition with the US Bankruptcy Court where they live. They will pay a filing fee of $338, which can be paid in four monthly installments. If they fail to fully pay the fee, the court will dismiss their case. According to data from the US courts, 10 percent of chapter 7 filers pay in installments.[10] Chris and Jessica can ask the court to waive the filing fee if their income is within 150 percent of the federal poverty line. Nationally, 4 percent of chapter 7 filers receive a fee waiver, although there is substantial variation around the country, with more than 16 percent and less than 1 percent receiving fee waivers in some judicial districts.

The filing of a petition initiates the case, although the word *petition* is something of a misnomer because the court does not need to "grant" the petition. Along with the petition, Chris and Jessica will file schedules prepared by their lawyer detailing all their assets, liabilities, income, and expenses. Chris and Jessica also will file a statement of financial affairs, a questionnaire about their prebankruptcy economic life. They will swear to the truthfulness of these documents under penalty of perjury. The information in this book uses these records to document the financial condition of the people who file bankruptcy.

Upon the filing of the petition, creditors must stop all debt collection activity against Chris and Jessica. Creditors can neither contact Chris and Jessica nor start or continue lawsuits. The sheriff cannot sell their house, even if it is in the middle of foreclosure. The repo man cannot haul off their car. Garnishment of wages ceases. This pause—known as the *automatic stay* because it happens without any order from the bankruptcy court—will provide important relief to Chris and Jessica. Overdue bill notices will no longer fill the mailbox, and the phone will not ring during dinner with a debt collector demanding payment. Importantly, Chris and Jessica now have time to negotiate with creditors about their most problematic debts.

The court clerk will assign Chris and Jessica's case to a bankruptcy judge. The case also will be assigned to a chapter 7 trustee. The trustee requires some explanation. Within the Department of Justice is an office known as the US Trustee Program. Among its duties is oversight and selection of chapter 7 and chapter 13 trustees. The nomenclature is confusing. A US Trustee is an employee of the Department of Justice. A chapter 7 or chapter 13 trustee is a private individual who often works for a law firm or in a solo law practice. The US Trustees select the chapter 7 and chapter 13 trustees—who are also known generically as *bankruptcy trustees*. Chapter 13 trustees are assigned to all chapter 13 cases in a geographic locale and for that reason are also known as *standing trustees*. There is usually a local panel of chapter 7 trustees who are assigned to individual chapter 7 cases in rotation.

Chris and Jessica's judge will only hear about matters their trustee brings before the court. It would be unusual for any creditors to be active in the case. The chapter 7 trustee may ask Chris and Jessica for further documentation, adding to the cost and hassle of filing. Thus, the chapter 7 trustee likely will play a bigger role in Chris and Jessica's case than the judge. The trustee will earn $60 for taking on Chris and Jessica's case, an amount that has not changed since 1994. The decision to become a trustee is not likely to have been motivated by the prospect of earning $60 per case. Instead, the trustee will be looking to earn the statutorily prescribed percentage of any recovery paid to creditors through the case. Only about 5 percent of chapter 7 cases yield any payment to creditors.[11] Thus, the fee structure incentivizes Chris and Jessica's trustee to make their case part of that 5 percent by questioning valuations they have put on assets, by hunting for undisclosed assets, or sometimes by filing a lawsuit to recover money or property Chris and Jessica transferred away on the eve of bankruptcy.

Within three to seven weeks after filing, Chris and Jessica will attend the meeting of creditors, known as the "341 meeting" after the section of the Bankruptcy Code that authorizes it. Their attorney also will attend, and their chapter 7 trustee will preside. Although any of Chris and Jessica's creditors can attend, it is extremely rare for them to do so. The trustee will ask Chris and Jessica more questions under oath about their financial affairs. The meeting will take place online. If the meeting is typical, it will last ten or fifteen minutes. Afterward, Chris and Jessica may feel like they have been to "court," but they have not. They have not appeared before a judge. Somewhat like a deposition in a lawsuit, they have only given sworn testimony to a private individual, the bankruptcy trustee, who will use that information to decide what steps the trustee wants to take in the case.

Most significantly, the trustee next will decide whether Chris and Jessica have anything of value the trustee can sell to raise money for creditors. The people who file bankruptcy come to court with little property of value. Also, bankruptcy law "exempts" some property from the process—for instance, clothing and household furnishings, retirement savings, and the equity in a car or a house (up to certain dollar amounts). Even if there is property, the costs of sale might not make it worthwhile for the trustee to pursue a sale. As typical consumers, it is improbable Chris and Jessica's case will be in the 5 percent that produce any payment for creditors.

After the 341 meeting, Chris and Jessica's involvement with their chapter 7 case is likely to be minimal. They will not see the bankruptcy judge or even the inside of a courtroom. There is no requirement that they do so. After filing bankruptcy, Chris and Jessica must complete a financial management course similar to the credit counseling they received before filing and of the same dubious utility.

In about six months and assuming no hiccups, Chris and Jessica will receive a court notice saying their debts have been "discharged." This forgiveness of debts is the central relief for most bankruptcy filers. For example, Chris and Jessica will no longer have to pay outstanding credit card or medical bills, and bankruptcy law forever bars their creditors from taking any collection actions whatsoever, under penalty of contempt of court. Some debts are nondischargeable, most notably alimony, unpaid child support, tax debts, or fraud debts. Chris's and Jessica's student loans will not be discharged unless they can show that paying them will lead to *undue hardship*, a demanding standard few filers are able to meet. If they have concealed information from the trustee or committed fraud in the bankruptcy case itself, the trustee might ask the court not to issue a discharge, but this very rarely happens in bankruptcy cases. With their discharge, Chris and Jessica will have the fresh start promised by bankruptcy. Of course, they will be responsible for their debts moving forward, but they will be free of their past burdens.

## SECURED AND UNSECURED DEBTS

Although bankruptcy will have discharged Chris and Jessica's personal liability on their loans, it does not eliminate any liens that might exist against their property. A debt with a lien is known as a *secured* debt. Classic examples are home and car loans. Some filers also might have liens that come from prebankruptcy collection activities or other prebankruptcy loans. Debts without liens are *unsecured*. Examples of unsecured debts are credit cards and medical debts.

Bankruptcy does not change the promise that Chris and Jessica made on their secured debts. Most importantly, an unpaid mortgage or car loan allows the bank to foreclose on the house or repossess the car. If Chris and Jessica want to keep their house or car, they must continue to pay those loans after they receive the discharge and after the bankruptcy case concludes.

Their fresh start has provided some help for their mortgage or car loans. With their unsecured debts discharged, Chris and Jessica likely can devote more of their income to their mortgage or car payments without falling behind on their daily expenses. Because the discharge forgives their personal liability, Chris and Jessica are not liable for any deficiency on their mortgage or car loan if they are "underwater," meaning the value of the home or car is less than the amount owed on the mortgage or car loan. Thus, if they do end up defaulting and losing their home or car, Chris and Jessica do not owe the lender anything more even if the lender is not able to sell the home or car for the full amount of the debt.

The breathing spell afforded by the automatic stay also gives Chris and Jessica time to deal with their problems on a mortgage or car loan. If they have not missed payments, they might simply continue making payments and let the loan "ride through" the bankruptcy case. Many creditors are happy with a performing loan rather than insisting on whatever technical rights they might have because of the bankruptcy filing. That is, creditors are often better off if Chris and Jessica can continue to perform their promise on the loan by making payments. The creditor's alternative of foreclosure or repossession will be costly and likely result in a low recovery. More likely, however, Chris and Jessica will have missed payments, meaning they will need to look to other options available in bankruptcy.

For a car loan in a chapter 7, Chris and Jessica have the option of *re-deeming* the car. They would pay the creditor the full value of the car, which eliminates the lien. The creditor has no choice but to accept payment, although the creditor could contest the value of the car. The difficulties of raising the cash and possibly fighting the creditor over the car's value make redemption an unattractive option. A filer who has the financial wherewithal to raise cash equal to the value of a car likely will not need to file bankruptcy. Only an exceedingly small percentage of filers (1 percent) propose this option.[12]

Another option for Chris and Jessica would be to *reaffirm* the car or home loan. A reaffirmation is an agreement between Chris and Jessica and a creditor to create a new, postbankruptcy debt. The new car loan or mortgage will occur on whatever terms to which they and their creditor agree. The creditor benefits because the agreement promises a greater return than either a repossession or a foreclosure. Chris and Jessica benefit by being able to retain their car or home, especially when their bankruptcy filing makes the prospect of acquiring a new car loan or mortgage unlikely or very expensive. There is a catch. Because it is a new debt, the bankruptcy discharge does not protect Chris and Jessica from the reaffirmed debt. If the reaffirmed loan becomes underwater at a later date, Chris and Jessica will be responsible for the deficiency.

The court must approve any reaffirmation agreement. Chris and Jessica's attorney must certify to the court that the attorney discussed the consequences of the agreement with them and believes that it will not impose an undue hardship on them. Among bankruptcy professionals, reaffirmation agreements can be controversial. Practices regarding reaffirmation agreements and undue hardship certifications vary widely around the country.

The wisdom of reaffirmation agreements is especially controversial in regard to home mortgages. Even if Chris and Jessica are behind on their mortgage, the automatic stay will have stopped any foreclosure process their creditor might have started. Chris and Jessica will have rights under state or federal law to catch up on their missed mortgage payments, up to a limit, and they can use the breathing spell provided by the automatic stay to do so. Chris and Jessica can get relief without creating a new debt through a reaffirmation agreement. These tools are not available, however, for car loans. If their car loan creditor insists on a reaffirmation agreement, they will need to sign one if they want to keep their car.

CHAPTER 13

If Chris and Jessica are typical filers, chapter 7 will bring less expensive, quicker, and broader relief. As noted previously, there are extralegal explanations for why they might end up filing chapter 13. Some people may use chapter 13 for legal reasons, and well-counseled filers will choose chapter 13 if they need to take advantage of one of these reasons.

Chapter 13 requires the filer to propose and the court to approve a repayment plan that lasts for three to five years. Through that plan, people can catch up on their mortgages, car loans, and other secured debts. Broadly speaking, whatever monthly income remains, after making those monthly payments to secured creditors and paying other household expenses, goes toward unsecured debts. Many filers have so little income that nothing goes to paying unsecured debts. The case ends upon completion of the plan. In exchange for binding oneself to the plan, people keep all their property.

If Chris and Jessica make this bargain, they take a big risk. Unlike chapter 7, through which they would almost certainly receive a discharge, Chris and Jessica will receive their discharge only at the end of the plan and only if they make all the plan payments. Of persons who file chapter 7, 95 percent receive a discharge, compared to only 33 percent of those who file chapter 13. Eight percent of chapter 13 cases are converted to chapter 7. These filers receive their discharge through chapter 7.

Bankruptcy law's requirements may account for the high plan failure rates, along with extralegal factors that influence people's chapter choice. Plans have little wiggle room for unexpected expenses, big life changes, or even some expected expenses. Filers struggling with a chapter 13 plan may convert to a chapter 7 or may ask the court to modify the plan to lower payments, but it is expensive and time-consuming to do so. These procedures also often occur long into a case, when the original attorney may no longer be in close communication with the filer. If Chris and Jessica's chapter 13 case is dismissed, it is as if they had not filed bankruptcy at all, and they are back at the mercy of their creditors. They may have paid for a while into a chapter 13 plan, with most or all of the payments going toward the higher chapter 13 attorney's fee, and have nothing to show for their filing. They will still owe the original debts they brought to bankruptcy, plus any interest that has accrued and any associated attorney fees.

Bankruptcy law may require Chris and Jessica to file chapter 13. Congress changed bankruptcy law in 2005 to require a "means test" to force people into chapter 13 when they have a supposed ability to repay creditors. The means test requires filers to use chapter 13 if they meet two conditions. First, their income must be above the state median for a household of the same size. Second, and after deducting monthly mortgage payments, car payments, child support, and household expenses, their income must allow payment to creditors above a statutory minimum. Generally speaking, that statutory minimum is about $250 per month (a figure that is periodically adjusted for inflation), although it could be a lower figure if Chris and Jessica's unsecured debts are less than approximately $60,000. Even if the means test directs a chapter 13 filing, filers can argue they have "special circumstances" to allow a chapter 7 filing.

At the time Congress imposed the means test, experts said there was little evidence that "can pay" debtors were abusing the system by filing bankruptcy.[13] Our data bear that out. The means test forces exceedingly few people into chapter 13. Of the chapter 7 filers in our data, only 8 percent had income above the state median income, and only 1 percent had enough income that they could pay the statutory minimum. The court allowed all of them to proceed in chapter 7, likely because of the "special circumstances" rule. Of the chapter 13 filers in our data, 24 percent had an income above the state median. Many of those would not have the income left to pay unsecured creditors the statutory minimum, but the bankruptcy schedules do not allow us to compute an exact number. Chapter 13 filers tend to have higher incomes than chapter 7 filers. If we conservatively assume that three times as many chapter 13 filers could meet the statutory minimum payment—the same ratio as those above state median income in chapter 13 as compared to chapter 7—then the means test forces only about 3 percent of all bankruptcy filers into chapter 13.

For some persons, chapter 13 offers special benefits that make it a better option. The paradigmatic cases are people with valuable property they might lose in chapter 7, especially if they have fallen behind on their home mortgage. Chris and Jessica cannot alter the terms of their mortgage, but they can catch up on missed mortgage payments through their chapter 13 plan. They can "cure and reinstate" the mortgage by making up the missed payments, stretched over three to five years. The same rules apply to missed car loan payments. So long as they continue to make payments during the plan, they will be protected from creditor actions. If they make all the payments, chapter 13 will have been a valuable tool, working exactly as designed to give Chris and Jessica a fresh start while minimizing harm to creditors. The more demands the chapter 13 plan makes on their income, however, the less likely they are to be part of the fortunate 33 percent of chapter 13 filers who make it all the way through the plan and receive a discharge. If Chris and Jessica are part of the larger group whose cases are dismissed, their mortgage and car lenders are likely to proceed with foreclosure and repossession.

Chapter 13 also has some provisions that address specific situations that can make it work well for a few filers. For example, chapter 13 discharges some debts that chapter 7 does not, most significantly civil fines such as parking tickets. If someone's car has been impounded for unpaid parking tickets, chapter 13 will allow them to get the car back without much hassle, catch up on any missed car loan payments, discharge the parking tickets, and keep their car after their bankruptcy case ends. Another chapter 13 provision allows a filer to pay tax debts in full without paying the interest. In both instances, the person must successfully complete the chapter 13 plan.

If Chris and Jessica file chapter 13, they will need to start making payments under their proposed plan within thirty days of filing and even before the court has approved the plan. If they miss any of these payments, the court will dismiss their case. If the court has not approved the plan—*confirmed* in bankruptcy argot—at the time of dismissal, they will receive a refund for any payments they made. Similar to chapter 7, a chapter 13 trustee will preside over a section 341 meeting and question Chris and Jessica about their financial affairs. Chris and Jessica will make their plan payments to the trustee, who will forward the payments on to creditors.

Chapter 13 trustees oversee all the cases in a geographic area, such as a city or a region of a state. They essentially run small businesses, with millions of dollars flowing through their offices and bank accounts each year. The expenses of this business, including an annual salary for the trustee and any employees, are funded by a percentage of the payments coming through the office. The US Trustee Program sets the percentage for each trustee, which is capped at 10 percent. The chapter 13 trustee will oversee all aspects of Chris and Jessica's case, including objecting to their plan if the trustee believes Chris and Jessica are not committing a sufficient portion of their income to it. Chris and Jessica, through their lawyer, can respond to the trustee's objections, and it is ultimately up to the court to decide. In some judicial districts, the chapter 13 trustee runs the financial management course Chris and Jessica must take before receiving a discharge. Some trustees take this obligation quite seriously and offer meaningful training to help people navigate their financial lives during and after the bankruptcy case. Most filers are not lucky enough to live in a judicial district where this occurs.

Even more than chapter 7 trustees, a chapter 13 trustee plays a major role in the outcome a filer will experience. Bankruptcy judges heavily rely on the chapter 13 trustees assigned to their courts. One scholar characterized it as a "superdelegation" of the bankruptcy court's authority, including one local practice she witnessed in which a chapter 13 trustee presided over an "unofficial" court hearing before the real court hearing began.[14]

Chris and Jessica's decision to file chapter 13 will shape their view of the bankruptcy system, likely more so than if they decided to file chapter 7, however they make that choice. If they are like most of the people who file bankruptcy, they first will face years of financial problems that lead them to struggle with paying their debts. The next chapter draws from people's stories of living with financial precarity to detail their prebankruptcy lives.

# 2 Struggling to Survive

I was let go from my job 3 days before my 10 year anniversary. It was devastating. I tried and tried but could not get work. My unemployment ran out, then my insurance ran out, then I used up my retirement money. I always had excellent credit even during the time of not working. Then [three years later], I ended up hospitalized and needing gallbladder surgery. The 1st hospital kicked me out after 6 days because I had no money or insurance. The medical emergency put me over 150K in debt. As the retirement $ began to run low I started using credit cards for my medicines, gasoline, food, etc. Not good. The rest is history. I finally have a job earning what I did before. Humiliating.

—Fifty-three-year-old single, biracial woman

People want to keep their promises, pay their debts, and maintain financial self-reliance.[1] Not doing so signals a lack of personal responsibility. Filing bankruptcy is nothing if not a failure to follow through on one's promises and an admission of needing help. For this reason, we should expect people to go to exceptional lengths to avoid it. Our data show that most people put off filing bankruptcy for years.

Many people who eventually file bankruptcy try to save face and stave off the inevitable. They postpone talking with a bankruptcy attorney for months or even years. During that time, they use a range of strategies to make good on their debts—many of which involve taking on more debt to pay old debts. They also forego some of life's basic necessities, such as medical attention, car repairs, and food, and they fall behind on rent and mortgage payments. For some, the stress of their situation causes physical and mental suffering.

Scholars have described the time before bankruptcy as living in a "sweatbox."[2] Another apt description might be a pressure cooker—with bankruptcy serving as the release valve. Our data necessarily come from bankruptcy filers, but those data illustrate the suffering of Americans in financial distress more broadly. Despite their dire stories, the people who file bankruptcy have one advantage over those who do not. All got at least some relief upon filing.

## REASONS FOR FILING

For decades, social scientists have warned of the increased financial precarity in the lives of Americans. Sociologist and anthropologist Katherine Newman described how extraneous and unpredictable events resulted in economic hardship and downward mobility among middle-class families—many of whom never recovered.[3] Political scientist Jacob Hacker detailed how changes in economic policies shifted the costs associated with health care, education, and retirement onto individuals.[4] More recently, sociologist Matthew Desmond chronicled how weakened unions, low wages, housing costs, and unequal banking and tax policies have allowed poverty to persist in the United States.[5]

As a result of these financial realities, many people experience economic fragility for much of their lives. One stumble may lead to an unrecoverable financial downfall. For example, in 2022, people with savings accounts held a median of $8,000 in those accounts, excluding retirement funds. More than half of households could not cover a $1,000 unexpected expense.[6] A new set of all-weather tires might cost $1,000. The average cost for a dental crown for people without insurance is more than a thousand dollars, as is the cost of a new refrigerator. Emergency veterinarian visits for the family pet often will cost more than a thousand dollars.

For the majority of households, these relatively small, unexpected expenses will significantly strain their budgets. They may fall behind on a rent or mortgage payment, leading to eviction or foreclosure. Others may have their cars repossessed, leaving them struggling to get to work or get their kid to childcare. Still others may face debt collection that results in wage garnishment, which will hinder their ability to pay their debts.

The leading financial causes of bankruptcy have held constant for decades: declines in income and medical expenses consistently top the list of people's reasons for filing.[7] We gave bankruptcy filers a list of eleven items and asked which among them contributed to their bankruptcy.[8] Seventy-eight percent said that a decline in income was a reason for their bankruptcy. This income decline could have resulted from a job loss, a reduction in hours at work, a parent taking time off to have a baby or care for a sick child, or a transition into retirement. A forty-six-year-old man described how job loss followed by a string of lower-paying subsequent jobs led to his and his wife's bankruptcy.

> I lost my job several years ago which was good pay and benefits. Since then I have had four jobs, each paying less and no benefits. After my last job was done, seven months ago, we have exhausted all emergency funds.... We maxed out credit cards hoping to hold on 'till I got back to work.... Me and my wife [decided] that even if I did find work it would take 5 years minimum to get back to "normal" and I could not get laid off, which has happened four times in five years (I am a carpenter). So we filed chapter 7.

Sixty-five percent of filers reported that their bankruptcy stemmed from medical issues, defined as either excessive medical expenses or medical problems that led to missed work. Even something seemingly as minor as a broken ankle can lead to bankruptcy, as evidenced by the comments of a World War II veteran.

> My wife fell and broke bones.... She was trying to seek employment but this incident put a stop to this. The hospital and doctor bills went to $120,000.00, which we could not pay out of my [retirement].... We were paying all of our bills until [this happened] but just had to file bankruptcy because we couldn't pay her hospital & doctor bills.

This couple's path to bankruptcy reflects the financial precarity caused by the confluence of linking health insurance with employment, the difficulties of holding a job while dealing with medical issues, and the costs of health care. Almost half of employees participate in health-care plans provided by their employers.[9] Tying health insurance to employment makes health insurance nonportable. An interruption in employment comes with a loss of insurance that will have to be remedied by someone finding another job or enrolling in an expensive health insurance plan, such as through COBRA.[10] Unfortunately, the increasing instability and unpredictability of employment since the late 1970s has exacerbated the potential for losing health insurance.[11] And a health crisis, either for oneself or for one's dependents, can result in the loss of a job. Without health insurance, and sometimes even with health insurance, that health crisis can cost tens of thousands of dollars. People's reasons for filing bankruptcy reflect these employment and health-care realities.

## HOW LONG THEY STRUGGLED

Filing bankruptcy is neither a trivial nor inconsequential decision. It might be considered one of those exclamation points that can occur over the life course, like getting divorced or having major surgery. In a perfect world, people would know when their financial futures are best served by cutting their losses via bankruptcy, like a dashboard light tells you to change the oil in the car. Obviously, there is no indicator light for one's financial life. Many people postpone filing bankruptcy, trying to stay financially afloat for years. Like the car engine that is damaged from running without enough oil for too long, for the people who eventually file bankruptcy, their personal and financial lives often have suffered significantly in the time leading up to their filings.

We asked people how long they seriously struggled with their debts before they filed bankruptcy.[12] For simplicity of presentation throughout our analyses, we group the responses into three categories—short strugglers, modest strugglers, and long strugglers. Table 2.1 reports how the responses break down into these categories and compares our current data to responses from people who filed bankruptcy in 2007. Consistently, very few filers seriously struggled for less than six months. The percentages of short and modest strugglers both have trended slightly downward since 2007.

The overwhelming majority of filers are long strugglers, people who fought to make ends meet for at least two years. They now make up

*Table 2.1.*   Time Frames in Which Respondents Seriously Struggled with Debt before Bankruptcy

|  | 2007 (%) | 2013–2023 (%) |
|---|---|---|
| Short strugglers | | |
| Not at all | 3 | 3 |
| Less than 6 months | 7 | 4 |
| Modest strugglers | | |
| 6 months to 1 year | 20 | 10 |
| 1 to 2 years | 27 | 20 |
| Long strugglers | | |
| 2 to 5 years | 31 | 37 |
| More than 5 years | 13 | 26 |

63 percent of bankruptcy filers. Most notably, since 2007 the percentage of filers who struggled for more than five years has doubled from 13 to 26 percent.[13]


## ALL THEIR BEST EFFORTS

During the months and years before people came to terms with the magnitude of their financial situation and filed bankruptcy, most employed multiple coping strategies to stay afloat. We provided people with a list of fourteen common things that they or their spouse or partner may have done during the two years before filing to make ends meet. Figure 2.1 depicts the most common coping strategies, by time spent struggling: accepting or borrowing money from family members or friends, putting necessities on credit cards, working more hours at a current job or seeking additional employment, pawning personal property, taking out payday or car title loans, and withdrawing savings from retirement accounts.

Unfortunately, most of these coping strategies likely worsened people's financial situations. To buy necessities, 65 percent of filers took out debt in the form of using a credit card. Although not nearly as expensive as

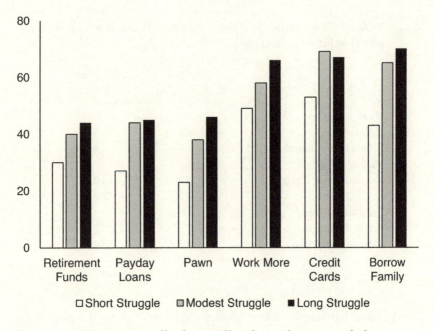

*Figure 2.1.* Coping strategies of bankruptcy filers during the two years before bankruptcy, by length of time spent struggling

fringe banking products, such as payday and title loans, credit cards come with annual interest rates nearing 20 percent and penalty interest rates, triggered upon late payments, of upward of 30 percent.[14] Paying for gas, food, electricity, or prescription medications with a credit card digs the financial hole even deeper. Nonetheless, during times of financial struggles, there may be little choice but to use credit cards for necessities. If the fuel gauge reads empty, and one needs to drive to work or get the kids to daycare, the gas goes on the credit card. The same happens when people are hungry or need a prescription filled. A thirty-nine-year-old married woman with two children wrote about paying off debt by taking on more debt.

> We can afford our house and bills, but medical bills and routine bills became too much. We took out loans to pay off credit cards that were full of utility payments and gas and groceries. . . . I lost my job after 14 years with zero

notice. As the main source of income in the house, we were screwed. We had to stop all payments to keep the house, car, and utilities on.

This couple took out loans to pay off credit cards from financial technology companies that specialized in debt consolidation and peer-to-peer lending. These companies can be thought of as offering new ways to take out a loan other than from a mainstream bank. They can create the same cycles of indebtedness as payday and car title lenders do.

Forty-two percent of filers turned to payday and car title lenders to make ends meet. These loans, which often come with interest rates upward of 600 percent annually, are financial disasters waiting to happen.[15] Borrowers routinely pay more in interest and fees than their initial loan. The average borrower uses more than a third of their income to pay the loan, and 90 percent of payday lenders' profits come from borrowers who take out five or more loans per year.[16] Twenty percent of car title loan borrowers lose their vehicles due to loan default.[17] Payday and car title loans also take a physical toll on many borrowers: those who rely on fringe banking report poorer health than those who do not.[18]

A sixty-six-year-old disabled man described his experience with a payday lender: "I needed to go to my mother's funeral in Puerto Rico. Pay Day loan tell me to call and they will work with me for the payment, but that was bull. . . . [T]hey took all the money that I borrow plus the interest from my bank account. . . . Pay Day loan Sucks."

An alternative tactic to taking out debt to pay debt was to get rid of property, at least temporarily. Forty-one percent of filers pawned personal property to make ends meet. Compared to payday and title loans, pawnshop loans can look less risky. The most people will lose is their property. But pawnbrokers generally only loan 20 to 60 percent of an item's value. People must pawn a lot to get a little cash. To retrieve the item, the borrower must pay not only the amount of the initial loan but also the interest that has accrued on the loan, which is generally around 200 percent. Some brokers also charge additional fees for insurance and storage.[19] As a result, pawning items often amounts to selling property for cash at a fraction of the property's value.

People also commonly withdrew or borrowed from retirement funds as a way to stay afloat during their time struggling. Forty-one percent of filers reported using this strategy. A middle-aged man combined this strategy with taking on debt during the years leading up to his filing. "Experienced a layoff from our jobs where both me and my spouse worked for the same company. After being laid off, it took some time to find new employment. During that time, we used our retirement savings along with credit cards to survive."

Using retirement savings may keep food on the table, gas in the car, and a creditor or two at bay, and it may initially appear to be a more practical way to pay for expenses than taking on more debt. However, withdrawing funds from a 401(k) plan or IRA before the age of fifty-nine and a half will result in the IRS levying a penalty of 10 percent as well as often paying income taxes on the withdrawal.[20] For example, a person who withdrew $10,000 and had a 22 percent marginal tax rate, as our median filer would, will pay a $1,000 penalty and $2,200 in federal taxes, leaving the individual with only $6,800 before state or local income taxes take another few hundred dollars. Employees also may borrow from their 401(k) plans (but not IRAs). Although most workers who borrow from their 401(k) plans pay back the loan with interest, default rates skyrocket to above 80 percent for workers who leave their employment.[21] The median bankruptcy filer in our data has changed jobs within the past three years, suggesting many present the higher risk of default. Using retirement savings has serious financial consequences and is not a free pass. It also reduces the money available for the person's final years, a time when age or health will make it increasingly difficult to find another job.

Rather than put expenses on credit cards or withdraw from retirement accounts, perhaps because neither option remains available, people may turn to their networks for help. Sixty-six percent of filers accepted or borrowed money from family or friends. If the money is a gift, there may be few financial downsides to this strategy. But if it is a loan, bearing or not bearing interest, then the person's total debt load continues to increase. Regardless of whether the money comes in the form of a loan or a gift, accepting help from family and friends may bring feelings of shame and vulnerability. It goes against people's desire to maintain financial self-reliance. Yet this is one of people's top three coping mechanisms, evidencing the lengths to which people will go to try to pay their debts in the years before they file bankruptcy.

In addition to turning to family and friends for help and putting necessities on credit cards, people's other most commonly used coping
mechanism was to work more hours or get another job. Sixty-one percent of filers indicated they used this strategy, which is considerably more
than the eighteen percent of all households that report working a "side
hustle."[22] This strategy has the most potential to improve a household's
financial situation. Despite how straightforward and effective this choice
might seem, working more comes with costs: increased daycare expense if
there are children in the home, decreased time with family, decreased lei-
sure time, and increased transportation costs. Working more hours is also
associated with poorer diets, decreased exercise, increased use of alcohol
and tobacco, and increased likelihood of heart attack (especially among
lower-income individuals) and stroke.[23]

Our data paint a picture of people who are determined to get caught up
on their debts and willing to try numerous methods to avoid bankruptcy.
There is nothing to suggest that they are eager to walk away from what
they owe. The data also show a not entirely unexpected trend. As reflected
in figure 2.1, the longer a household postpones filing, the more likely they
are to employ coping strategies and the more strategies they will employ.
Unfortunately, for people who file bankruptcy, the various strategies, including even working more hours, ultimately fail. Although bankruptcy
will help with their debts through the discharge, their time struggling
often has diminished their assets, such as through pawning and liquidat-
ing retirement accounts, which decreases their postbankruptcy financial
security and their ability to benefit from the discharge.

## CONSEQUENCES OF DELAYING BANKRUPTCY: SUFFERING ASSET DEPLETION, PRIVATIONS, AND STRESS

In the months and years before bankruptcy, people work hard to regain
some financial stability. Our data suggest that, despite their best efforts,
this time instead is marked by loss and suffering. People's financial situations further deteriorate the longer they postpone filing. They experience
serious deprivations in their day-to-day lives. And the stress of their indebtedness causes substantial emotional and physical injury.

*Asset Depletion*

Table 2.2 shows how financially strained people become by the time they file. For example, their total unsecured debts—credit cards, medical bills, and student loans—are between $40,000 and $50,000. Most filers' debt-to-income ratios are over two-to-one, meaning that they have twice as much debt as their annual income. To put it another way, they would have to put all their income toward their debts for two years to pay it. Across the board, bankruptcy filers are in bad financial shape.

Comparatively, long strugglers face dreadful financial situations. Short and modest strugglers have thousands of dollars more in assets, which decreases their debt-to-asset ratios as compared to long strugglers. These assets make their recovery after bankruptcy more likely to be successful. Long strugglers also bring considerably more unsecured debt with them to bankruptcy. As shown in figure 2.1, long strugglers put necessities on credit cards to make ends meet, which may have caused credit card balances to balloon through accumulated interest, in turn increasing unsecured debts.

Two other data points reflect the financial chaos that comes with struggling longer: the percent of homeowners and the percent with liens on their homes.[24] Especially compared to modest strugglers, fewer long strugglers are homeowners, possibly because they were forced to sell their

*Table 2.2.*   Median Financial Characteristics, by Length of Struggle

|  | Long Strugglers | Modest Strugglers | Short Strugglers |
|---|---|---|---|
| Total assets | $28,707 | $44,597 | $40,803 |
| Secured debts | $18,503 | $31,711 | $27,214 |
| Unsecured debts | $51,791 | $41,668 | $40,564 |
| Total debts | $102,769 | $100,640 | $100,675 |
| Annual income | $47,334 | $45,792 | $49,014 |
| Total debts/assets (ratio) | 2.42 | 1.72 | 1.74 |
| Total debts/annual income (ratio) | 2.22 | 2.23 | 2.18 |
| Homeowners | 38% | 46% | 38% |
| Homeowners with liens | 12% | 7% | 8% |

homes or experienced foreclosure. Long strugglers are almost twice as likely to have liens on their homes, suggesting legal actions by creditors.

## Privations

Our survey provides an unparalleled opportunity to explore what people cut from their budgets prior to bankruptcy, as they struggled to pay their debts. We asked filers what they and others in their households went without in the two years before bankruptcy and provided them with a list of fourteen common privations.[25] Filers who responded to our survey could choose as many privations as they or others in their household experienced. Bankruptcy filers, and many of their family members, including children, experienced substantial privations. Table 2.3 reports the distribution of these sacrifices.

People were most likely to go without health care. We asked people if they went without one of four types of health care: dental care, doctor visits or surgery, medication or prescriptions, and mental health care. Seventy-three percent of filers indicated that they went without one of these things.

Among these four privations, 63 percent of people reported that someone in their household went without dental care. Among older Americans, about half do not have dental insurance. Medicare does not cover dental

Table 2.3.   Privations Prior to Bankruptcy, by Length of Struggle

|  | Long Strugglers (%) | Modest Strugglers (%) | Short Strugglers (%) |
|---|---|---|---|
| Any health care | 77 | 67 | 54 |
| Dental care | 68 | 57 | 42 |
| Medical attention | 56 | 45 | 31 |
| Prescriptions | 45 | 37 | 22 |
| Mental health therapy | 33 | 22 | 15 |
| Car maintenance | 74 | 66 | 45 |
| Late mortgage or rent | 68 | 57 | 39 |
| Retirement savings | 53 | 46 | 33 |

care and without that coverage, it may simply be too costly.[26] Insurance providers estimate costs of between $700 and $2,100 for a root canal and between $500 and $2,500 for a crown.[27] An eighty-year-old widow wrote that her radiation treatments for cancer severely damaged her teeth, but since she did not have dental insurance, she could not afford the much-needed dental work. A single mother of four who worked as a paralegal used another option to deal with her dental issues. "Root canals and crowns were not covered by [my insurance], so I had to just have them pulled."

Fifty-two percent of filers indicated that they or someone else in the household went without medical attention, such as doctor visits or surgery. For example, a retired woman who brought in extra money by doing laundry for others wrote: "Unable to afford routine care such as pap smear, lab work, mammograms etc. I broke my foot & could not afford care. Treated self & now have foot deformity." A thirty-five-year-old man who worked in a bakery described the medical treatment he could not afford: "The metal pins in my leg and arm from surgery need to be removed. They are causing pain and numbness but I can't afford to have them taken out."

Filers also went without prescription drugs. Forty-one percent indicated that they were unable to afford medications, such as insulin, seizure medication, blood pressure medication, and prescriptions for ADHD and depression. Given that prescription medications sold in the United States are, on average, 240 percent more expensive than in peer nations, such as Austria, Japan, the United Kingdom, and Germany, this privation is not unexpected.[28] A sixty-one-year-old single woman, who filed for medical reasons, wrote: "Have chronic illness, went without asthma medications for 2 years, no insurance, meds cost over $600 a month."

Finally, 29 percent of filers said that they or someone in their household went without mental health care. A sixty-five-year-old single woman with more than $50,000 in unsecured debt wrote that the most important thing she went without before filing was "[m]ental health care. I feel that excessive spending was manic behavior related to chronic depression. Finances spiraled out of control." If she had access to therapy, one must wonder whether she would have needed to file bankruptcy.

After medical care, a close second privation was to skip car maintenance or repair, which 70 percent of filers reported going without. As discussed in chapter 3, federal transportation policies have turned the United

States into a "car-centered society."[29] Most people have little to no access to reliable public transit. Skimping on car maintenance is risky. It saves money in the short term, but in the long term, it could cost even more to fix or replace a car that is necessary to get to work, to get the kids to day-care, or to get groceries.

An equally risky privation was paying the mortgage or rent late, which 63 percent of filers indicated that they did. For some, this privation re-sulted in homelessness or moving in with family or friends. A man in his late twenties wrote that to earn more money, he worked odd jobs, doing things that he otherwise would not do, "even dangerous things," when he was unhoused.

> I went homeless for a month, sleeping in whatever unlocked building lob-bies I could find or staying in the cheapest AirBnb/motels I could find be-cause I couldn't afford to renew the lease on the place I was living in. I also couldn't afford to immediately put security deposits and such upfront for a new place, and there weren't many affordable places to begin with. So I just went homeless until I could save up enough money to perhaps secure a se-curity deposit on a rental.

Fifty percent of filers indicated that they discontinued contributions to their retirement accounts. For some, they not only stopped making contri-butions, but they also combined this privation with the coping mechanism of withdrawing money from their retirement accounts. A married woman in her late fifties, whose court records listed nothing in retirement sav-ings, wrote: "Cashed out a previous employer account and took a huge tax penalty." Her husband, also of retirement age, is self-employed. Because they have nothing in retirement, they both likely have many years of work ahead of them.

In addition, 28 percent of filers indicated that they or someone in their household took the desperate step of going without food in the two years prior to filing. A comment written by a woman who is disabled, is married, and has a teenaged child is reminiscent of the Dust Bowl or Great De-pression era. The most important things that she and her loved ones went without before filing were: "Shoes, toilet paper, soap, shampoo. Had to eat cheap food like bread, potatoes, and cabbage. We never got meat except bologna or canned meat."

Table 2.3 again illustrates that the longer one postpones filing bankruptcy, the more they will suffer. The difference between long and short strugglers' use of most privations is generally at least twenty percentage points. The discrepancy increases to almost thirty percentage points for paying the mortgage or rent late and foregoing car repairs and maintenance.

## Stress

Research describes the physiological and psychological consequences of stress. For example, Mayo Clinic reports that periods of stress cause the release of high levels of adrenaline and cortisol. The constant exposure and overexposure of these hormones affects the brain, body, and immune system, resulting in numerous mental and physical health problems: anxiety, depression, diabetes, headaches, fatigue, inability to concentrate, loss of sexual desire, frequent infections or illnesses, muscle pain, insomnia, obesity, autoimmune diseases, PTSD, heart disease, heart attack, high blood pressure, stroke, and cognitive impairment.[30] People under considerable stress also experience reduced mental "bandwidth" that interferes with focus. Among older people, stress correlates with "lower cognitive scores and a faster rate of cognitive decline."[31]

Specific to financial precarity, economic hardship taxes people's minds and impedes their ability to make wise financial decisions.[32] Indebtedness, specifically, is highly stressful. Struggling with debt triggers a range of negative emotions, such as "fear, frustration, anxiety, and despair."[33] Debt-caused stress prior to filing bankruptcy can also result in damaged or destroyed marriages.[34] And owing unsecured debts, like payday loans, credit card debt, and student loans, is considerably more stressful than owing secured debts, like mortgage and car loans.[35]

Debt-related physical and emotional distress prior to filing is quite common. We asked people: "Before the bankruptcy, did you have any physical, mental, or emotional health problems that were *caused or made worse by the stress of the debts*?" Fifty-two percent of respondents said they experienced physical or emotional distress because of the strain of the debts. Thirty-five percent said the same was true for a spouse or partner.[36]

Our respondents left us over one thousand heart-wrenching descriptions of their physical and emotional trauma before filing bankruptcy. Examples of mental health problems from the stress of the debts included depression, anxiety, panic attacks, anger and rage, bipolar episodes, hopelessness, fear, uncontrollable bouts of crying, and even thoughts of suicide. People described physical problems such as sleeplessness, fatigue, hives, migraines, seizures, lack of sexual desire and sexual dysfunction, changes in appetite resulting in extreme changes in weight, intestinal issues, shingles, drug and alcohol abuse, heart palpitations, trouble breathing, diabetes, high blood pressure, exacerbated fibromyalgia and rheumatoid arthritis, heart attack, stroke, and cancer.

A thirty-nine-year-old man who worked as a retail store manager described his depression and rage.

> I would have weeks to months at a time where I got so depressed that I couldn't function. My performance at work suffered, my relationships suffered, and I was hopeless. On my days off, I would lay in bed and do absolutely nothing until I had to go to work again. I would also get incredibly angry and I would hold it all in for the sake of everyone around me. My hopelessness and anger finally exploded and I screamed at my boss and threatened him in front of his boss and other employees. I was fired immediately. After that I would lay in bed and hope that something would kill me.

Others shared that emotional stress led to suicidal thoughts or suicide attempts. A man in his midthirties wrote: "Hard to sleep, hard to eat, thoughts of suicide, stomach ulcers, headaches. Just HELL." Another man about the same age actually tried to end his life: "Attempted suicide which resulted in a spleen removal and extended stay in the hospital and then psychiatric ward; untreated depression and anxiety; alcoholism."

For some people, emotional distress caused stomach problems and eating issues—either losing or gaining large amounts of weight. The same individual who described being homeless and sleeping in unlocked building lobbies wrote: "I've gained 80 pounds in just the last two or three years and I now have a non-alcoholic fatty liver and high cholesterol because the stress and depression of all of this makes it difficult to focus on exercising, eating right, etc. . . . Let alone I often can't afford good food."

Other filers indicated that stress caused or worsened high blood pressure. A middle-aged woman described her reaction to the stress in the following way: "Anxiety, panic attacks, insomnia. I have been on blood pressure meds for about 5 years but within the past two years placed on a beta blocker to slow my resting heart rate." She continued: "Please just know that it got to a really bad place. Sometimes I thought I might be worth more to my children and grandchildren if I were not here. I do not feel this way any longer."

Some people had even more extreme physical responses to debt. A woman in her mid-fifties wrote that after her first stroke, she fell behind on her bills, including her mortgage. She thought that her second stroke resulted from the stress of being unable to catch up on her mortgage and afford her medications. The second stroke left her disabled, and she was not able to return to work.

A sixty-year-old woman described the most catastrophic response to the stresses of the debts: "My husband went into ER. Stroke or aneurysm. He was brain dead. 54 years old. One year prior he had a kidney transplant. All of the stress of the house, car, and bills were too much."

Once again, comparing physical and emotional distress among filers shows that the more time spent struggling to pay debts, the greater the likelihood people experienced new or worsened illnesses. Specifically, 30 percent of short strugglers and 45 percent of modest strugglers reported worsened health problems. In contrast, among long strugglers, 58 percent reported worsening health problems. People reported that their spouses and partners experienced a similar trend: 21 percent of short strugglers' spouses and partners, 31 percent of modest strugglers' spouses and partners, and 39 percent of long strugglers' spouses and partners endured health declines. The longer one tries to repay their debts, the more likely they are to suffer, and often in destructive ways.

Debtors' various hardships speak to the often asserted claim that many people who file bankruptcy are opportunists. In signing the onerous 2005 amendments to the bankruptcy law, President George W. Bush stated: "In recent years, too many people have abused the bankruptcy laws. They've walked away from debts even when they had the ability to repay them."[37] Opportunists would not sacrifice essential needs, suffer extreme physical and mental distress because of the strain of the debts, or seriously struggle for years when faced with such hardships.

## WHY RESIST? WHY CONCEDE?

The time prior to filing bankruptcy can be packed with financial hardship and extreme physical and emotional distress. People who struggle to pay their debts the longest suffer the most. Financial precarity seemingly breeds more financial precarity. As such, when it becomes apparent that repaying their debt is improbable, and people begin to make sacrifices, turn to multiple coping mechanisms, and experience health consequences, why do more people not prioritize themselves and their loved ones over their creditors and file bankruptcy sooner? That is, why do long strugglers make up the largest group of filers? Research shows that people want to make good on their debts and find pride in financial self-sufficiency. Our data show that many people who ultimately cannot live up to their promises and must file bankruptcy feel ashamed and guilty.

### Shame, Guilt, and Fear

In our survey, we gave people a list of major emotions and asked how much they agreed or disagreed that they experienced each of them at the time of their bankruptcy filing. Their responses provide insight into potential reasons that they postponed filing. People commonly felt shame, guilt, and fear. Regardless of how long they struggled, at least half of filers indicated that they felt these emotions "somewhat" or "a great deal" (as opposed to "not at all" or "a little bit"). The only exception was the fear of short strugglers. Table 2.4 breaks down filers' reported emotions by their length of struggle and shows the longer people struggled, the more likely they were to report these negative emotions.

Filers' reports of feeling shame and guilt likely relate to their inability to make good on their debts. Financial security and self-sufficiency are central components of the American dream.[38] Filing bankruptcy means reneging on obligations. It means breaking promises.

A couple who wrote about their feelings upon filing bankruptcy were both well educated and worked as therapists.

> We have taken a Dave Ramsey course which was very enlightening however the min payment hurdles were so overwhelming that we were never able to gain traction. . . . Filing was not a decision that was made lightly. Guilt,

*Table 2.4.*  Filers' Emotions, by Length of Struggle

|  | Long Strugglers (%) | Modest Strugglers (%) | Short Strugglers (%) |
|---|---|---|---|
| Shame | 68 | 61 | 54 |
| Guilt | 62 | 57 | 51 |
| Fear | 53 | 54 | 44 |

shame, failure, fear for our future, and feelings of dread were dealt with on a daily basis. We have/are working hard to lay a foundation of better fiscal responsibility and are sharing those changes w/ our kids. We are grateful for a "clean slate" and do not ever want to be our old selves again.

While not as common as either shame or guilt, filers also feel substantial fear before filing. This is reflected in this comment from a sixty-six-year-old widow: "I put off doing this [filing bankruptcy] a long time, I was ashamed, afraid, suspicious . . . felt it wrong to not pay bills." For most people, the bankruptcy system is wholly unfamiliar and intimidating. The required paperwork is complicated and overwhelming and demands considerable personal information; interactions with attorneys and judges, all people whose social status is elevated and who have considerable control over debtors' futures, is required; and individuals' personal and financial failures become public.[39]

Filers might also fear what may come postbankruptcy. Bankruptcy law cannot solve the problems that led many people into the financial spiral that resulted in filing. It does not cure medical issues. It does not fix employment problems. It neither provides additional education to boost income potential nor discharges student loans. Mortgage and car loan payments will continue. Everyday expenses will remain. Chapters 3 and 7, which discuss homeownership and single women's filings, respectively, detail further people's trepidation about what might transpire with their ability to remain financially afloat postbankruptcy.

Table 2.4 shows that long strugglers were more likely to report feeling shame, guilt, and fear upon filing bankruptcy. Short strugglers were the least likely to report feeling these three negative emotions. Taken together, this may explain, in part, why those who seriously struggled to pay back their debts for two or more years despite suffering financial, physical, and mental hardships postponed bankruptcy for so long.

## Capitulation

Powerful negative emotions seem to have delayed most of our respondents from filing bankruptcy for months or years. Our data suggest that calls from debt collectors and legal actions, such as wage garnishments, pushed people to finally seek relief from the pressure cooker of their financial struggles.

Annually, debt collectors contact more than seventy million Americans— about one-third of consumers—most often about credit card or medical debt. Debt collectors can contact people by phone, mail, email, text, or social media platforms, such as Facebook and Instagram.[40] Debtors often say that they feel harassed or threatened by collectors, many of whom contact borrowers multiple times a week, refuse to honor requests to stop calling, and often call at inconvenient times during the day.[41]

Seventy-seven percent of bankruptcy filers cited debt collection as a precipitator of their filing. People who wrote their story of bankruptcy reported similar experiences with debt collectors. A married couple in their late forties, who had been seriously struggling with their debts for at least five years, described their reaction to collection calls.

> We always thought we could get ourselves out of this, we never wanted to file bankruptcy. Filing bankruptcy for us is like a sense of failure. We needed to file so the phone calls would stop, collection people have no heart. We had to file so we could put more food on the table, get the medication every month that is needed.

If collection calls fail to produce results, creditors and debt collectors may file a lawsuit, typically in state court, to compel payment. If the court finds the debtor liable for the debt, likely the default result if the debtor does not appear at the hearing, the court may order wage garnishment. At any given time in the United States, about one in one hundred employees' wages are being garnished. The average garnishment lasts five months and amounts to 11 percent of the employee's gross earnings—more than most households spend on food each month. Researchers studying the financial effects of wage garnishment have commented that "[t]he magnitude of these collections raises the possibility that unexpected wage garnishment could severely strain workers' budgets and cause them to fall behind on other bills, thus potentially perpetuating a cycle of debt."[42]

Based on the stories they wrote, for some filers, the threat of wage garnishment trumped their shame, guilt, and fear. Their stories also suggest that researchers' predictions about the potential for wage garnishment to result in complete financial collapse are not unfounded. A married woman in her late twenties, who made $35,000 per year before taxes and who reported seriously struggling to pay her debts for five years or more before filing, wrote.

> I lost hours at work and fell behind. Then family members that lived with us and shared bills passed away and made it hard for us to just make the rent. I started getting lots of calls from creditors and they started garnishing my wages. I barely make it on what I make, so I had no choice but to file.

Wage garnishment led to tragedy for a forty-four-year-old man. "I should've filed for bankruptcy when I had my first judgements. My family wouldn't have had to suffer during my garnishments. I could've afforded an oxygen machine for my mother." His mother had been diagnosed with stage 5 kidney disease and needed oxygen. The doctors postponed admitting his mother to the hospital, so he needed to purchase the oxygen machine to use at home. He could not afford the machine, and his mother died.

## SURVIVING IN THE SWEATBOX

The reasons that people turn to bankruptcy for help have held constant for decades: declines in income and costs associated with medical care. Chapters 4 and 5 discuss how medical care has grown costlier as well as how earning a living wage has become more precarious. We link these leading reasons for filing bankruptcy to the loading of financial risk onto households. People also seriously struggle to repay their debts longer. They apparently are not rushing the bankruptcy courts to stiff their creditors.

Instead, consistent with people's drive to fulfill their promises, to be financially self-reliant, and to show personal responsibility, when they file, they feel shame and guilt, suggesting that these emotions play a role in their postponement of bankruptcy. Indeed, it is creditors' actions—debt collection in and out of courts, as detailed in chapter 9—that, in part, push people to finally file bankruptcy.

People's time in the sweatbox is often exceedingly difficult. They fall further into debt and sacrifice some of life's most important necessities, such as health care and food, because they simply cannot afford the expense. People suffer extreme physical and emotional hardship: sleeplessness, migraines, seizures, drug and alcohol abuse, diabetes, high blood pressure, heart attack, stroke, depression, anxiety, rage, bipolar incidents, and suicidal ideation. Because most households in the sweatbox cannot afford health care, these crises likely go untreated.

Those who postpone filing bankruptcy often enter it with relatively few assets, especially if they have struggled longer. Their depletion of assets, combined with the inability of bankruptcy law to fix their life issues, such as health problems and unaffordable mortgage payments, leaves many fearful of what may come. Subsequent chapters in this book explore how federal and state policies across housing, education, employment, health care, retirement, and lending have imbued people's financial lives with precarity, and bankruptcy law's inability to alleviate that precarity. Although there are ways to make bankruptcy law a more effective solution to people's problems, repairing the tattered social safety net and prioritizing people's financial security are necessary to prevent so many families from spending significant portions of their lives struggling to survive.

# 3 Staying Home and Going Places

> I had credit cards and was doing fine paying them. Then
> I bought a house but the associated expenses were more
> than expected and it became impossible to keep paying
> enough on the credit cards to pay them down because of
> the interest rates going up. I kept a strict budget and
> managed for about a year until an unexpected car accident
> which put me an extra grand in the hole. This made my
> choice for bankruptcy.
>
> —Thirty-eight-year-old, divorced Latina woman

The two most expensive assets that most people will purchase during their lives are homes and cars. Economic and government policies have promoted homeownership and created pathways for funding those purchases, leading people to strive to purchase primary residences rather than rent. Two-thirds of households in the United States own their homes, about 60 percent of which have a mortgage.[1] For decades, federal, state, and local government policies have prioritized driving as the primary means of transportation, compelling the vast majority of people to purchase cars. The rate of car ownership in the United States has remained at around 85 percent for the past two decades.[2] People typically purchase cars with the help of a hefty car loan.[3] Consistent with the push toward homeownership and the necessity for having cars, homes and cars make up the bulk of the property owned by most bankruptcy filers.

This chapter details what the people who file bankruptcy with houses and cars show about the effects of US housing policies and the car economy on individuals and families. It does so by disaggregating the bankruptcy cases in our dataset by those 3,007 filers who own houses and cars

(36%), those 343 filers with houses but who do not own cars (4%), those 4,031 filers who own cars only (48%), and those 928 filers who do not own houses or cars (11%). Fewer of the people who file bankruptcy own houses than the general population. In contrast, bankruptcy filers own cars at the same rate as the population.

For those people who file and own houses, regardless of whether they own cars, their finances show the economic resources that make purchasing a house possible, even if that purchase was a stretch at the time. They cite the typical precipitators of bankruptcy, such as health issues and job loss. But their decisions about how to handle their financial struggles and when during those struggles to file bankruptcy seem to be shaped by worries about keeping their houses and holding onto the American dream of homeownership.

Those filers who own cars, with or without accompanying homeownership, have cars of relatively low value, owe significant amounts on those cars, and hold little equity in those cars. Through their bankruptcies, they seek to hold onto their most valuable and thus often most reliable car. Their use of bankruptcy suggests that the nearly universal imperative of owning a car that transportation policies have imposed on people living across the country—from most cities to suburban towns to rural areas—does not dissipate in the face of financial problems.

## ASPIRING TO HOMEOWNERSHIP

Homeownership is central to the American dream, and US housing policies have long encouraged people to invest in houses. Owning a home can buy access to what people may deem to be better neighborhoods and better schools for their children, and, presumably, to long-term financial stability.[4] Homeownership also has become a marker of middle-class status. People will strive to purchase a house, and they will stretch, even overstretch, their budgets by taking on mortgage loans to do so.

People understandably aspire to homeownership. Mortgage loans generally are considered "good debt"—debt that has the potential to increase one's net worth or future income. Research has found that owning a house has social, psychological, and emotional benefits for children; that homeowners invest more in their property than renters; and that home-owners have a greater sense of community and tend to be more involved in their neighborhoods. Homeownership additionally can serve as forced savings, and for most people the bulk of their wealth consists of equity in their house.[5] Because prices for most houses have appreciated over the long term, many people have benefited financially from homeownership.[6]

The recent history of government policies pushing people toward home-ownership traces back to the late 1980s. At that time housing prices had soared, but wages had stagnated. People had less income to put toward saving for a down payment on a house and ongoing mortgage payments. Still, the government extolled homeownership's benefits. To address the unaffordability of houses, the federal government encouraged lenders to innovate their loan offerings, thereby allowing people who were ineligible for a conventional thirty-year, fixed-rate mortgage that required a 20 per-cent down payment and at least a good credit score to purchase houses via alternative mortgage loans. These innovations included low or no down payment requirements, low initial monthly payments, adjustable interest rates, and high interest (subprime) rates.[7]

Although the Great Recession's foreclosure crisis sparked a push to tighten lending requirements, many of these innovations that allowed people to attain their homeownership dreams in the 1990s and 2000s re-mained available into the 2020s. For example, in 2023 the typical down payment for first-time home buyers was 6 percent.[8] This means that people can stretch to homeownership by taking out conventional mort-gages and mortgages with features that increase their cost. A study analyz-ing homeowners with mortgages found that 28 percent are *cost burdened*, defined as spending more than 30 percent of their incomes on housing costs.[9] Although mortgages continue to be sold to people as good debt, and many mortgages may be good debt, the dream of homeownership still constrains budgets, may add to financial stress during times of troubles, and may lead to financial hardships over time.

## The Financials of Homeownership

The people who file bankruptcy who own houses must balance the po-tential benefits of homeownership against the associated costs of houses,

*Table 3.1.*   Finances of Bankruptcy Filers with Homes, by Car Ownership and Chapter (Medians)

|  | CHAPTER 7 | | CHAPTER 13 | |
|---|---|---|---|---|
|  | *Homes & Cars* | *Homes, No Cars* | *Homes & Cars* | *Homes, No Cars* |
| Total assets | $193,922 | $171,697 | $210,699 | $203,264 |
| Home value | $160,980 | $167,960 | $174,043 | $184,275 |
| Home equity | $14,584 | $18,848 | $19,143 | $30,141 |
| With other real property | 8% | 10% | 13% | 13% |
| Total car value | $10,354 | – | $13,456 | – |
| Total car equity | $1,577 | – | $1,309 | – |
| With retirement assets | 43% | 30% | 37% | 22% |
| Retirement assets | $15,476 | $14,711 | $11,889 | $8,803 |
| Total debts | $245,074 | $222,247 | $232,369 | $211,021 |
| With home loans | 89% | 88% | 89% | 89% |
| Total home loans | $142,230 | $130,176 | $144,039 | $132,257 |
| Total car loans | $7,164 | – | $11,836 | – |
| Total unsecured debt | $60,143 | $51,050 | $34,562 | $17,104 |
| Debt-to-asset ratio | 1.24 | 1.30 | 1.07 | 1.03 |
| Employed | 71% | 63% | 76% | 53% |
| Annual income | $57,360 | $44,664 | $70,668 | $52,302 |
| Debt-to-income ratio | 4.16 | 5.21 | 3.16 | 3.47 |

NOTE: N for homes and cars, ch. 7 is 1,522. N for homes, no cars, ch. 7 is 174. N for homes and cars, ch. 13 is 1,473. N for homes, no cars, ch. 13 is 165. Home value is market value of residential real property.

including the perils of mortgage debt and upkeep expenses. As summarized in table 3.1, they enter bankruptcy with finances showing that they had achieved a level of resources sufficient to purchase a home, even if doing so was a stretch. The table disaggregates those filers with houses who own cars from those without cars. Although few people enter bankruptcy with homes but without cars, their finances differ sufficiently to merit reporting them separately. Overall and at the median, homeowners who file bankruptcy have houses worth $168,196, owe $140,333 on home mortgages, and have $17,028 of equity in their houses.

As detailed in chapter 1 of this book, chapter 13's legal protections are particularly useful to retain homes. People with houses, regardless of car ownership, file chapters 7 and 13 effectively evenly. Fifty-one percent are in chapter 7; forty-nine percent are in chapter 13. In comparison, among people without a house, three-quarters file chapter 7 and one-quarter file chapter 13. Table 3.1 also disaggregates bankruptcy filers with homes by chapter 7 and 13. It reports retirement assets only for filers with retirement assets.[10]

That filers with homes had the financial wherewithal to purchase houses, even if doing so was a stretch, is most evident in the details of the assets they bring with them to bankruptcy. Compared to filers without a home, they are more likely to have real property in addition to the houses they live in. Less than 4 percent of filers who do not own a home enter bankruptcy with other real property, meaning that filers with houses own other real property at three times the rate of filers without houses.

Compared to people who file bankruptcy who do not own a home, filers with homes are also more likely to have retirement assets, and their retirement assets are worth more. Thirty percent of people without a home enter bankruptcy with retirement assets. Among filers without houses, chapter 7 filers with a car and retirement assets have the most retirement assets, a median of $5,049. This is a fraction of the value of homeowners' retirement assets.

In addition, although they are as likely to be employed when they file bankruptcy, people who enter bankruptcy without houses have less income than filers with houses.[11] Those people without homes who file chapter 7 make a median of $45,505, and those who file chapter 13 make a median of $59,656. Bankrupt homeowners have more resources—assets and income—than bankrupt nonhomeowners.

Although filers with homes have more resources than other people who file bankruptcy, their financial resources pale compared to homeowners in the general population, as reported by the Federal Reserve. The median homeowner in bankruptcy has an annual income of $62,256, a total debt-to-income ratio of 3.61, and a net worth of negative $36,076. In contrast, the median homeowner generally has an annual income of $94,039, a total debt-to-income ratio of 0.98, and a positive net worth of $396,500.

Our bankruptcy filers demonstrate that homeownership, so often touted as the marker of financial security, is a stretch for many. The fixed expense of a monthly mortgage and other expenses of homeownership can break a household budget.[12]

This chapter's opening story serves as a good example. That debtor's homeownership expenses proved more than she had anticipated. Despite keeping a strict budget, the house's associated expenses put her behind on credit card payments, which made it difficult to make room for the added expenses of a car accident. When she filed chapter 7, she owed one mortgage lender $181,000 on a house worth $157,000. Her car, worth $13,000, likewise was underwater; she owed the car lender $15,000. Prior to filing, she had held the same job for eleven years and made $62,000 per year before taxes. She wrote "raises at work were less than inflationary and change in living situation" as reasons for her bankruptcy.

People who are relatively financially better off also overextend in pursuing homeownership and the social identity that one might believe accompanies being a homeowner. A couple, both around forty years old, with one teenager, acknowledged as much. "Bought too much of a house. Bills went up, no raises. He gambled. I drank a lot. Bought lots of things that weren't needed. Took trips when we couldn't pay for them. Relied heavily on credit cards." When they filed chapter 13, they owned a house worth $237,000, on which they owed $225,000. Their only car, worth $30,000, was $4,000 underwater. But they had $88,000 in retirement assets and made a combined $145,000 per year before taxes.

On our survey, they indicated that to make ends meet prior to filing, they stopped contributing to retirement accounts and "traded down on vehicles," which might explain the underwater car loan. They noted that they very much felt shame and guilt upon filing. Still, they thought that their debt problems were somewhat out of their control, that they acted responsibly in owning up to their debt problems, and that they deserved a fresh start in their financial lives. Homeownership and its attendant costs and ambitions are complicated. People are tied to their homes, emotionally and physically.[13]

The homes that people bring with them to bankruptcy in chapter 7 and chapter 13, as summarized in table 3.1, at the median are worth about the same. Filers also hold similar amounts of equity in their houses, and they have similar household employment rates. If they do not own a car, however, they are less likely to be employed, especially if they file chapter 13. Age does not explain the lower rate of employment. Those people with houses and no cars are not significantly older, such as of retirement age, than those people with houses and cars. As discussed later, car ownership is key to maintaining employment, which may explain the lower rate of employment among homeowners without a car.

The most noticeable financial disparities are that those homeowners in chapter 7 owe more unsecured debt and have less income, increasing their debt-to-asset and debt-to-income ratios. Those homeowners in chapter 7 without a car, relative to other bankrupt homeowners, own relatively less expensive homes and make the least income, which leaves them with the highest debt-to-asset and debt-to-income ratios. They might be striving, and possibly struggling, the most to keep their houses.

Otherwise, homeowners who file chapter 13 are more likely to enter bankruptcy in the wake of a state court foreclosure action, which makes sense given that chapter 13 is considered to be the bankruptcy chapter better suited to save a house from foreclosure. Thirteen percent of chapter 13 filers with a home list a foreclosure action in their bankruptcy paperwork, as compared to six percent of chapter 7 filers. Overall, only 9 percent of bankrupt homeowners file following a foreclosure action.[14]

*Holding onto the Home*

Homeowners' bankruptcies and the time leading up to their filings display one uniting theme: people want to keep their houses. The demographics of homeowners skew toward married or partnered couples, single women, white persons, and at least one filer having obtained a bachelor's degree or higher. Some of these characteristics, such as couples and higher educational attainment, increase the potential for having the financial resources to stretch to purchase a home. Others characteristics, such as gender and race, reflect disparities in the housing market and the desire to purchase and retain homes for children. Chapters 6 and 7 of this book detail the financial circumstances of Black persons and single women, including with children, who file bankruptcy, and focus on barriers to and incentives toward homeownership.

Across these demographics, homeowners enter bankruptcy following similar life events, particularly declines in income and medical issues. In addition, and predictably, homeowners cite unaffordable mortgage payments and foreclosure as precipitators of their filings. These precipitators accompany the uniting theme of homeowners' bankruptcies and the time leading up to their filings of wanting to keep their houses.

For example, the financial problems of a white couple in their thirties with four children started with the birth of their two youngest children, who were only one and two years old when the couple filed chapter 13. The mother took some time off work, but then the father got sick. They never recovered from the combined loss of income and increased medical expenses. "Filing was our only option to keep our house and vehicles and get as fresh a start as possible." Prior to filing, they went without medical attention, therapy, dental care, and car repairs; paid their mortgage late; and stopped contributing to their retirement accounts. They also looked for more work, in the form of the mother going back to work, put necessities on credit cards, and borrowed from family and friends.

Like this couple, homeowners reported going without things (privations) and trying to make ends meet by taking actions (coping mechanisms) that might allow them to hold onto their houses and their social status as homeowners in the years leading up to their bankruptcies. The top five privations of homeowners, regardless of filing chapter, were the same as for nonhomeowners: medical attention, dental care, not keeping up with car repairs, stopping contributions to retirement accounts, and paying the mortgage late. More than 45 percent of filers reported trying each of these privations.[15] This is true for filers with or without cars and with or without houses. Some people at some point presumably gave up on their cars or their houses. Others did not.

In contrast to privations, homeowners' coping mechanisms differed noticeably from nonhomeowners'. Figure 3.1 shows filers' use of six other coping mechanisms that stand out among homeowners for their *infrequency* of use as compared to filers without houses. The figure reports coping mechanisms for all homeowners and nonhomeowners, with or without cars.[16]

Compared to nonhomeowners, homeowners were less likely to work more, although the difference is the least noticeable when only comparing

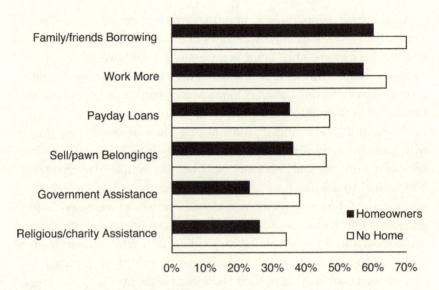

*Figure 3.1.* Coping strategies of bankruptcy filers during the two years before bankruptcy, by homeownership

filers based on homeownership. Car ownership matters here. Homeowners without cars were the least likely to report working more, only 41 percent, compared to 56 percent of filers without cars and without homes. This may reflect the increased difficulties of surviving without a car in most places in the United States where homes, rather than apartments and other rental properties, are located. Relatively few people enter bankruptcy owning a home but not a car—only 4 percent of filers. Some of these people may live in places where cars are not absolutely needed, although not having one makes life more complicated.

For example, a white couple in their midthirties filed chapter 7 while owning a house worth $320,000, on which they owed $200,000, but no car. They already were struggling before they had their two children, who were one and ten years old when they filed. "Wasn't getting paid enough at work to cover household expenses plus bills from credit cards. Then had 2 kids and between daycare and bills and spending money for children, couldn't afford much." They indicated that they went without car maintenance during the years before they filed, suggesting that they gave up their car.

They lived in a place where they could reasonably get other places via public buses that would connect them to commuter rails. The journey would not be nearly as direct as if they drove. But traveling to work, dropping the kids off at daycare, or getting groceries seemed feasible. They were among the minority of filers with homes and no cars who reported taking on more work to make ends meet.

Homeowners' relative lack of using the other coping mechanisms detailed in figure 3.1 suggest that they tried to stay away from using fringe lending networks or publicly asking others, including the government, for help. To seek out help from any of these places signals that one has slipped down society's socioeconomic rungs. Bankrupt homeowners' coping mechanisms may reflect a resolve to adhere to beliefs about the higher social status that accompanies homeownership. Not only do people want to keep their houses, but some also may hold tight to the full dream of the middle-class status that comes from homeownership.

In addition, one-third of bankrupt homeowners reported obtaining loan modifications, refinancing home loans, or taking out home equity loans in the two years preceding their filings. Eight percent of filers who did not have a home at the time of filing still reported making these efforts during the two years before bankruptcy. These filers tried and failed to save their homes through such a deal in the years leading up to their bankruptcies.

The story of a divorced forty-year-old white woman with one preteen dependent illustrates the attempts to save a home. She wrote that she "just got in over my head with credit cards and debt. I began to take cash from credit cards to pay monthly bills. I tried to get a debt consolidation and help from different places. No one would help me because my debt/ratio was out of proportion." She also "tried to refinance my home and I couldn't get help there either. After months of struggling and trying everything I knew to try, I finally realized bankruptcy was my only option." When she filed chapter 7, she listed her house as having a market value of $63,000. She owed a single mortgage lender $62,000. Going along with her comment that she filed after months of struggling, she indicated that she seriously struggled with her debts for least one year but less than two years before she filed bankruptcy.

How long she struggled before filing aligns with what other homeowners have done. Overall, homeowners struggled for slightly less time

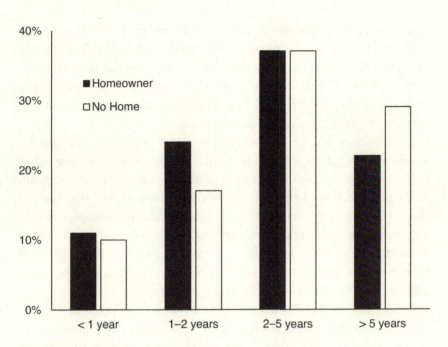

*Figure 3.2.* Time spent "seriously struggling" with debts by bankruptcy filers, by homeownership

than filers who did not own a home. As figure 3.2 illustrates, homeowners were more likely to report struggling for less than two years and less likely to report struggling for more than five years.[17] The average homeowner reported struggling three fewer months than a nonhomeowner. Hidden in the aggregate data, however, is an important reason. Among those filers who told us that they "very much agreed" that foreclosure was a reason for bankruptcy, they reported struggling seven fewer months than a nonhomeowner. Saving a house from foreclosure can rush people into bankruptcy court, similar to how debt collection generally leads many people to capitulate and file bankruptcy, as we discuss in chapter 2 of this book.

## Fearing Loss of the Home Despite Bankruptcy

For those people who file bankruptcy while still owning a house, retaining that home is both a feature and a worry of their case. People tend to value things that they own more highly than if they had not ever owned them, termed the *endowment effect* in psychology and behavioral economics. People exhibit loss aversion.[18] Stated differently, it is worse to have something and lose it than never to have had it.

Losing a house also is the loss of a marker of middle-class status, which comes as a blow to one's social identity. It potentially requires relocating neighborhoods. Children may have to switch schools, and even if they do not, they might be uprooted from their neighborhood social circles. Based on research about the effects of foreclosure, adults likewise suffer—from the stress of moving and from the displacement from a familiar space.[19] Homeowners have much to lose, and they may feel anxiety about the threat of the potential loss. This is part of what Barbara Ehrenreich, in her 1989 study of the psychology of the middle class, dubbed the "fear of falling."[20]

This fear of falling may be partially what pushes homeowners to file bankruptcy slightly sooner during their struggles than do nonhomeowners. It also shows up in the emotions that homeowners report feeling upon filing. Bankruptcy law does not solve the root problems that lead to financial struggles. It will discharge most unsecured debts, but the mortgage will remain. Attendant costs of homeownership, such as maintenance and property taxes, also will remain. People may rightly worry about what it will take going forward to maintain their status as homeowners.

We asked people the extent to which (not at all, a little bit, somewhat, a great deal) they felt certain emotions when they filed bankruptcy. Among the people who filed while still owning a house, fear stands out as one of five emotions with which homeowners with cars responded notably differently than filers without houses. They were more likely to feel "a great deal" of fear. They also felt more anger, had more guilt, were less thankful, and were less happy when they filed.[21]

Unease about the place of homeownership in their lives may have guided these emotions. They may also have felt anger about how much it costs to maintain homeownership and at the situations that led them to be unable to keep up with mortgage payments. For example, a widowed Black woman indicated she felt a great deal of anger, shame, depression, and fear when she filed chapter 13. Her financial problems stemmed from employment, but her filing came down to keeping her house.

I was already working with a salary that was too low. My [employer] then told me he could no longer afford to pay me. He offered me $[6,100] severance pay if I agreed to [a noncompete]. I did not sign it. I was in a lose/lose situation. He owed me for 12 weeks vacation but would not give it to me in a lump sum. If he had, I would have been able to keep up my mortgage payments, qualify for the Obama Housing Program, and not have to file bankruptcy. YES, I am angry!!!

Even if they feel anger, people also feel guilty for buying into what they have been told about the benefits of homeownership and for being unable to fulfill the "happy homeownership narrative" in which they live comfortably and stress-free in their houses, a narrative they have been taught that they should be able to fulfill.[22] They are less thankful and happy because mortgage debt and other homeownership costs still loom large. And they fear that all their efforts will have been for naught because they will lose their houses in the end anyhow.

## KEEPING A CAR

In most places in the United States, lack of public transportation options makes having a car essential to access work, education, medical care, childcare, family, and other life necessities. Even after the pandemic increased the number of people who work from home, 68 percent of people drive to their jobs. Car ownership increases the probability of employment, the number of hours someone will work, and income. Eighty-eight percent of households use cars to get food. Having access to a car correlates with ability to get health care.[23]

The stories written by bankruptcy filers bear out these realities. A single, Black twenty-year-old mother of three young children described the consequences of not having a car: "I was a new mom. After my car was repoed I was evicted because I couldn't work. Due to me not having a vehicle. Soon I became homeless because no matter where I worked my checks were getting garnished. I couldn't get a place because I had numerous evictions." She looked for government assistance. "I was accepted into public housing which saved me and my kids. I went back to school and got a job." She filed chapter 7 with one car worth $2,800, which she owned free and clear of loans. Her bankruptcy centered on discharging unsecured debt so that she could continue to pay the $12,200 she owed in student loans, while also keeping her car so she could hold down a job.

Like this mother, people generally do not own a car because they cannot afford a car, not because they have deliberately opted to live an idyllic, green "car free" lifestyle.[24] For most people, foregoing a car is done out of financial necessity. This is true for people living in all but a handful of cities in the United States. Transportation policies have prioritized cars as people's primary means of transport so dramatically that getting around most places requires a car. Getting around includes traveling within a town, city, or suburban area, from town to town, and from state to state. Unless someone lives in areas around Boston, Chicago, District of Columbia, Miami, New York City, Philadelphia, San Francisco, and a select few other metropolitan areas, the United States is largely inaccessible without a car. Even people living in those cities will find it difficult to travel elsewhere.

Federal and state policies have allocated much more money to roads, highways, and interstates than to trains, commuter rails, and buses. Traffic regulations, land use laws, environmental regulations, and tax law incentivize car ownership.[25] The combination of poor street design and reliance on cars makes walking on the roads in many areas of the country dangerous.[26]

As a result, 85 percent of households own at least one car. But the same policies and laws that require car ownership do little to regulate or subsidize the cost of purchasing those necessary cars. And cars are expensive. In 2023, on average, a new car cost about $48,000, and a used car cost around $27,000.[27] According to the Survey of Consumer Finances, in 2022 the median value of all vehicles owned by households in the United States was $28,000.[28]

To fund those purchases, most people take out car loans, many of which come with hefty interest rates and other fees.[29] Between 2000 and 2023, car loan debt grew by 39 percent, even after adjusting for inflation and population growth.[30] During these years, the subprime car loan market grew to account for one-quarter of the car loan market.[31] By 2020 car loans comprised about 9 percent of household debt, making the car loan market the third largest consumer credit market after home loans and student loans.[32] In 2022, again according to the Survey of Consumer Finances, 35 percent of households had car loans. For households that had a car loan, the median amount owed was $15,000.[33] Cars also come with gas, insurance, road tolls, registration, and maintenance costs, which as of 2023 could total $5,000 to $10,000 a year.[34]

Car loans are secured loans, and thus lenders can repossess cars if debtors miss payments and default. Unless people reach deals with their lenders to get their cars back, lenders will sell those cars. If the sale price is less than what is owed to the lender, the lender can pursue the debtor—the person who previously owned the car—for the difference, called a *deficiency*. The lender will do so through debt collection, including state court actions seeking to garnish people's bank accounts and wages.

On our survey, people wrote about how car lenders pursued them for deficiencies, including how wage garnishment arising from car repossessions pushed them to file bankruptcy. A single Black mother filed chapter 7 because of car-related debt collection. "I had a car company garnishing my wages making it hard for me to afford the cost of living and taking care of my 3 kids." Chapter 9 of this book considers in more detail how debt collection forces people to invoke the protection of bankruptcy courts.

Those who file bankruptcy demonstrate the paradox of car ownership: having a car may be necessary to avoid poverty, but reliable cars are expensive, and a car loan may lead to repossession and further debt collection. In total, 85 percent of filers have cars. The median bankrupt household owns one car. Joint filers, at the median, own two cars. It appears that very few people shed their cars before they file bankruptcy. Instead, they seek to use bankruptcy to keep at least one of their cars—typically the most valuable car.

Table 3.2 summarizes the finances of people who file bankruptcy while owning cars, disaggregated by homeownership and filing chapter. At the median, car owners file bankruptcy with cars worth a total of $10,485 and owing $9,969 in total car loans. The most valuable car is worth $9,125 against a loan of $8,742, again at the median.

People with cars but without houses enter bankruptcy in what looks like worse financial situations than homeowners. They hold less equity in their most valuable cars, have lower incomes, and have higher debt-to-asset ng HOME AND GOING PLACES 71

*Table 3.2.* Finances of Bankruptcy Filers with Cars, by Homeownership and Chapter (Medians)

| | CHAPTER 7 | | CHAPTER 13 | |
|---|---|---|---|---|
| | Cars & Homes | Cars, No Homes | Cars & Homes | Cars, No Homes |
| Most valuable car | | | | |
| Value | $8,603 | $7,254 | $10,982 | $12,009 |
| Cars with liens | 56% | 59% | 65% | 85% |
| Amount owed | $5,657 | $5,811 | $9,689 | $14,803 |
| Equity | $1,154 | $1,000 | $649 | ($1,588) |
| 2nd most valuable car | | | | |
| Value | $3,457 | $2,950 | $4,326 | $4,867 |
| Cars with liens | 36% | 37% | 45% | 66% |
| Amount owed | $0 | $0 | $0 | $3,849 |
| Equity | $1,283 | $1,180 | $1,250 | $224 |
| Total value, cars | $10,354 | $8,115 | $13,456 | $13,403 |
| Total owed, cars | $7,164 | $6,543 | $11,836 | $16,414 |
| Total equity, cars | $1,577 | $1,213 | $1,309 | ($1,475) |
| Total assets | $193,922 | $16,856 | $210,699 | $21,476 |
| Total debts | $245,074 | $64,015 | $232,369 | $61,401 |
| Debt-to-asset ratio | 1.24 | 3.61 | 1.07 | 2.86 |

NOTE: N for cars, no homes, ch. 7 is 2,892. N for cars and homes, ch. 7 is 1,523. N for cars, no homes, ch. 13 is 1,129. N for cars and homes, ch. 13 is 1,473. The table reports medians for all filers for all financial variables, which is why the median amount owed for the second most valuable car is $0 for all but chapter 13 filers without homes.

ratios. This further confirms that bankrupt homeowners have more resources than bankrupt nonhomeowners.

Seventy-two percent of people who own cars but not houses file chapter 7, which makes sense because bankruptcy law provides ways for people to keep their cars and pay car loans going forward through chapter 7. Absent another legal or financial reason to file chapter 13, such as an impending home foreclosure, chapter 7 likely can save the car with less expense than chapter 13. Chapter 6 of this book discusses Black households' overrepresentation in chapter 13, and how that racial disparity connects with the median negative total equity in all cars of chapter 13 filers who own cars but not houses.

Bankruptcy filers' cars are worth less than those owned by the median household in the United States. They are more likely to owe on car loans, owe more on those car loans, and hold less equity in their cars than the general population. People still seek to hold onto their cars through their bankruptcy cases, seemingly because they need cars to survive and trying to obtain other cars outside bankruptcy does not present a better financial option.

### Reaffirming the Loan on the Most Valuable Car

Based on their bankruptcy schedules, households specifically want to keep their most valuable car, which likely is their most reliable car. People who file chapter 7 have four options to deal with cars on which they owe car loans. They indicate which option they choose on a form called the Statement of Intention. (Chapter 13 filers will handle the disposition of their cars and car loans in their repayment plans.) First, the debtor can surrender the car to the lender and face no postbankruptcy liability. If they owe anything to the lender after accounting for the value of the surrendered car, what they owe will be discharged. (Outside of bankruptcy, of course, they would remain liable for what they still owe to the lender.) Second, the debtor can redeem the car by paying the entire amount of the car's value to the lender. This amount may be less than the amount outstanding on the car loan, which makes redemption attractive. But most people do not have enough money to redeem. They have filed bankruptcy, after all.

Third, the debtor can keep the car by entering into what is called a reaffirmation agreement with their car lender. The reaffirmation agreement essentially renews the car loan, binding the debtor to a new car loan postbankruptcy. The filer gets the discharge for most of their unsecured debts, which presumably will help them pay the reaffirmed car loan postbankruptcy. Fourth, the debtor can retain the car while continuing to pay on their prebankruptcy car loan without entering into a reaffirmation agreement, provided that their car lender does not make a fuss about how the loan is being handled in the bankruptcy case. This is colloquially called a *ride-through*.

*Table 3.3.* Intended Disposition of Cars in Chapter 7, from Statements of Intention

| | Most Valuable Car (%) | 2nd Most Valuable Car (%) | 3rd Most Valuable Car (%) |
|---|---|---|---|
| Surrender | 14 | 24 | 24 |
| Redeem | 1 | 2 | 1 |
| Reaffirm | 64 | 56 | 45 |
| Retain/no intention listed | 21 | 19 | 30 |

Of these options, the first three are explicitly allowed by bankruptcy law, and the fourth is supposedly prohibited by bankruptcy law. Retention via ride-through will not work if the lender insists on its rights under bankruptcy law. Many people who file chapter 7 still retain their cars without entering into reaffirmation agreements because lenders often will not make a fuss if the loan is being paid. If the lender does insist on its rights, entering into a reaffirmation agreement will ensure the filer keeps the car.[35] Table 3.3 details the intended disposition of chapter 7 filers' three most valuable cars as provided on their Statements of Intention.

The more valuable the car, the more likely people are to go through the process of obtaining a reaffirmation agreement. The relative use of reaffirmation versus ride-through and surrendering cars evidences a desire among the people who file bankruptcy to guarantee that they will have at least one car in their postbankruptcy lives. What people wrote about their road to bankruptcy tells of filings motivated by safeguarding car ownership.

## The Imperative of Keeping a Car

People's stories about the connection of cars and bankruptcy generally described their inability to balance budgets with car loan payments and other debt payments, some of which arose from the cars themselves. For instance, the Latina woman from this chapter's opening story traced her financial problems partly to a car accident. She indicated that she would file a reaffirmation agreement to keep her car. She also wrote that the most important thing she went without prior to bankruptcy was car repairs and maintenance. Based on where she lived, she likely used the car to get to her job as an accountant, the salary from which she needed to hold onto her house.

Similarly, a sixty-five-year-old woman's troubles began with a car accident.

> My car (12 years old) was paid off and was in excellent condition. I was in an auto accident caused by driver running a red light and car was complete loss. Insurance claim was only enough for a down payment of about $[4,500] on a new car. Now I had a car payment of $[600] a month plus higher insurance and state auto fees. . . . I was using credit line at credit union and credit cards to supplement extra money needed each month. . . . I was under so much stress prior to filing, with sleepless nights and physical ailments. As soon as I decided to file, 1 million pounds was lifted off me.

She likewise lived in a place where a car seemed necessary to complete daily activities. When she filed chapter 7, she owned one car worth $19,000, on which she owed $22,000. She indicated that she would file a reaffirmation agreement to keep the car.

For these two women, although they kept their cars via reaffirmation agreements, bankruptcy's discharge may not be enough to keep them financially afloat in future years such that they can continue to pay those reaffirmation agreements. Their car ownership will continue to remain precarious, as will the homeownership of many of the people with houses who file bankruptcy. Homeowners have a good chance of surviving financially if they lose their houses, although they may take a blow to their sense of self-worth. Given transportation policies, the loss of a car may amount to a devastating life event.

# 4 Staying Alive

Three years before the bankruptcy my wife was hit by a
motorcycle and was disabled. So we took a blow to our
income at that time as she is a nurse and has long term
disability and draws 50% of her income. As we had just
recovered from that, I had two heart attacks 30 days apart
with no history of any health problems other than a little
hypertension which I was being treated for. I had a triple
bypass then another heart attack as they messed up the
bypass. . . . After being off work so long and just going back
on light duty part-time I had used all of our savings and to
add to it I had $27,000 in medical bills that insurance did
not pay. I had nowhere to turn. It was not that I did not
want to pay anyone, I just needed time to be able to get
myself together which no one wanted to give me.

—Fifty-six-year-old white man

In modern society, the health-care system is intimately woven into our
everyday lives. We are birthed into the institution. We turn to it for vac-
cinations, for treatment for injuries—such as cuts from kitchen knives
and broken bones from falls from bikes and trees—and for treatment for
illnesses—such as pneumonia and more complex ailments, like the heart
bypass described in the opening quote. We come to it for routine continuing care and to get our medications. Ultimately, within this system, we will
age and die.

Modern society has made significant medical advances. Perhaps the
greatest accomplishment of the past century is the US increased life expectancy, with most people expected to survive to almost eighty years old

instead of merely their mid-fifties, the average life expectancy in 1900.[1] But though we may feel an imperative to heal the suffering and push the boundaries of medicine, the United States has fostered an extremely costly health-care system—the costs of which are often foisted onto the people who are hurting.

At the end of 2021, twenty million Americans owed $250 or more in medical debt, despite more than 90 percent of the population having health insurance. In total, adults owed medical debts of $220 billion.[2] Of that, $88 billion was in collections, affecting about 20 percent of people in the United States.[3] Additionally, half of adults report that health care is difficult to afford, and one in four says that they have gone without health care in the past year because they could not afford it, even if they had insurance. Health-care costs consistently rank among voters' top concerns.[4] The health-care system introduces extraordinary precarity into the lives of many people and pushes some to file "medical bankruptcy."

## MEDICAL BANKRUPTCY

Legally, there is no such thing as medical bankruptcy. Rather, medical bankruptcy is a catchphrase that describes a bankruptcy precipitated by either medical expenses or a loss of income due to illness or injury. People may say that they filed a medical bankruptcy when medical bills chiefly brought about their need for debt relief. Because the term *medical bankruptcy* is commonly used when discussing bankruptcies stemming from medical expenses and medical-related income losses, we also use the term here.

For decades, scholars affiliated with the CBP have reported on the relationship between bankruptcy and medical struggles.[5] Research conducted in 2001 concluded that almost half of all bankruptcy filings qualified as medical bankruptcies.[6] By 2007, data suggested that more than 62 percent of filers did so for medical reasons, and three-quarters of them had health insurance.[7] This chapter serves as a sequel, of sorts, to that research.[8]

We asked people who filed bankruptcy if either "medical expenses, including doctor bills, hospital bills, and prescriptions" or "medical problems that caused you, or your spouse or partner, to miss work" were reasons for their bankruptcies.[9] Sixty-five percent of filers "very much" or "somewhat" agreed that one of these reasons contributed to their filing. In other words, two-thirds of bankruptcy filings include a medical reason. Another way to state this is that only 35 percent of people in bankruptcy did not indicate that their financial problems stemmed at least in part from a medical issue.

Among those people who cited a medical reason, 30 percent indicated that *only* medical expenses—doctor bills, hospital bills, prescriptions— were a reason for their bankruptcy. Twelve percent specified that *only* missing work—to heal from their own health issues or to care for an ill partner or child—was a reason for filing. Fifty-seven percent reported that *both* reasons led to their filings. In the rest of this chapter, we use *medical bankruptcy* as shorthand for filers who cited either or both as reasons for their bankruptcy.

## WHO ARE MEDICAL BANKRUPTCY FILERS?

Medical bankruptcy pervades bankruptcy courts. Across every demographic category, six out of ten filers generally cite a medical contributor to their need to turn to bankruptcy court for help. Whether one is young (under thirty-five), middle-aged (between thirty-five and sixty-four), or a senior (sixty-five or over), essentially two-thirds of people file for a medical reason. Sixty-three percent of young people, sixty-six percent of middle-aged people, and sixty-three percent of seniors file medical bankruptcies.

Health-care costs affect people differently across age categories. Younger individuals may need to purchase health insurance on the open market because they are ineligible for employer-provided health insurance, or they may choose insurance plans with higher deductibles to keep premiums affordable. They thus may go uninsured or face high medical bills despite insurance coverage. People in the middle age range are members of the "sandwich generation" or the "club sandwich generation." The sandwich generation is responsible for their own children and their aging parents. The lives of those in the club sandwich generation are even more complicated. They may be responsible for their own children, their grandchildren, and their aging parents.[10] As the number of people in a household grows, so too does the likelihood of medical bills and the need to take time away from work to care for others who are sick. Seniors face increased health issues and often live on fixed incomes. Even though they may have Medicare, the coverage is not adequate, as detailed in chapter 8.

Marital status likewise does not especially alter the likelihood of filing for medical reasons. Whether a filer is single or married, the percent of medical bankruptcies hovers around two-thirds. Sixty percent of single men, sixty-two percent of single women, and sixty-nine percent of married people cited medical contributors to their bankruptcies. The slightly larger number of medical bankruptcies among married filers is not surprising. Having two adults in the household increases the risk of illness or injury and a corresponding uptick in medical bills. If both adults are employed, they will have established a lifestyle based on two incomes.[11] When one misses work, income will necessarily decline, pushing the couple toward bankruptcy.

Attaining a four-year college degree appears to provide modest protection against medical bankruptcy. Fifty-nine percent of those households that have a member with a bachelor's degree, compared to sixty-seven percent of those that do not, file medical bankruptcies. A college degree may lead to a job with comprehensive health insurance and a higher income and thus the ability to pay for medical expenses more easily; perhaps more importantly, the job may include paid sick leave. People without college degrees may be employed in more physically taxing or dangerous occupations, leading to an increased likelihood of illness or injury, and they may be less likely to have employee-provided health insurance. Still, regardless of education level, the percentage of medical bankruptcies remains high.

The likelihood of filing medical bankruptcy differs somewhat by race. Even so, again, around six out of ten filers cite a medical reason for their bankruptcy. White filers are the most likely to enter bankruptcy for medical reasons. Specifically, 67 percent of white households file for medical reasons. The percentages for Black and Latine households are lower—63 percent and 59 percent, respectively.[12] In general, adults of color, except for Asians, are less likely to have a primary care provider, less likely to receive mental health services, and more likely not to have seen a doctor in the past year because of the cost.[13] These circumstances may decrease their incurrence of medical debt. Conversely, if white adults are more likely to seek care from physicians and to seek treatment for mental health issues, they likely are incurring medical debt.

*Table 4.1.*  Financial Characteristics of Bankruptcy Filers, Medical and Nonmedical (Medians)

|  | *Medical Bankruptcy* | *Nonmedical Bankruptcy* |
| --- | --- | --- |
| Pretax annual income | $46,464 | $47,148 |
| Unsecured debt | $47,720 | $47,252 |
| Debt-to-income ratio | 2.2 | 2.3 |
| Significant decline in income | 56% | 51% |
| Primary petitioner employed | 65% | 70% |

Regardless of medical reasons, filers share similar financial circumstances, as summarized in table 4.1. They enter bankruptcy with virtually identical income, unsecured debt, and total debt-to-income ratios. This suggests that people generally have a financial breaking point regardless of the reasons behind their hardships. But as compared to nonmedical filers, more medical filers experienced a significant decline in their income in the two years prior to filing, and the primary petitioner was less likely to be employed. Medical problems could be behind both hardships.

Table 4.1 does not include a summary of total medical debt because there is no reliable way to calculate the amount of that specific type of debt from the information disclosed in bankruptcy court records. Because people may pay their medical debts with credit cards on which they also charge other needs, it is not possible to isolate medical expenses charged to those credit cards.[14] For example, a debtor's bankruptcy court records may include a Visa card balance, but there is no way to know whether and to what extent the balance represents an emergency room visit or several weeks' worth of groceries. However, the stories written by bankruptcy filers demonstrate the size of some of the medical debts charged to credit cards.

## THE PRECARITY OF INSURANCE AND RESULTING MEDICAL DEBT

Currently seventy-two countries have universal health care. The United States is not among them.[15] This distinguishes the United States as the only developed nation without universal health care. Instead, in the United States people must access health care through a labyrinth of public and private health insurance. The US patchwork of public insurance programs comprises Medicare, available to seniors and certain people under the age of sixty-five with disabilities; Medicaid, available to individuals with low incomes and with disabilities; and the Children's Health Insurance Program, available to children in low-income families.[16]

People in the United States otherwise must rely on private health insurance. They either get insurance through their employers or buy it on the open market. In 2021 about 55 percent of Americans were covered by private employer-sponsored health insurance.[17] Employer-sponsored programs typically require employees to pay a portion of the insurance premium. For single person coverage, employees, on average, pay 17 percent of the premium, which is about $1,300 per year. For a family policy, the employee portion averages 28 percent of the premium, or approximately $6,100 annually.[18] Among people with employer-provided health insurance, almost 30 percent are underinsured because they cannot afford the high out-of-pocket bills.[19]

Under the Affordable Care Act, enacted in 2010, people who do not have health insurance, either through their employer or via a public program, must be allowed to purchase it, privately, through the health insurance marketplace.[20] Nonetheless, a small portion of the population, about 8 percent, remains without health insurance.[21] The leading reason is the cost.[22]

Among people who file bankruptcy, the percentage who are uninsured is notably higher than the percentage of uninsured among the general population—both before and after bankruptcy. During the two years prior to filing, 41 percent of medical filers and 37 percent of nonmedical filers went without health insurance. Stated differently, although almost six out of ten medical bankruptcy filers had health insurance prior to filing, they still sought the help of bankruptcy because a medical issue caused them to incur bills or lose income. By the time of filing, more people had secured health insurance—75 percent of medical and nonmedical filers alike—although a full quarter remained uninsured and at risk if they or someone in their household needed health care. Even with this increase in coverage, the percentage of uninsured people among bankruptcy filers remains substantially higher than that among the general population.

The US health insurance system is known for both its cost and its complexity, a messiness that some filers described well. The experience of a sixty-two-year-old single woman who had insurance before and at the time of her bankruptcy highlights how even with coverage people are at risk of incurring large debts that can propel them into bankruptcy. Annual deductibles, copayments, and loopholes can add up to tens of thousands of dollars, as it did for her. Her annual deductible was $2,000, and she was also responsible for copayments. These out-of-pocket expenses averaged about $300 a month, which seems problematic given that her monthly income when she filed bankruptcy was barely over $1,800. Those costs, coupled with an unexpected bill from her surgery, left her little choice but to file bankruptcy.

> Then I had a surgery at the end of the year, which should have been totally covered, but because my employer changed insurance on January 1, the old insurance refused to cover it all and the new insurance refused because they did not pre-approve the surgery. So I had $35,000 that did not get covered. So, I absolutely had no way out but bankruptcy.

She filed owing more than $70,000 in unsecured debt, which, on her modest salary, would be difficult, if not impossible, to pay.

Being uninsured altogether is even riskier. A sixty-one-year-old married man, who had been living for years without health insurance, reported that he had seriously struggled to pay debts for between two to five years prior to filing. He also indicated that he had experienced a significant decline in income in the two years before his bankruptcy. Based on his story, his income decline probably occurred because of his multiple illnesses.

> Had ... surgery. Working ... (maintenance worker). Had no health insurance. Struggled to make ends meet. [One year later]: Had [another] surgery from falling. ... Had no health insurance. Struggled more to make ends meet. [One year later]: Developed Type 2 diabetes, was hospitalized and almost died due to the stress. I lost 60 pounds in three weeks. Had no health insurance. ... [Two years later]: Struggled with my health, medical bills, creditors until I couldn't take it anymore.

Not having medical insurance did not exempt him from needing attention for his multiple medical issues. By the time he and his wife filed bankruptcy, they owed more than $82,000 in unsecured debt, most of which almost certainly originated with medical bills.

Health insurance serves only as a partial defense against medical debt. Loopholes and gaps in coverage can cause bills to mount. Even with full coverage, treatments can be so expensive that debts pile up to the point where people believe bankruptcy is their best option. And health insurance does not protect against the loss of income that may accompany medical crises.

## MISSING WORK, TEMPORARILY AND PERMANENTLY

Illness may cause someone to miss work because they are sick or because they must care for other family members. In some instances, a medical situation may be so serious that they or their loved one never recover such that they can return to work. Income loss because of health issues is another reason for filing bankruptcy. That is, it is another measure of medical bankruptcy.

If the time away from work is brief, the sick individual or the person taking care of another family member may not lose their job, and the family may be able to manage despite a few smaller paychecks. When an employee is absent for a longer period, however, the result may be devastating: a significant loss of income, or the loss of a job and, therefore, the loss of health insurance.

Parenthood stood out among bankruptcy filers' narratives as increasing the risks of missing work and missing out on income. A married couple, parents to two children, a five-year-old and a newborn, struggled financially when the wife took time off from work to have the baby, which reduced their household income by approximately $3,000 a month. When the infant was hospitalized two months later, the mother took more time away from work and lost another two weeks of income. "We filed 20 years ago due to medical bills and now this time is basically due to medical bills." Despite having health insurance prior to and at the time of filing, the combination of medical bills and missed income left them unable to manage their debts.

Even when an employee receives partial pay during an absence from work, that money may not be enough to keep the family financially afloat.

A married white woman, mother to two teenaged children, was hospitalized for ten days. Afterward, she spent "nine months out of work with half pay." Not long thereafter, one of her children became sick and "almost died." She missed work for ten days while her child was in the hospital and then another month to care for her child at home. Between the series of illnesses that resulted in considerable time away from work and the corresponding loss of income, the family was unable to financially recover. More generous paid sick leave may have helped to keep this family afloat. However, federal law presently does not guarantee paid sick leave to anyone.[23]

While it may seem inaccurate to describe this mother as lucky, she was. She had a job to return to after her health crisis and again after caring for her son for over a month. Lengthy illnesses such as hers often result in both unemployment and a loss of health insurance. A forty-five-year-old Black man described how an injury left him without a job or money to buy health insurance. "I injured my knee away from work. . . . I had to have surgery on both knees and was out of work and that meant no insurance and I could not afford the [COBRA] plan, so I went through the clinics to get assistance. All the while falling deeper in debt." He wrote that the most important thing he could not afford prior to filing bankruptcy was "surgery and medical bills." He still did not have insurance when he filed bankruptcy. Hopefully, after he recovers from the knee surgery, he will find employment that provides health insurance.

In his narrative, he mentioned that he could not afford COBRA (Consolidated Omnibus Budget Reconciliation Act). This program provides that employees be allowed to continue their health insurance coverage after leaving employment, including following job loss. It allows for continuation of the same benefits, but the individual must assume the entire cost of the policy—the amount the employer and the employee paid—plus a small administrative fee.[24] In 2022 the average cost for individual coverage was about $7,900 annually. For a family, it approached $22,800 a year.[25] For someone freshly unemployed, this cost is potentially prohibitive, leaving them and their family without income and without health insurance.

People face an even greater financial catastrophe when an illness or injury is so severe that they can never return to work. Their income loss is permanent, and their only ways to get health insurance are to buy it themselves or qualify for public insurance. A fifty-nine-year-old married Latino father of three children experienced this unfortunate situation. Because of his extreme illness, multiple physicians told him not to return to work. "Lost my job after 15 years of employment with the same company. Lost medical insurance, all income, and have been struggling ever since." He and his family members were without health insurance prior to and at the time of filing. For health insurance coverage, Medicaid likely is his best option.

Going without health insurance, for these two filers, amounted to a forced privation in the years leading up to their bankruptcy filings. To try to make ends meet while dealing with health issues and related income losses, bankruptcy filers cut a variety of expenses from their budgets. As with going without health insurance, some of these expenses included health care itself.

## GOING WITHOUT WHEN SICK

As described in chapter 2, those who file bankruptcy go without everything from higher education and contributing to retirement to health care, food, and utilities in the years leading up to their filings. We asked bankruptcy filers what they went without during the two years prior to their filings and provided them with a list of fourteen common items. Table 4.2 disaggregates filers' privations by those people who indicated their bankruptcies had medical contributors versus those people with bankruptcies precipitated by nonmedical problems. Compared to other bankruptcy filers, medical bankruptcy filers were more likely to experience every privation.

Most medical bankruptcy filers, and at a much higher percentage than other bankruptcy filers, went without some form of health care. Dental care stands out as the type of health care that all filers, but especially medical filers, were most likely to go without. Most health insurance, including Medicare, does not cover dental care. Without that coverage, it makes sense that people who are struggling financially would be more likely to forego trips to the dentist.

*Table 4.2.*  Privations, Medical and Nonmedical Filers

| | Medical Bankruptcy (%) | Nonmedical Bankruptcy (%) |
|---|---|---|
| Health-care-related privations | | |
| Dental care | 68 | 54 |
| Medical attention | 58 | 41 |
| Prescriptions | 50 | 26 |
| Mental health care | 33 | 22 |
| Any of the above | 79 | 63 |
| General privations | | |
| Car repair or maintenance | 74 | 64 |
| Late mortgage or rent payment | 65 | 60 |
| Retirement contributions | 52 | 46 |
| Food or vet care for pets | 44 | 29 |
| Home, auto, life insurance | 39 | 32 |
| Health insurance | 35 | 31 |
| Food | 32 | 20 |
| Further education | 32 | 24 |
| Move out of home | 26 | 25 |
| Utilities | 19 | 14 |

Medical bankruptcy filers were also considerably more likely to go without medical attention, prescriptions, and mental health care than other filers. Across every type of medical care, medical privations among medical filers were a double whammy. These were people who filed because of medical problems while *simultaneously* being unable to afford the medical care that they or family members may have needed.

The remaining nonmedical privations suggest a similar trend among bankruptcy filers. To varying degrees, people who file in the wake of health problems go without more in the years prior to filing than others. Some differences are relatively small. Medical and nonmedical bankruptcy filers alike made late mortgage or rent payments, withdrew from their retirement accounts, went without insurance, moved out of their homes, and did without utilities. But people facing health problems struggled more than others to afford car repairs, care for their pets, buy food, and advance their education.

Among these privations, foregoing car repairs, going without food, and moving out of the home are the most concerning. Reliable transportation aids in getting to doctor appointments. Healthy food aids in recovering from illness. And recuperating from surgery or illness is best done in one's home, not under the stress of finding a new living situation.

The struggles and privations correlated with medical debt extend to people who have not filed bankruptcy. In 2022, 43 percent of adults in the United States indicated that they could not afford dental care.[26] That same year, more than one-third of Americans indicated that they had not filled a prescription because they could not afford it.[27] People in the United States who have unmanageable medical bills go without necessary household items, spend down their savings, borrow from friends and family, and take on other debts to pay doctor and hospital bills.[28] They also skip paying other bills, postpone buying homes or attending college, or move to more affordable housing.[29] Sacrificing to pay for health care is a national phenomenon.

## THE LONG-HAULERS

The people who file bankruptcy and cite medical contributors to their bankruptcies will benefit from the debt discharge, which will free them from medical debts and other unsecured debts that they have incurred while dealing with their health issues and related income losses. Ideally, people will regain their financial footing postbankruptcy. Although there is limited longitudinal research regarding how people fare after they file, findings from an earlier iteration of the CBP suggest that 65 percent of filers were financially better off approximately one year after their bankruptcies. The remaining 35 percent indicated that their financial situations were the same as or worse than when they initially filed (27% and 8%, respectively). The leading reasons for the lack of postbankruptcy financial recovery included income and job problems, medical problems—especially chronic illness—and old age.[30]

The stories shared by filers suggest that chronic medical conditions have the potential to undermine their postbankruptcy financial recovery and are likely to challenge their finances long after they receive the discharge. (Chapter 2 includes additional analysis of the results of our survey question asking people to describe how the stress from the debts caused or worsened any physical, mental, or emotional health problems.) The chronic conditions that people wrote about run the gamut from physical through mental health issues that could threaten financial recovery after bankruptcy.

The following two stories showcase the types of chronic conditions that could compromise financial recovery. A man, who had been with the same partner for thirty-two years, reported a small amount of unsecured debt and a mortgage on the home. He was not employed and was not seeking work because his partner, who was fifty-seven at the time he filed, required full-time care.

> [Partner] fell and hit his head. Severe brain trauma. He also had a seizure and had to have CPR 2 times. The last time he was gone too long and suffered brain damage. His kidneys and liver shut down, produced a poison in his system, which damaged the brain. That's 3 times of trauma to the brain. I now sit home and take care of him. He can't be left alone. He falls a lot, is dizzy, and can't remember minute to minute. I have to do what I have to do to keep him safe.

In assuming the role of a full-time caregiver to his partner, he will not be able to return to work. Because his partner likely will need ongoing medical attention, unless he qualifies for Medicare or Medicaid, medical bills probably will pile up again. Without another source of income, their financial future appears quite rocky.

The second example is a stay-at-home mom to two young boys with autism. She wrote that "insurance did not want to cover services" for her sons' care and that she opted not to work "because of all of [her sons'] appointments." The situation with her boys, coupled with her partner's recent job loss, pushed the couple into bankruptcy. During the two years before they filed, everyone in the household had health insurance. But by the time of their bankruptcy, they had lost their health insurance, and with it, any hope for coverage for their sons' autism care. If her sons' father finds employment, that will help their postbankruptcy situation, but they will have to continue fighting insurance to cover the boys' care. Without that coverage, the family will once again face medical costs, which have the potential to undermine the financial reset afforded by bankruptcy.

The situation is the most dire for those people who cannot work and lack other support. For instance, a middle-age, single man did not have insurance during the two years before filing or at the time of filing. He became sick five years prior to filing. Two years into his illness, he was no longer able to work. "I have (mental ill/severe/suicidal), chronic kidney disease, 3rd stage liver disease, with multiple cysts growing in both with no health insurance, unable to afford operation." He applied for Supplemental Security Income but was denied several times. At the time of his bankruptcy, he still had not been approved. He filed owing about $150,000 in total unsecured debt, of which $17,000 was student loan debt.

In the short term, filing bankruptcy will help with the bulk of his unsecured debt. But the most pressing issue is long-term financial stability. Given his extensive and chronic mental and physical health problems, coupled with his inability to work, the future does not look promising. Bankruptcy cannot improve his health or provide him with employment.

In addition to writing generally about their financial problems and paths to bankruptcy, people described how the stress from their debts caused or worsened physical, mental, or emotional health problems. Among the medical bankruptcy filers, 59 percent indicated that the stress of debts worsened the mental or physical health of themselves or their partners. Medical bankruptcy begets more health issues. These people already confronted medical hardships before they filed. Many had juggled these health problems for years. In the years leading up to their bankruptcy filings, the stress of their debts, some of which were medical debts, compounded their health problems.

People commonly listed depression, anxiety, and panic as symptoms that the stress caused or worsened. For some, depression may lessen or resolve with the debt discharge. For others, the debt discharge may do little to ease their symptoms. Some people wrote that they developed PTSD because of panic and anxiety. Others developed eating disorders and gained or lost large amounts of weight. Treating eating disorders, which are considered chronic conditions, is a long-term process, and fewer than half of people with bulimia or anorexia recover.[31]

Bankruptcy filers also commonly listed experiencing hypertension or high blood pressure. Others wrote that they developed diabetes or that their existing diabetes worsened. Although symptoms of Type 2 diabetes can be reversed, it is a chronic illness. It cannot be cured, and the risk of increasing blood sugar levels is permanent.[32] Some filers also insisted that, because of the stress, they experienced heart disease, heart attacks, and strokes—the damage from which can last a lifetime. A single woman in her early seventies, who owed over $140,000 in student loan debt, wrote: "Heart problems that was worse because of the stress."

People additionally mentioned that stress from their debts caused or worsened illnesses related to the immune system, such as fibromyalgia, lupus, and multiple sclerosis. A married woman in her late thirties with two young children wrote that her "[i]mmune system is shot due to stress and sleeplessness, causing Epstein Barr virus to become chronic and causing Hashimoto's autoimmune disease." But for the stress of debts, she may not have developed a chronic illness. But now that illness cannot be cured by filing bankruptcy.

Several people wrote that the stress of the debts led to alcohol, drug, and gambling addictions, such as a seventy-year-old woman who described how the stress caused sleeplessness and prompted dependency on sleeping pills. Addictions are chronic illnesses, and often the entire household suffers. And finally, the stress of debts destroys some couples' relationships, leading people to separate or divorce.

Those medical bankruptcy filers facing chronic illnesses or injuries represent the instances in which bankruptcy's discharge is the most likely to fail to provide long-term relief. These cases elucidate the failure of the US health-care system to live up to the uniquely human imperative of taking care of each other. We may have advanced medical science such that some people can live longer and more fulfilling lives. But the United States has created a medical and health-care system that leaves people struggling under massive amounts of debt, which in some instances serves to replace one illness with another rather than heal people to the best of our ability.

# 5  Staying Out of the Red

I stopped paying my credit cards because I was unable to
keep up with balance due and additional late fee charge.
My employer at that time was reducing work hours and
closing extra days at the office. I did try numerous times to
apply elsewhere and seek full time employment but did not
succeed. I was using credit cards to purchase clothes, food,
pay bills, doctor appointments, rent, car services, and for
entertainment purposes. I felt overwhelmed with bills.
I ended up getting pregnant and lost my baby at 6 months,
so medical bills started to pile up. That's when I seeked an
attorney. Credit debt collectors were calling and harassing
me daily. I lost insurance through [the Affordable Care
Act] because I no longer was able to afford premiums.
I now found a full time job and I am hoping to learn how
to manage my money better than before.

—Single Latina in her thirties

It is not surprising that people turn to debt to deal with the vagaries of
employment and education. When they experience unemployment or underemployment, or do not make a living wage, they may put expenses on
credit cards. For those who turn away from the traditional job market,
they may use credit cards or unsecured loans to launch businesses or keep
businesses running. When they ponder their career prospects, they may
decide to pursue higher education despite its costs and take out student
loans. This chapter focuses on the unsecured debt that people rack up
trying to keep up. Many aspects of how people make a living cause them
to turn to unsecured debt.

Employment, workplace dynamics, and education in the United States have shifted markedly since the 1970s. Jobs in the manufacturing sector have decreased, replaced by more jobs in education, health, professional and business services, and other service-oriented sectors. Many of these jobs require additional education beyond high school or on-the-job training. Employers offer fewer benefits, such as employer-sponsored health insurance and retirement plans. More people work part-time jobs, temporary jobs, or in alternative arrangements, including as independent contractors. This makes employment less stable and income more volatile and contributes to wage stagnation.[1] It also leads some people to try self-employment and start their own small businesses.

Concurrently, higher education is touted as "the gateway to the middle class."[2] Federal policies provide pathways to borrow to pay for associate's degrees, bachelor's degrees, and professional degrees. More people now move on to higher education after high school, often taking out hefty student loans as the cost of public, private, and for-profit educational institutions continues to increase.[3]

At the same time, income inequality in the United States has increased significantly, with overall wages barely keeping up with inflation. In the thirty-five years between 1979 and 2013, accounting for inflation, low-wage workers' hourly wages decreased by 5 percent, middle-wage workers' hourly wages rose by 6 percent, and very high wage workers experienced a 41 percent increase in pay. Although a college degree raises income and improves employment prospects, for many people it still does not provide enough money to keep up with student loans and live comfortably. Instead, people report not buying homes, getting married, or having children because of student loans.[4]

Incurring unsecured debt to smooth consumption may be necessary, and some of the debt may even seem productive because it promises to increase future earning potential. But the confluence of income inequality, stagnant wages, persistent underemployment, and expensive higher education may cause many people to struggle to pay these unsecured debts. They may live with their finances in the red for significant portions of their lives. The finances and stories of the people who file bankruptcy evidence the effects of reliance on unsecured debt to make up for insufficient income because of job loss or underemployment, to try self-employment, and to pay for higher education.

## UNSECURED DEBT TO DEAL WITH DECLINES IN INCOME

As detailed in chapter 2, one of the leading precipitators of people's bankruptcy filings is a decline in income. This decline may result from job loss or from a reduction in hours at a current job. In the years leading up to bankruptcy, some people may cycle through several different jobs. The people who file bankruptcy are more likely to be unemployed and actively seeking employment than the general population, and filers reported income fluctuations in the years prior to bankruptcy. Both unemployment and underemployment seem to lead people to incur debt such that they enter bankruptcy with more unsecured debt than other filers.

### Unemployed and Using Credit Cards

Nine percent of bankruptcy filers who responded to our survey reported that they were unemployed but seeking work at the time of filing, the same definition as used by the United States Bureau of Labor Statistics (BLS) in computing the unemployment rate. During the same time as our study, the BLS reported an average unemployment rate of just over 5 percent, making bankruptcy filers 80 percent more likely to be unemployed. Whereas the BLS focuses on the unemployment of individuals, our concern is the economic unit of the American household. In an era of underemployment and stretched household budgets, financial strain will happen if either income earner in a two-person household becomes unemployed.[5] Therefore, we aggregate and count a household as having unemployment if either person in a two-person household is unemployed. For the sake of simplicity, we refer to filing households with an adult who is unemployed and actively seeking work as *unemployed households,* and to other households as *employed households.*

Unemployed households enter bankruptcy with more unsecured debt: $93,472 as compared to $83,346 for employed households. Being unemployed correlates with incurring unsecured debt. The relationship is not merely because those who are employed have more income. In a regression controlling for income, any household unemployment—at least one unemployed adult who is actively seeking employment at the time of filing—remains a significant predictor of unsecured debt. Specifically, unemployment increases the households' amount of unsecured debt by an average of 26 percent even after controlling for income.[6]

At almost every decile of household income among filers, the value for unsecured debt is higher if at least one adult is unemployed and actively seeking employment. Unemployment at the time of filing bankruptcy links with higher amounts of unsecured debt. A lack of income leads people to take out unsecured debt, such as putting expenses on credit cards.

Filers' responses about why they turned to bankruptcy for help reflect the income strain of unemployment. Ninety-two percent of unemployed households stated that a decline in income contributed to their bankruptcies, compared to three-quarters of employed households.[7] Unemployed households also used more coping mechanisms to try to stay financially afloat in the years preceding their filings than did other households—a median of six versus five. Two-thirds of unemployed households relied on credit cards to make ends meet, the same as employed households. Unemployed households pawned their property, borrowed or accepted help from friends and family, turned to charity and government assistance, and moved more often than other households.

The stories written by people who entered bankruptcy while unemployed illustrate their decisions to incur unsecured debt and, for some, their eventual need to seek assistance beyond taking on debt, such as from government or a charity. A white couple in their midforties filed with $94,000 in unsecured debt, all of which was owed to credit card lenders. "Our reason for filing is my husband lost his job of over 26 years. We had to start using credit cards for groceries, gas, medical, etc."

A Latine couple, both in their forties, with two children, filed owing $28,000 in unsecured debts, mostly to credit card or retail card lenders. "My husband works construction which is seasonal. So if work is slow or it rains or gets too cold no work. Which in turn meant smaller paychecks and we weren't able to keep up with our bills. Our situation arised due to too much credit card debt." When they filed, her husband was employed, and she was seeking work. She wrote that, prior to filing, to make ends meet her husband would "do some maintenance work on buildings in the neighborhood for a few dollars." In the years leading up to bankruptcy, in addition to using credit cards and working more hours, this couple turned to government assistance and borrowed from family and friends.

Perhaps counterintuitively, 69 percent of unemployed households reported that they had worked more hours or had gotten another job in the two years before they filed bankruptcy, compared to 60 percent of employed households. That an adult in the household was unemployed at the time of filing signals more persistent employment problems, including part-time or temporary work, in the years prior to bankruptcy. Unemployed households reported shorter job tenures. About half of unemployed households changed jobs in the year before filing bankruptcy, compared to less than one-third of employed households. Bankruptcy data demonstrate how the working relationship between employers and employees in the United States has shifted in the past forty years to the benefit of employers, resulting in job instability, income volatility, and underemployment.

*Underemployed and Using Credit Cards*

In addition to unemployment, underemployment leads households to deplete savings and turn to credit cards to pay for everyday expenses. Underemployment occurs when a worker holds a job that does not match their skill or training, is not employed full-time and wants to work full-time, or works part-time for fewer hours than they have available to be scheduled.[8] Underemployment leads people to earn less than their potential income, leaving them struggling financially. It also leaves them perpetually looking for better and more work.

The BLS measures underemployment as workers employed part-time, but who want full-time jobs. Under this measure, underemployment was at around 6 percent following the Great Recession and slowly decreased to about 3 percent before the COVID pandemic. But researchers criticize this measure for failing to account for all people who want to work more. In the years leading up to the pandemic, researchers estimated true underemployment at roughly twice as high—between 8 and 11 percent.[9] Factoring in people working in the gig economy, the percentage of people underemployed could be even higher.

Why underemployment surged in recent decades relates to employers' ability to decrease the number of stable jobs and workers' inability to fight back against changes in job structure. Particularly vulnerable are part-time workers, whose employers have the greatest ability to set their hours, including decreasing hours and shifting schedules. Employers have cut benefits, such as retirement plans, in full-time jobs.[10] Part-time positions offer even fewer benefits, such as health insurance or paid leave, a situation that increases workers' financial vulnerability. The part-time work dynamic also is stressful. Research has shown it can lead to anxiety, depression, and physical pain.

In recent years, the employment market has structurally shifted toward more extensive use of part-time workers, decreasing the availability of full-time positions that provide employees with more stability. This shift has affected Black, Latine, and single women the most.[11] (Chapters 6 and 7 consider how disparities in the employment market increase Black households' and single women's use of bankruptcy to deal with financial problems.)

Underemployment—or the abandonment of full employment—is linked with wage stagnation and income inequality, particularly for low- and middle-income workers, who are the workers whose wages have stagnated the most. The decline of unions and collective bargaining in the United States since the late 1970s also has correlated with rising income inequality and wage stagnation.[12] Considered together, people's employment now yields less income in terms of money needed to meet expenses, provides less ability to save money for emergencies or in case of job loss, leaves more workers at the whims of employers, and is more likely to subject people to income fluctuations.

What the people who file bankruptcy report about their prebankruptcy lives shows the instability now built into the employment market. We asked debtors whether their household income changed during the two years before their bankruptcy. Fifty-four percent of filers reported that their income decreased significantly during those two years, signaling periods of unemployment or underemployment prior to filing. In contrast, only 5 percent of people stated that their incomes increased significantly during those two years. The rest of filers said that their incomes stayed about the same.

Consistent with unemployed households, those filers reporting that their household income significantly decreased enter bankruptcy with 17 percent more unsecured debt than those who reported that their income increased significantly. If income decreasing is a proxy for gaps in employment, including working part-time and underutilization of people's skills, again, these gaps correlate with incurring unsecured debt.

The relationship remains even after a regression controlling for filers' income. At the same income level, a filer who stated that their income decreased significantly prebankruptcy had 22 percent more unsecured debt on average than a filer who stated that their income stayed about the same.[13] At almost every decile of household income among filers, the amount of unsecured debt is higher if the filer reported that income decreased significantly before bankruptcy. Fluctuations in employment, whether they be gaps because of complete unemployment or reductions in hours or pay, lead people to take out unsecured debts, such as putting expenses on credit cards.

Those filers who reported that their household income decreased significantly were much more likely to indicate a decline in income as a contributor to their bankruptcy than were other filers—95 percent versus 56 percent.[14] This makes sense. A decrease in income, if unresolved, may become a precipitator of needing bankruptcy relief.

Additionally, those people with significant prebankruptcy decreases in income reacted to their bankruptcies differently than others. Fifty-five percent of filers whose income decreased significantly agreed "a great deal" that their debt problems were the result of circumstances outside of their control, compared to forty-one percent of other filers. Because employers can exert control over workplace dynamics and can set workers' hours and pay, people may experience the financial spirals that ultimately land them in bankruptcy court as external to them. Although these filers tried to deal with the decreases in income, their efforts proved ineffective, which many viewed as no fault of their own.

Compared to other households, those households with significant income decreases in the years leading up to their bankruptcies were more likely to work more hours or get another job, sell or pawn belongings, receive government assistance, receive charitable assistance, and move in with family and friends. Two-thirds of filers who experienced significant income declines turned to credit cards to make ends meet, compared to 64 percent of other filers.

Households with significant income declines also tried more coping tactics—a median of six as compared to a median of five for other households, which likely reflects the financial problems that come with severe income loss. If people had the ability to save money while fully employed to weather income declines, or if people's underemployment was not persistent, then perhaps they would not have pursued so many ways to try to make ends meet. But what people wrote about the effects of fluctuations in their income and employment situations indicate that years of underemployment reverberated through their finances.

This chapter's opening story illustrates the mounting problems that underemployment can have on finances. Although that bankruptcy filer held a job, her limited hours led her to put what seemed like primarily necessary expenses on credit cards. Because she could not keep up with her credit card payments, extra fees and interest caused her monthly payment amounts to increase. To try to balance her budget, she trimmed out health insurance, which may have led to higher medical bills. When she filed chapter 7, she owed $40,000 on student loans, $9,000 to medical providers, and $15,000 on credit cards.

She ended her story by declaring that now that she had found full-time employment, she was "hoping to learn how to manage my money better than before." But her self-diagnosis is off. Money management skills were not the primary issue or possibly not even a problem at all. She did not make enough money because she was underemployed and could not find full employment despite her numerous attempts.

Similarly, a sixty-five-year-old divorced Black woman listed the reason for her filing as "not able to find a job that paid a decent wage." She was laid off from a position that she had held for a significant period of time—twelve years—and then cycled through a few subsequent jobs.

> [After being laid off, I] was able to secure another job right away and after three months that job closed due to insufficient licensing. After being let go from that job it was very difficult to gain employment and started using my emergency saving. I was able to find a part-time job as a caregiver at six hours a week. In the meantime still using my savings trying to pay rent, student loan and all my bills. I then cashed in an IRA and finally tapped into my 403B. I remained unemployed for 19 months before finally being offer a position at a university. The pay is very low but its income coming into the house. I have been interviewing for other positions but no takers.

After her savings, including her retirement savings, ran out, she made ends meet by putting expenses on credit cards and seeking government assistance. By the time she filed bankruptcy, she owed $44,000 on student loans and $37,000 on credit cards.

Other people commented on the changing nature of employment. One took a position as a "clerk" after she could not find a job that provided enough working hours in her field following her employer's retirement. "Middle class employment has been taken down [to] poverty level. Can't find FT [full time] employment in our area. All dentists are hiring part time only unless you are already in an established private practice. . . . Doctors/corporations hire part time only so they don't have to pay health benefits. It sucks!" That "clerk" position came with a decrease in income.

Another switched jobs from traditional employment to commission-based work. "I started a new job and my income declined which caused me to get behind on my bills. My new job was based on commission and my income was up and down all the time." Part of why her commission-based income fluctuated so much was "car problems," which prevented her from meeting quotas, which decreased her compensation.

This person's reference to commission-based work reflects employers' changing the nature of their workers' jobs from full-time employment that comes with benefits paid by the employer to contract work. Fourteen percent of workers report independent contracting as part of their job.[15] This contract work relieves employers from providing workers with benefits—such as medical insurance, paid days off, and retirement accounts—and saddles the "independent contractor" with finding and paying for these benefits themselves. For employers, this decreases the cost of employment. For people, it increases the fixed costs of life, often without an increase in income to pay those costs. The clerk who worked on commission listed her employment status as self-employed.

Beyond those jobs that employers have relabeled as self-employment, some people may decide to remove themselves from the employment market altogether and start their own small businesses. They may take out debt to start those businesses or to keep those businesses alive.

## UNSECURED DEBT TO TRY SELF-EMPLOYMENT

Self-employment rates in the United States have been stable at around 10 percent in recent decades.[16] The rate is higher if one counts independent

*Table 5.1.*   Finances of Self-Employed Bankruptcy Filers vs. All Other
Bankruptcy Filers (Medians)

|  | *Self-Employed* | *All Other Filers* |
| --- | --- | --- |
| Total assets | $47,480 | $33,269 |
| Total debt | $171,039 | $100,163 |
| Unsecured debt | $67,819 | $45,544 |
| Annual income | $46,332 | $46,584 |
| Debt-to-asset ratio | 2.50 | 2.06 |
| Debt-to-income ratio | 3.39 | 2.15 |

contractors, gig workers, and those individuals who engage in self-employment irregularly as they cycle through traditional part-time or full-time employment. Historically, studies of self-employed individuals found that they were more likely to be white, male, and comparatively higher educated than the general population, although the shifting nature of employment may have lessened some of the demographic skews of self-employment.[17]

Nine percent of bankruptcy cases include a filer who reported self-employment, either full-time or part-time, at the time of bankruptcy.[18] This percentage is the same as the 9 percent of bankrupt households who reported full-time self-employment in 2007. It is lower than the 14 percent of bankrupt households who reported any self-employment, either full-time or part-time, in 2007.[19] As summarized in table 5.1, the finances of self-employed bankruptcy filers demonstrate that starting and sustaining a small business can lead to high unsecured debts—higher than other filers.

Among self-employed filers, median unsecured debts are almost 50 percent higher than other filers, which contribute, in part, to self-employed filers' higher median total debts. Although households reporting some self-employment enter bankruptcy with almost identical incomes as other households, that income has to cover significantly more debt, which is noticeable in self-employed filers' higher debt-to-income ratio. Narratives from debtors discussing their small businesses suggest that unsecured debts prompted their struggles.

The demographics of self-employed bankruptcy filers generally match studies of self-employed individuals. Forty-four percent of self-employed households include at least one adult who had earned a bachelor's degree or higher, as compared to twenty-seven percent among bankruptcy filers overall. Although there are no meaningful racial or ethnic differences among self-employed households, single women filers are the least likely to have reported self-employment. Five percent of single women are self-employed at filing, compared to nine percent of single men and twelve percent of married or partnered filers.

In the years leading up to their bankruptcies, self-employed filers are most likely to go without those items that do not relate to the precipitators of their bankruptcies. Compared to other filers, they were much less likely to indicate that medical expenses or missing work for medical reasons were contributors to their filings. Consistently, self-employed debtors' privations center on shaving health-care expenses from their budgets.

The self-employed also focus on work in the years leading up to their filings and eventually succumb to insufficient income. Compared to other debtors, self-employed filers were more likely to try to find more work in the two years before they filed—72 versus 61 percent. Finding more work could be trying to get back into mainstream employment or continuing to grow their businesses. Their efforts, though, proved insufficient. Eighty-nine percent of self-employed filers indicated a decline in income was a reason for their bankruptcy, compared to 76 percent of other filers.

What people wrote about self-employment as an aspect of their bankruptcies suggests some felt pushed into self-employment because of a lackluster job market. The wife of a married couple who filed chapter 13 wrote about the transition from mainstream to self-employment. "When my husband lose his job and start to work been self-employed and try other type a business [that] don't work well. Our income become really low and we try to work with our bank to consolidated our debt." When their mortgage company did not accept the debt consolidation plan, they filed bankruptcy owing $54,000 in unsecured debt. By the time they filed, her husband had secured full-time employment and had given up on self-employment.

In contrast, the husband of a married couple pursued dreams of building a business. "I left a good paying job at Wal-Mart. I dreamed of running my own business and expanded my E-Bay hobby into a full time operation. I was sucked in by an online loan company. . . . Struggled with making the payments and continued to take advances to pay the bills." He blamed the online lender, which he termed "predatory," and his chosen area of business for the failure. "Competition became fiercer by the day and it became hard to make any money to pay suppliers." He listed himself as self-employed and as seeking work.

Based on their bankruptcy schedules, his business suffered operating losses during the two years prior to bankruptcy, and he and his wife owed unsecured debts of $253,000, including $72,000 to the predatory online lender, when they filed. Some of the other unsecured creditors, based on their names, were lawn and garden product suppliers. He had gambled big on his dream, it had not panned out, and he and his wife were left owing lots of unsecured debt.

Although starting a business can be productive for some people—and a smashing success for a select few—it ends in failure for many. A portion of those failures end up in bankruptcy, which shows just how much the self-employed put on the line. Even among people who file bankruptcy, they are in more of a hole, with sizable unsecured debts and no greater income with which to cover them. A bankruptcy filing helps cushion the blow, but the bankruptcy files show the reality of being self-employed does not reflect the mythical tales of fame and fortune that come from entrepreneurship studies. The typical self-employed person owns a modest business and is trying to make a living. In many instances, self-employment is not a choice but an attempt to deal with unemployment or chronic underemployment.

## UNSECURED DEBT TO PURSUE HIGHER EDUCATION

Among the general population and people who file bankruptcy, small-business owners have higher educational attainment than the average adult.[20] Educational attainment in the United States, generally, has been climbing over the past decades, largely in reaction to the government's creation of pathways to allow people to continue their education after high school. These pathways are twofold.

First is the availability of higher education through public, nonprofit, and for-profit institutions, such as community colleges, state universities, and specialized technical programs. The share of adults with bachelor's degrees or higher rose from 17 percent in 1980 to 33 percent in 2015. Second is the availability of funds to attend these institutions, which is crucial because pursuing higher education is costly. Between 1980 and 2020, the average price for an undergraduate degree, including room and board, rose 169 percent.[21] Government data say that the total cost of a four-year degree, net of financial aid, averages $57,080 at a public school and $111,800 at a private school. At the same time, the median earnings for employed persons during the time they are most likely to be paying student loans—ages twenty-five to thirty-four—is $60,470.[22] That figure does not include people who are unemployed and obviously have even lower incomes.

Although higher education yields economic benefits, research finds that those benefits are tempered for some people, particularly Black and women students, as discussed in chapters 6 and 7. Education's income bump accrues the most upon completion of a bachelor's degree, exacerbating the debt and income problems of those who fail to finish their academic programs.[23] The people who file bankruptcy show how pursuing education may not generate income benefits and instead results in more struggle to make ends meet, with a mountain of unsecured obligations in the form of student loans.

Bankruptcy filers fail to launch with respect to their educations in two ways. Either they do not complete their degrees, or if they complete their degrees, they do not find jobs with income that matches their level of education.

As detailed in table 5.2, those who file bankruptcy are more educated than the general population but are less likely to have earned a bachelor's degree. More bankruptcy filers have started higher education than the general population, but they fail to complete their programs or they earn an associate's degree. Thirty-eight percent of adults in the United States have earned a bachelor's degree or higher. In comparison, 28 percent of bankruptcy filers had one or more adults in the household with a bachelor's degree or higher.

Dropping out of a degree program, despite an outlay of money for the uncompleted education, does not yield the income boost that finishing and getting the degree does. As summarized in table 5.3, among the general population, in 2022, at the median, only finishing some college

*Table 5.2.*    Education of Bankruptcy Filers, Primary Survey Respondent, vs. US Population, 2021

|  | Primary Filers (%) | US Population (%) |
|---|---|---|
| No high school degree | 6 | 9 |
| High school degree | 32 | 28 |
| Some college or associate's degree | 38 | 25 |
| Bachelor's degree | 15 | 24 |
| Graduate or professional degree | 9 | 14 |
| Other | 1 | — |

NOTE: If a joint petition was filed, education for the primary survey respondent is reported. We have educational data for 2,284 respondents. Data for the US population are from US Census Bureau, "Census Bureau Releases Data."

*Table 5.3.*    Median Income of Bankruptcy Filers, Primary Survey Respondent, vs. US Population, 2022, by Educational Attainment

|  | Bankruptcy Filers | US Population |
|---|---|---|
| No high school degree | $32,970 | $29,706 |
| High school degree | $41,736 | $36,931 |
| Some college or associate's degree | $47,136 | $43,988 |
| Bachelor's degree | $56,592 | $64,982 |
| Graduate or professional degree | $64,980 | $85,680 |

NOTE: If a joint petition was filed, education for the primary survey respondent is reported. Data for the US population are from the US Census Bureau, "Median Earnings by Educational Attainment."

gained an individual an extra $7,000 per year in income. Completing the degree bumped income by another $19,000. Among the people who file bankruptcy, as evident in table 5.3, the income benefits of education are even less.

Bankruptcy filers make less than the general population when they earn a bachelor's degree and considerably less when they earn a graduate or professional degree. These income figures reflect the chronic underemployment that some people may experience that leads them to eventually turn to bankruptcy for help. Higher education bumps the income of bankruptcy filers but not as much as for those in the general population with the same education.

Income, of course, is critical to keeping a household financially solvent. For people who have attempted to improve their income prospects with higher education, in addition to not getting the expected earnings bump from the education, they also may have to worry about paying student loans. One-fourth of households enter bankruptcy owing student loans.

The more education that people undertook, the higher the amount of student debt they entered bankruptcy owing. The median student loan amount owing for those filers who completed some college is $24,539. In comparison, the median student loan amount owing for filers with bachelor's degrees and with graduate or professional degrees is $66,844 and $115,949, respectively.

Some filers wrote about how student loans, combined with unemployment and underemployment, affected their ability to make ends meet. A fifty-year-old single white woman listed the reason for her bankruptcy as "laid off three times," but also identified her student loans as the catalyst of her filing. She had held her initial job for eight years before her employer downsized, eliminating her position. "I collected unemployment benefits for about 6 months then took a temporary job at a rate of over $2/hour less than I had been making. About 2 months into the temp assignment, they hired me full time. A little over one year later, I was laid off." She again collected unemployment until she found "a seasonal job at $2/hour less than I had been making in my previous job. The seasonal job was extended to last about a year."

When she filed chapter 7, she had been laid off from that third job for a month. But by that time, she had seriously struggled with debts for at least two years. She specifically mentioned the drain of her student loans, which totaled $61,000 and bore an $800 monthly payment. "Since . . . I was first laid off, I struggled to pay student loans. . . . Had I not had these student loans, I am confident that I would not have had to file bankruptcy." The monthly payment on her student loans amounted to 40 percent of her after-tax income. To make ends meet, she put expenses on credit cards, as evident in her unsecured debts, which she owed predominantly to credit card companies.

Student loans likewise featured in the narratives of bankruptcies written by some other filers discussed in this chapter. These stories necessarily came from people who filed bankruptcy. They sought the bankruptcy system's help, in part, for the debt discharge. When they emerged from bankruptcy, they would face the same employment market, including the possibility that they would again become or remain underemployed. But at least they would not be bogged down with tens of thousands of dollars in credit card and medical debt.

For people to discharge their student loans, however, they must prove that those loans are an "undue hardship," which is a burdensome task such that student loans are very rarely discharged.[24] Even with guidance issued by the Department of Justice and the Department of Education designed to assist debtors considering seeking student loan discharges, bankruptcy filers face an uphill battle in obtaining relief from their student loans.[25] Most people who file bankruptcy owing student loans will emerge still owing that debt.

Bankruptcy's undue hardship standard to receive a student loan discharge fails to recognize that pursuing higher education simply may not work out for some people. Some students will fail to finish the degree. They may drop out to help family. Or they may decide the program itself is not worth finishing. Some people will finish the program, but their degree will not yield the expected income benefits regardless of how many years they look for a job. Yet there is effectively no system that recognizes that some people will gamble on higher education, incurring the unsecured debt that the federal government has created pathways to take on to do so, and still find themselves, over the long term, unable to pay their student loans and maintain a basic standard of living. This is again another instance of the systemic loading of risk onto individuals.

## FEELING SET UP TO FAIL

Bankruptcy filers' efforts to stay out of the red when dealing with disruptions in employment, coping with fluctuations in income, pursuing

entrepreneurship, and bettering themselves through higher education signal larger problems with the risks associated with the employment market
and the costs of education that US policies have foisted onto American
citizens. That the working relationship between employers and employees
has shifted, wages have stagnated, and higher education has become more
expensive while yielding less useful degrees has not gone unnoticed. The
wife of a couple who filed chapter 7 lamented the state of the job market
in the United States.

> I'm not sure how to explain it . . . being here in America is a lot better than
> in my country but the financial issues are so hard to make ends meet. . . .
> [E]verything cost expensive and without an income or stable job it is so
> hard. Better make sure that your job pays good and stable. I feel so de-
> pressed even though I'm writing [these] words. It is hard living this way.
> Why does everybody have to suffer? It is supposed to be easy for everyone
> that is trying to make a living. Pardon my words. They just come out of my
> down depressed feelings. God bless America.

Widespread movements to ensure that employees have paid time off,
to provide employees with more comprehensive medical and maternity
leave, to increase the minimum wage, to cancel some student loan debt,
and to reform the education system such that pursuing higher education
is less expensive or less necessary to make a living wage reflect this sen-
timent. Until policies realign employers' and employees' interests, and
higher education returns to being less of a gamble, people will continue
to accrue unsecured debt to smooth periods of unemployment and underemployment and to attempt to gain skills to increase their income. Staying
out of the red will continue to prove challenging. And there will be little
but bankruptcy's debt discharge to help people reset their finances as they
try to find jobs that pay more money and provide more security.

# 6  Blackness of Bankruptcy

> In 2009 I got laid off of my job of 10 years. For the next two
> years I was unemployed. In 2011 I got a job making approx.
> 1/2 my salary at my job I lost in 2009. The house went into
> foreclosure. I applied for a modification I was refused. I
> liquidated my 401K in an attempt to save the house. The
> lawyers for Wells Fargo took thousands of dollars from
> me but continued with the foreclosure. I finally filed a
> chapter 13 to save the house.
>
> —Black couple with two children

Surviving as a Black person in the United States stands apart for its financial and societal difficulties. From slavery to Jim Crow laws to banking and credit policies that "redlined" them out of opportunity, Black persons have been repeatedly denied their civil and economic rights.[1] Research continues to find racial disparities in access to nearly every aspect of life, including education, employment, health care, housing, lending, and police interactions.[2]

In the realm of finance, Black persons pay more across credit products—for home loans, auto loans, credit cards, and education loans.[3] They have less access to mainstream banks and banking products and thus are more likely to use high-cost alternatives, like check-cashing outfits and payday lenders.[4] Creditors also target Black persons more often than others for debt collection lawsuits.[5] Research links these disparities with historical and continued discrimination as well as structural and systemic racism.[6]

The uniqueness of the Black experience in the United States shows up in the bankruptcy system in three ways. First, the percentage of Black households among bankruptcy filers is twice their incidence in the US population. Second, more Black households than non-Black households file chapter 13 rather than chapter 7. Third, Black households arrive at bankruptcy court with financial profiles and issues that evidence their broader financial and societal struggles.

To detail these disparities, this chapter compares the 621 bankruptcy cases in our dataset filed by Black households to other bankruptcy filers. The data suggest that discrimination can push Black households toward the bankruptcy system, and that system both fails and succeeds in helping with their financial troubles. (We count a two-person household as Black if either person so identifies. Only 6 percent of our Black respondents reported living in a household in which their spouse or partner is not Black.)

## BLACK HOUSEHOLDS' OVERREPRESENTATION IN BANKRUPTCY

Although 14 percent of the population identifies as Black, Black households make up 27 percent of the households that file bankruptcy. Their overrepresentation is offset by an underrepresentation of white persons in bankruptcy. Among the households that file bankruptcy, 64 percent are white. In comparison, 76 percent of the population identifies as white.[7]

The overrepresentation of Black households in bankruptcy holds across the country and has persisted for decades.[8] In places where more Black people live, such as Alabama, in which 27 percent of the population is Black, even more households that file bankruptcy are Black. Black households make up 55 percent of the households from Alabama that file bankruptcy. In places where fewer Black people live, such as Ohio and Illinois, where the Black population is close to the national average of 14 percent, still more households that file bankruptcy are Black—22 and 42 percent, respectively.[9]

Black households' higher than expected bankruptcy filing rate, detailed below, parallels the economic disparities they encounter in nearly every aspect of their lives. These disparities make it more likely that they will confront financial problems, and they make it harder to accumulate savings to weather those financial problems. As a result, Black households are more likely to struggle with debt, which in turn increases the possibility that they will consider filing bankruptcy. The breadth of racial disparities across institutions in the United States also suggests that when they turn to bankruptcy for assistance, Black persons may find a system that itself is infected with the structural racism that has persisted throughout US history.

## BLACK FILERS' OVERREPRESENTATION IN CHAPTER 13

Across all households that file bankruptcy, about two-thirds file chapter 7 and one-third file chapter 13.[10] The balance between chapter 7 and chapter 13 filings, however, differs significantly based on debtors' race, as illustrated in figure 6.1. Seventy-two percent of white and seventy-three percent of Latine households file chapter 7. For white, Latine, Asian, and other households, filing chapter 13 can be thought of as somewhat atypical, a choice that should be motivated by specific financial or legal reasons. In contrast, for Black households, filing chapter 7 is relatively less likely,

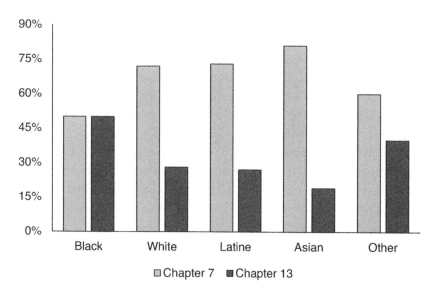

*Figure 6.1.* Racial and ethnic demographics of bankruptcy filers, by chapter 7 or chapter 13

and filing chapter 13 is typical. Fifty percent of Black households file chapter 7, the quicker and less expensive chapter, through which more than 95 percent of debtors receive a debt discharge. The other half of Black filers are in chapter 13, the slower and more expensive chapter, through which less than 40 percent of debtors receive a debt discharge.[11]

Given the US history of racial discrimination, it is not particularly surprising to find racial differences in the bankruptcy system. That this chapter's analysis focuses on Black bankruptcy filers as compared to all other filers is not to discount that people of other ethnicities face bias or prejudice in the economy and society. For instance, studies have shown that Latine borrowers are targeted for high-cost home loans.[12] But Black persons' experience in the United States is unique, including how often they file bankruptcy and which bankruptcy chapter they file.

### Searching for an Explanation for the Racial Disparity in Chapter Choice

As with their overrepresentation in the bankruptcy system, Black filers' overrepresentation in chapter 13 has endured for decades. Prior studies, including our own, have raised and ultimately rejected the possibility that financial, legal, demographic, and locality reasons explain why Black persons file chapter 13 more often than others—that is, reasons that would make choosing chapter 13 a logical choice or at least not based on race. These earlier studies relied on regression modeling, which controls for confounding variables—factors other than their race that might lead someone to file chapter 13.[13]

We built a new regression model that replicates the models that we and other scholars have used in prior research to study Black filers' overrepresentation in chapter 13, including relying on the same controls that might plausibly correlate with someone filing chapter 13.[14] The controls fall into four categories: legal and financial circumstances, attempts to renegotiate debt, demographic information, and local legal culture.

Chapter 13 provides some benefits. As a matter of law, filing chapter 13 may be beneficial for people who have previously filed bankruptcy; who owe priority and nondischargeable debt, such as child support and certain taxes; and who owe fines and fees, such as parking tickets. Foremost among the financial benefits is chapter 13's ability to protect valuable assets, such as homes. In addition, when people fall behind on debt payments, they report that they try to negotiate with their creditors. Given the barriers that Black persons find in lending markets, including the home mortgage market, they similarly may face difficulties in negotiating with mortgage and other lenders, which may lead Black households to file chapter 13 more frequently than others to keep their homes.

Certain demographic characteristics, such as age, marital status, and educational attainment, may positively correlate with a households' financial means. For instance, a married couple may make more money. If a household has more financial means, they may be better able to pay the higher attorney's fees that accompany chapter 13, which may correlate with filing chapter 13. The financial resources that may accompany these demographic characteristics alone also plausibly may correlate with filing chapter 13. Black filers may be more likely to have these characteristics, and thus their demographics may explain their higher chapter 13 filing rate.

Nationally, the rate at which people file chapter 13 versus chapter 7 in a given jurisdiction varies substantially, a situation that has persisted at least since the Brookings Institution published David Stanley and Marjorie Girth's study in 1971 that first noted the variation.[15] Prior literature has linked the variation to local legal culture—the interactions among bankruptcy judges, trustees, and debtor attorneys that create shared expectations, which lead to subtly guiding people's choices about which chapter to file.[16] Places with high chapter 13 rates are located in the South, where over half of the Black population lives.[17]

Table 6.1 presents the regression model's results. Full results are in the appendix. To show the effects of each set of variables separately, we entered them separately, starting with the legal and financial circumstances that may lead a household to file chapter 13, then adding debt renegotiation attempts, then adding demographic characteristics, and finally adding local legal culture.

Many of the controls are statistically significant, including income, prior bankruptcy filing, and the chapter 13 rate in a district. This is expected. Bankruptcy law provides particular benefits and has certain requirements; some filers should take advantage of those benefits, and some should be funneled into chapter 13 by those requirements. For example,

*Table 6.1.*  Logistic Regression on Probability of Filing Chapter 13

|                                 | *(1)* | *(2)* | *(3)* | *(4)* | *(5)* |
|---------------------------------|-------|-------|-------|-------|-------|
| Black household                 | 2.73* | 2.62* | 2.51* | 2.39* | 1.64* |
| Controls for                    |       |       |       |       |       |
| Legal & financial circumstances |       | yes   | yes   | yes   | yes   |
| Attempts to renegotiate debt    |       |       | yes   | yes   | yes   |
| Demographic information         |       |       |       | yes   | yes   |
| Local legal culture             |       |       |       |       | yes   |
| Model statistics                |       |       |       |       |       |
| N                               | 2,088 | 2,088 | 2,088 | 2,088 | 2,088 |
| McFadden pseudo $R^2$           | .04   | .28   | .29   | .29   | .34   |

NOTE: The table reports odds ratios. An asterisk (*) denotes statistical significance at the 5% level. The word "yes" indicates whether a particular vector of control variables was in the equation, not necessarily whether they were statistically significant. Due to extreme outliers, the financial variables were Winsorized at 3.5 standard deviations. The complete results, with odds ratio, are in the appendix.

other work has found that some Black persons file chapter 13 to avoid suspension of their driver's licenses, which chapter 13's broader discharge of some fees and fines can help prevent.[18] Even in the presence of controls, the race of the filing household remains significant, as multiple prior studies also have found.[19] Across studies spanning nearly twenty years, the evidence is overwhelming that confounding factors cannot explain away the substantial difference in Black households' chapter 13 filing rate.

Scholars have returned to local legal culture's influence on people's chapter choice and looked specifically at attorneys' interactions with their clients to explain why Black households file chapter 13 more frequently than other households. Using a hypothetical vignette about a couple thinking about filing bankruptcy, one of this book's authors, Robert Lawless, along with legal scholar Jean Braucher and psychologist Dov Cohen, found that attorneys recommended that a couple with names and a church affiliation consistent with a Black couple file chapter 13 more often than a couple with names and a church affiliation consistent with a white couple.

The financial and legal situation made filing chapter 7 and 13 equally plausible. Nothing else about the couple or their situation varied.[20]

Following that study, Lawless and Cohen, along with psychologist Faith Shin, surveyed consumer bankruptcy attorneys and asked them for their estimates about the rates at which Black bankruptcy filers end up in chapter 7 or chapter 13. One would expect the expert opinions to reflect the reality on the ground. Instead, attorneys reported believing that Black households were twice as likely to file chapter 7 as white households, but as shown in figure 6.1, the opposite is true—they are twice as likely to file chapter 13.[21] Those closest to the system could not see the disparity.

Around the same time as the follow-up survey of bankruptcy attorneys, we published research that focused on the amount and timing of fees that people pay their bankruptcy attorneys. Consistent with what we found then, Black households continue to disproportionately file chapter 13 on a "no money down" basis, under which a debtor pays nothing to their attorney prior to filing, and the entire attorney's fee is paid through the chapter 13 plan, essentially using chapter 13 to finance their attorney's fees. Again, even after controlling for confounding financial and other variables, race matters. As compared to similarly situated white filers, Black filers were more likely to be in a "no money down" chapter 13, and this disparity widened in places with high chapter 13 rates. Stated differently, how filers pay their attorney drives some of the racial disparity in the use of chapters 7 and 13.[22] Money matters in the provision of bankruptcy services to Black filers, the same as it does in the sale of goods, services, and credit to Black persons.

## Why Race Matters in Chapter Choice

Linking local legal culture and attorneys to racial disparities in chapter 13 filings that remain partially unexplainable returns to the US history of policies and practices that have resulted in racial disparities across multiple settings. In the contexts of housing and lending, scholars have connected these disparities to steering and stereotyping. *Stereotyping* refers to expectations about how members of a group, such as Black persons, will behave or a group's preferences. It is a fixed part of life and happens daily, particularly in the categorization and processing of substantial amounts of information.[23]

Bankruptcy law and the bankruptcy process, particularly chapter 13, are complex. Attorneys play a crucial role in helping people decide to file bankruptcy at all and which chapter to file. Subtle preconceptions about which chapter is the better choice for particular clients will guide recommendations and discussions. For some filers, those recommendations may amount to steering to chapter 13. For others, discussions may result in choosing chapter 13. Consumer bankruptcy often is a volume practice. Over hundreds of thousands of interactions, a skew in the demographics of who files which chapter will become detectable and will remain not fully explicable by financial, legal, and other factors. This has remained true for the racial disparity in chapter 13 across the country for half a century at least; research data before then are nonexistent. Even in judicial districts in which the vast majority of households file chapter 7, Black households are less likely to file chapter 7 than other households.

The racial disparity in chapter 13 matters. Attorneys charge almost $3,000 more at the median to assist with a chapter 13 case—$1,456 for chapter 7 versus $4,483 for chapter 13. If Black households filed chapters 7 and 13 at the rates of non-Black households, over the eleven years from 2013 to 2023 they cumulatively would have saved nearly $5 billion in attorney's fees.

Not only do Black households pay more for bankruptcy, they receive less. Across all households and even including those cases later converted to chapter 7, 41 percent of chapter 13 cases result in a debt discharge, as compared to 95 percent of chapter 7 cases. Black filers' chapter 13 cases are even less likely to yield a discharge than other filers' chapter 13 cases. Among chapter 13 cases, the court dismisses 59 percent of those filed by Black households, as compared to 40 percent filed by white households.[24] A dismissal leaves the debtor with the same financial problems they started with and returns them to the mercy of debt collectors and the state court collection process. Blacks are thus more likely to pay for legal services and a proceeding and leave without its primary benefit.

For Black filers, bankruptcy can be "rent-to-own." Rent-to-own companies target lower-income customers, including Black customers, and have been criticized as unduly expensive and deceptive.[25] In a rent-to-own transaction, a person commits to renting an item, such as a piece of furniture or an appliance, and does not actually own the item until it is completely paid for. With rent-to-own, people pay two to three times what they would if they had purchased the item outright. Those who do not complete the installment payments will never own the item they rent, even though they pay a significant portion of the item's outright value. A filer who used chapter 13 to finance their attorney's fee and ended up with their case dismissed similarly paid two to three times what they would have otherwise and, like a rent-to-own transaction, did not get what they paid for.

In addition, dismissal should increase the likelihood that the debtor will need to turn to bankruptcy for help again. Black filers indeed are more likely than others to file bankruptcy yet again. Twenty-six percent of Black households list a prior bankruptcy, compared to eleven percent of other households. A second bankruptcy case adds even more expense, is stressful, and requires more time and energy. Bankruptcy consumes more of Black people's lives.

That Black persons are overrepresented in chapter 13 is not to say that every Black person in chapter 13 should have filed chapter 7. As explained in chapter 1 of this book, chapter 13 offers financial and legal benefits distinct from the debt discharge, such as potentially keeping a home. Similarly, using chapter 13 to finance a more expensive attorney's fee may be financially wise if the alternative is eviction from a rental unit or repossession of a car. Some Black filers also may make too much money relative to their expenses to legally qualify for chapter 7. All these facts can be true for non-Black filers as well, but study after study has identified race as a determinant of bankruptcy chapter choice.

Regardless of the exact mechanisms behind their overrepresentation in chapter 13, Black individuals and families face a racially skewed bankruptcy system. How the bankruptcy system operates is yet another instance of racial injustice in the United States. Black persons will find this injustice, even if it goes unperceived, when they turn to bankruptcy to deal with the fallout from a multitude of other racial injustices. The financial profiles of Black households in bankruptcy show both the economic problems that lead them to bankruptcy and the extent to which bankruptcy law, in its current form, can assist Black filers in the distinctive financial struggles that they face.

RACIAL WEALTH INEQUALITY AND BLACK HOUSEHOLDS'
HEIGHTENED FINANCIAL PRECARITY

The racial wealth gap stands out as the largest economic disparity between Black and white persons in the United States. It conveys the accumulation of more than a century and a half of explicit exclusion from capital and labor markets following emancipation and the later obstruction of equal opportunities to build and maintain wealth through disparities in access to housing, education, employment, and credit. As of 2019, the median white household held eight times more wealth than the median Black household. The median Black household owned $24,100—$165,000 less than the median white household. On average, Black households had 15 percent as much wealth as white households, with an absolute dollar gap of $838,220.[26]

Wealth is an integral part of prosperity. It provides financial and emotional security. It cushions people from the vagaries of life and of the economy. It fuels professional and social growth, providing capital to start a business, relocate for a better job, or purchase a home in a desired location.

Immediately following emancipation, the racial wealth gap was nearly sixty to one. Between 1860 and 1970, it slowly diminished. During those years, the reduction of the wealth gap did not occur nearly as quickly as it could have and should have. But then something happened. Since the 1980s, not only has the reduction stalled, but in recent decades the racial wealth gap has widened.[27]

Housing policies, exclusion from mainstream consumer financial markets, income inequality, and education funding contribute to the perpetuation of the racial wealth gap.[28] Each make it difficult for Black persons to save money and build equity, cumulatively making it nearly impossible for the racial wealth gap to dissipate. Over recent decades, each exacted a toll on Black households' finances that has driven wealth of Black and white households further apart. Each also increases a Black household's likelihood of experiencing financial precarity, of facing problems with credit, and of looking to bankruptcy to deal with debts.

People bring the barriers they find with housing, consumer credit, income, education, and taking care of their families with them to the bankruptcy system. Most of these drivers of the racial wealth gap are evident when comparing Black filers to other filers. Table 6.2 provides that

*Table 6.2.*   Finances of Bankruptcy Filers, by Race and Chapter (Medians)

|  | Black Filers, Ch. 7 | Other Filers, Ch. 7 | Black Filers, Ch. 13 | Other Filers, Ch. 13 |
|---|---|---|---|---|
| Total assets | $20,103 | $27,112 | $33,174 | $134,686 |
| Homeowners | 30% | 34% | 45% | 64% |
| Home value | $140,000 | $157,448 | $129,580 | $167,400 |
| Home equity | $5,000 | $15,214 | $22,552 | $21,397 |
| With retirement assets | 30% | 35% | 26% | 40% |
| Retirement assets | $7,3388 | $9,287 | $3,471 | $9,510 |
| Total personal prop. | $13,830 | $16,514 | $17,100 | $23,153 |
| Total debts | $92,362 | $94,572 | $88,390 | $162,196 |
| Total home loans | $129,129 | $132,743 | $108,874 | $130,058 |
| With student loans | 43% | 24% | 30% | 25% |
| Student loans | $42,610 | $31,553 | $44,058 | $31,047 |
| Total unsecured debt | $53,955 | $52,470 | $28,607 | $37,505 |
| Debt-to-asset | 3.43 | 2.52 | 1.87 | 1.30 |
| Annual income | $42,822 | $42,468 | $47,742 | $61,332 |
| Debt-to-income | 2.15 | 2.26 | 1.98 | 2.37 |

NOTE: Home value is market value of residential real property.

comparison, emphasizing disparities in homes, retirement, and student loans. Later, we discuss possible reasons for the similarities in income among filers of all races despite well-documented racial income disparities outside of bankruptcy.

The table disaggregates chapter 7 and chapter 13 because Black filers are overrepresented in chapter 13, and chapter 13 filers differ from chapter 7 filers regardless of race. Half of Black filers find themselves in chapter 7 and half find themselves in chapter 13. The table reports home values, home equity, and home loans only for filers with homes, retirement assets only for filers with retirement assets, and student loans only for filers with student loans. Table 6.3 (found in a later section) focuses specifically on cars and car loans.

Other filers' total asset values exceed Black filers' total asset values, which aligns with racial differences in accumulated wealth. The difference also is evident when comparing total personal property values and debt-to-asset ratios. Black filers have fewer assets to cover their debts. Perhaps most noticeable are the disparities in homeownership and how they contribute to asset values and debt-to-asset ratios.

## Housing and Financial Insecurity

For most people, homeownership is the primary tool for building wealth. It also is a source of pride and grounds people in a community. Higher homeownership rates are associated with more positive outcomes for communities as a whole and for the people who live in them.[29] Although owning a home will not work out for everyone, many people have followed the path of homeownership to achieve at least some financial stability. But housing discrimination—from purchase to mortgage extension, appraisal, and sale—has placed obstacles in the way of the Black community to achieve the same level of financial stability as others.

### KEEPING THE HOME

The federal government has explicitly promoted homeownership as a wealth-building tactic since the New Deal programs of the 1930s. These programs established federal agencies and regulators that brought about low-cost credit to facilitate the purchase of houses. This low-cost credit, however, went predominantly to white families. Their purchases helped create segregated white suburbs and Black urban centers, with explicit redlining entrenching segregation and making it more difficult for Black persons to achieve their goal of homeownership even when they had the ability to make down payments. Houses in white neighborhoods became more valuable and appreciated more rapidly than houses in Black neighborhoods. Federal laws ultimately banned redlining, and the Supreme Court struck down racially restrictive property covenants, but neighborhoods across the United States remain largely segregated.[30]

As a result, the Black homeownership rate remains notably lower than the white homeownership rate—as of 2024, 46 percent compared to 74 percent.[31] Houses in predominantly Black neighborhoods also are undervalued, along with simply being worth less.[32] They are appraised at roughly 20 percent less than what their values would be if they were located in predominantly white neighborhoods, amounting to a cumulative loss of equity of approximately $156 billion.[33] When people put their houses up for sale, appraisals in majority-Black locations are nearly twice as likely to come in at under the contract price as homes in majority-white locations.[34] This affects final sale prices and limits wealth accumulation. For a Black home-owner struggling to pay the mortgage, it also makes selling the house less profitable, potentially leaving a deficiency to worry about.

The finances of the people who file bankruptcy show the monetary results of the Black community being steered to less desirable neigh-borhoods where housing values appreciate more slowly and being dis-criminated against in the appraisal process. As detailed in table 6.2, the value of people's primary residences is low for all filers, but it is even lower for Black filers. When Black homeowners wrote about their bankruptcies, they described how keeping those houses was at the top of their list of pri-orities and was a primary motivation for their filings.

A Black woman who filed chapter 13 alone listed her house as worth $67,000. "If you look at my bankruptcy file, you will see that I filed to re-tain my home. I lived in this house for 21 years and I am almost close to paying it off. To lose it was not an option." She owed her mortgage lender $22,000, so she was somewhat close to paying it off. She was among the 30 percent of chapter 13 filers who successfully complete their repayment plans. Just over five years after she filed bankruptcy, she received a dis-charge. She paid the remainder due on the mortgage through the plan and seemingly succeeded in retaining her home.

The house of a widowed Black man—a doublewide mobile home on a third of an acre of land—was worth a similar $71,000. Despite the home being underwater because he owed his mortgage lender $88,000, he wanted to keep it. "I was going to lose my house. Thank god for bankruptcy court and the people that helped me to get to bankruptcy court and my lawyer for his help. Thank god for helping me save my home." He likewise was one of the fortunate chapter 13 filers who completed their plans. After three years of payments, including over $28,000 to the mortgage lender, he received a discharge, and presumably remains living in his home.

## FIGHTING THE MORTGAGE LENDER

The bankruptcies filed by these two Black homeowners are outliers in terms of the equity that they held in their homes. Although the median home equity among Black chapter 13 filers is higher than among other chapter 13 filers, as shown in table 6.2, Black chapter 7 filers have significantly less home equity than other chapter 7 filers. Black chapter 7 filers' lower home equity reflects disparities that Black homeowners find in the mortgage market.

Although the 1968 Fair Housing Act and the 1974 Equal Credit Opportunity Act made it illegal for lenders to discriminate, and the Home Mortgage Disclosure Act (HMDA) requires lenders to disclose data about how they distribute credit, lenders still treat Black borrowers differently, and they pay more for mortgages. The Great Recession, which wiped out 53 percent of Black net worth, exemplifies this continued discrimination.[35]

In *Homeownership and America's Financial Underclass*, legal scholar Mechele Dickerson details how homeownership became a flawed promise, particularly for the Black community. Throughout the 1990s and early 2000s, overall housing prices increased by more than 50 percent, making it difficult for families of all demographics to afford houses and prompting the government to encourage lenders to diversify their loan products. Lenders began offering more expensive products—such as mortgages with high interest rates (subprime mortgages), with lower down payment requirements, with negative amortization, and with adjustable interest rates—ostensibly to people who otherwise would not have qualified for traditional mortgage loans.[36] Lenders used the opportunity to sell these more expensive products to target Black borrowers.[37]

During these housing boom years, 50 percent of mortgage loans issued to Black borrowers were subprime, compared to 20 percent of loans issued to white borrowers. Studies have confirmed that mortgage brokers disproportionately steered Black borrowers to higher-cost loans. For example, whereas 5 percent of higher-income white borrowers received subprime mortgages, 23 percent of higher-income Black borrowers received subprime mortgages.[38] By 2006, half of all loans made to Black borrowers were high-cost, compared to fewer than one-fifth of all loans made to white borrowers.[39] As a result, Black borrowers had higher mortgage debt, and during the Great Recession Black borrowers had a higher risk of defaulting on their mortgages and losing their homes.[40]

Discrimination in the mortgage market persists, with studies showing that lenders still charge otherwise equal Black borrowers higher interest rates, and that Black homeowners carry more expensive mortgages.[41] When Black homeowners file bankruptcy, this reality is reflected in the finances of chapter 7 filers: they hold little equity in their houses. At the mean, Black homeowners who file chapter 7 have a loan-to-value ratio of 0.94, meaning they hold 6 percent equity. In comparison, other homeowners who file chapter 7, at the mean, enter bankruptcy with a loan-to-value ratio of 0.86. They hold 16 percent equity in their homes, almost three times as much as Black chapter 7 homeowners. The low equity increases Black chapter 7 filers' debt-to-asset ratios. They have less ability to pay their debts with what they own, part of which is attributable to expensive mortgages.

Additionally, Black homeowners are more likely to confront other problems from their higher-cost mortgages, such as falling behind on payments. Black filers wrote about their experiences with mortgage lenders. This chapter's opening quote about losing a job and years later filing chapter 13 after a failed home loan modification attempt specifically identified Wells Fargo. After the Great Recession, Wells Fargo's mortgage modification policies resulted in multiple lawsuits. In 2022 it agreed to a $3.7 billion settlement with the Consumer Financial Protection Bureau (CFPB) over consumer abuses, including abuses related to its mortgage modification practices.[42]

When she filed chapter 13, a single Black woman with dependents pointed to her mortgage and foreclosure as among the reasons for her filing. "Mortgage people changed hands several times and mismanagement came into play. I stopped the foreclosure on my house several times myself. The lenders wanted more, doubling the amount of money, making me fall behind in mortgage payments. Only way to save my home was to file bankruptcy." She indicated that prior to filing, she tried to work with her creditor and had obtained a loan modification. She ended her story with: "I also was sick and out of work for 2 months with surgery. So I still struggle paying a high amount to the trustees, but it did save my home at least for now." The court dismissed her case for failure to make plan payments within a year of filing.

The husband of a Black married couple, both in their early sixties, filed chapter 13 when they fell behind on multiple debts. "Deep in debt. Got behind on house payment. Went into foreclosure on home. Payday loans and other types began to pile up. Rather than lose the home, filed bankruptcy. House, car note, etc., were too much. Had to save my home." He too pointed to the mortgage and foreclosure as reasons for the filing. Keeping the house, though, seemed to be of the utmost importance.

## Car Loans and Other Debts

When he filed chapter 13, this same filer also owned one car, worth $7,000, on which he owed $14,000, meaning that he held negative equity in the car. That his car was underwater is consistent with the median Black chapter 13 filer entering bankruptcy owing more on all car loans than the collective value of all their cars. Regardless of chapter, at the median, Black filers hold no equity in their most valuable car.

Table 6.3 details cars and car loans among bankruptcy filers, by race and chapter. Across all households, filers owned, at the median, one car. Joint filers, at the median, owned two cars.

Black filers are less likely to own cars than other filers, and they own cars at a slightly lower rate than the general population's approximately 85 percent vehicle ownership rate.[43] They own cars worth, at the median, about the same as other filers. But they are more likely to take out car loans and owe significantly more on those loans, particularly on their most valuable car. That car is likely what they rely on to get them to work and to take care of their family, and the car that they enter bankruptcy hoping to keep.

The car and car loan markets are in some ways like the home and home loan markets, and they are subject to similar temptations and tendencies to discriminate. Historically, Black consumers have paid more for cars and Black borrowers have paid more for car loans than other borrowers.[44] Black borrowers continue to pay more for car loans, are more likely to be sold subprime car loans, and experience higher rates of loan default.[45] A recent study found that, when controlling for creditworthiness, Black applicants' car loan approval rates are 1.5 percent lower, and that minorities pay interest rates that are seventy basis points higher.[46] These disparities mean that Black borrowers take out more expensive loans to finance the purchase of their cars. These more expensive car loans show up in the amount Black filers owe on car loans and the equity they hold in their cars.

*Table 6.3.* Bankruptcy Filers with Cars, by Race and Chapter

|  | Black Filers, Ch. 7 | Other Filers, Ch. 7 | Black Filers, Ch. 13 | Other Filers, Ch. 13 |
|---|---|---|---|---|
| Car owners | 77% | 86% | 89% | 92% |
| Car owners with houses | 27% | 32% | 39% | 59% |
| Medians, car owners | | | | |
| Most valuable car | | | | |
| Value | $7,551 | $7,195 | $10,844 | $11,205 |
| Cars with liens | 68% | 54% | 80% | 70% |
| Amount owed | $9,762 | $3,125 | $12,704 | $11,075 |
| Equity | $0 | $1,309 | ($793) | $549 |
| 2nd most valuable car | | | | |
| Value | $2,714 | $2,997 | $4,646 | $4,177 |
| Cars with liens | 41% | 36% | 70% | 51% |
| Amount owed | $0 | $0 | $3,719 | $596 |
| Equity | $1,265 | $1,228 | $298 | $956 |
| Total value, all cars | $8,500 | $8,401 | $12,429 | $13,311 |
| Amount owed, all cars | $11,456 | $4,678 | $14,002 | $13,783 |
| Equity, all cars | $0 | $1,805 | ($654) | $969 |

NOTE: The table reports medians for persons who own cars. N for Black chapter 7 filers' most valuable car is 235 and for 2nd most valuable car is 69. N for Black chapter 13 filers' most valuable car is 262 and for 2nd most valuable car is 91. N for other chapter 7 filers' most valuable car is 1,038 and for 2nd most valuable car is 405. N for other chapter 13 filers' most valuable car is 396 and for 2nd most valuable car is 203.

Other debts also may accrue from car ownership. Unpaid parking tickets and other government-assessed fees and fines can lead to cars being booted or impounded, a practice for which Chicago made national news, and to license suspension.[47] Chapter 13's broader discharge gets rid of some fees and fines, such as parking tickets, which in turn helps with license suspensions. Police officers disproportionately give traffic tickets to Black motorists.[48] More parking tickets are issued in predominantly Black neighborhoods.[49] Black drivers have higher rates of license suspension. In North Carolina, for instance, the rate is four times higher than that of white drivers.[50] These racial disparities appear in bankruptcy through the example of Black car owners who file chapter 13 owning little other than a car. They appear to file bankruptcy solely to try to save a car.[51]

The disparities also come out in the stories told to us. A single Black woman who filed chapter 13 had three children, one of whom was old enough to drive, and owned three modest cars that were all five to nine years old. The most valuable car was worth less than $9,500, and all three were subject to liens. She had missed payments, meaning the loans were in default. She was underwater on all three cars by a combined amount of $18,000. If the cars were repossessed, she would still owe at least that much (and probably more given that repossessed cars usually sell for only a fraction of their value). She also owed $7,000 in parking tickets. "I filed bankruptcy mainly for parking tickets that my family member got. I drive a lot taking my adopted children back and forth to school. Also during errands during the day. Couldn't afford to have my license suspended, nor afford the debt that had accrued to pay." Her repayment plan contemplated keeping two cars and surrendering the third.

As demonstrated by the narrative of the Black husband who filed to save the family home, getting behind on the home loan and car loan sometimes also can lead to taking on other types of debts, such as, in his situation, payday loans. Other Black filers also wrote about this cycle of debt. A single Black woman entered chapter 7 with $20,000 in unsecured debts. "A lot of pay day loans, credit cards and [finance] company that you can get money in one day with high payments and high interest rates."

Lenders target the Black community for high-cost products, like payday loans and auto title loans, making Black households particularly susceptible to a debt spiral if they lose their jobs or face health problems or if life simply spins out of control.[52] (The next chapter considers the intersection of bankruptcy and the even more specific marketing of payday loans to Black women.) These products both are more expensive and come with higher risks of default than credit cards. Likewise, studies have found that credit card lenders charge Black borrowers higher interest rates.[53] Taking out unsecured debt in general is more expensive for Black borrowers.

Nonetheless, Black persons must turn to unsecured debt to smooth breaks in income or if expenses increase, such as because of a medical issue, more often than white persons, because they have less savings and less ability to accumulate savings. Their greater reliance on credit products contributes to their financial precarity and increases their risk of defaulting on at least one debt, which puts them on a path to turning to the bankruptcy system for a debt discharge. That they generally pay more across credit products only worsens their financial precarity.

## Income and Education

Part of the reason the wealth gap persists relates to racial disparities in income, the employment market, higher education, and student loans. Black bankruptcy filers' finances both do and do not exhibit these inequalities outside of bankruptcy. In the following we reflect on the reasons for this. The next chapter compares these disparities at the intersection of race and gender.

### INCOME AND EMPLOYMENT

In 2019 the median Black worker made about 25 percent less per hour than the median white worker. Racial disparities in education, experience, and location only explain a portion of the difference, leaving an unexplained gap of 15 percent.[54] The wage gap differs when comparing Black and white men and Black and white women, with Black men and women making relatively less than their white counterparts.[55] The Black worker unemployment rate also historically is twice as high as the white worker unemployment rate.[56]

Black bankruptcy filers have approximately the same income as other filers. In table 6.2, Black chapter 13 filers have lower incomes, but that datapoint only reflects the racial disparity in chapter choice discussed earlier. Black persons end up in chapter 13, which requires payment of future income, despite having lower incomes than other chapter 13 filers. Aggregated across both chapters, Black filers have only a 4 percent lower income than white filers, a smaller difference than outside of bankruptcy. In an (unreported) regression, the income gap completely disappears once we control for education, experience, and location. Black households in bankruptcy were actually less likely to report unemployment than white households, 10 versus 13 percent.

Given the well-documented income and employment disparities outside of bankruptcy, we were surprised not to see similar disparities among bankruptcy filers. It is also a fact, as discussed previously, that Black persons are overrepresented among bankruptcy filers. What connects those facts are the additional stressors on the incomes of Black households, examples of which appear in our data. Fifty-seven percent of Black filers reported using high-cost payday loans, compared to thirty-seven percent of other filers. Black filers were 37 percent more likely to have a car repossessed, which can mean trouble getting to work and increased transportation costs. Black filers were 46 percent more likely to indicate financially helping family or close friends. Relatedly, Black filers were 11 percent more likely to have dependents under the age of twenty-three. These and other demands on the income of Black filers help to explain the higher filing rate as well as the lower wealth accumulation despite similar incomes shown in table 6.2.

Our filers also wrote stories that reflect other academic findings about the financial experiences of Black households. For example, Black employees are more likely to experience disruptions in their work schedules and income volatility.[57] Echoing these findings, a Black single woman who filed chapter 7 wrote.

> I filed bankruptcy due to my income decreasing. I was making almost $5,000 a month until the spring of 2017. It changed and I couldn't afford to pay all of my bills anymore. I tried to figure things out to make them better, like finding a part-time job or another full-time paying what I was making, but nothing came through and I had to pay what was important. Kept getting calls from bill collectors. I also tried to work out plans to get me caught up, but I still couldn't afford it. . . . It really sucks when your income changes and you don't know what to do.

When she filed, she was employed as a customer service representative, and her gross annual income was $39,000, which roughly matches the median income of Black chapter 7 filers.

Another study found that Black households are almost twice as sensitive to income shocks as white households, which the researchers attribute to the racial wealth gap.[58] The story written by a divorced Black woman who filed chapter 7 illustrates the difficulties brought about by a lack of savings. "I've always been employed, salaried, which means my income stays the same no matter how many hours I work, so when an emergency arises, such as needing a vehicle or medical expenses, it throws me in a loophole. Where do I get the extra money to make a car payment?" She had worked for the same employer for nineteen years when she filed chapter 7. At the time, she made $37,000 per year, before taxes. Her primary asset was her car, worth $12,000, and on which she owed $34,000. She owed $32,000 on unsecured debts.

Like most of the people who file bankruptcy, she had no retirement savings, despite being forty-nine years old. Black filers are even less likely than other filers to enter bankruptcy with retirement savings, and if they have retirement savings, they have less than other filers with retirement savings, as detailed in table 6.2. The relative lack of retirement savings likewise connects with the racial wealth gap. It is difficult to allocate income to retirement savings when income barely covers everyday expenses. Also, like other people who file bankruptcy, some Black filers who did have retirement funds wrote about how they liquidated their accounts to pay debts before turning to the bankruptcy system for help.

## EDUCATION AND STUDENT LOANS

Student loans, which play a particularly pernicious role in the lives of the Black community, also place stress on Black households' income. Black students are more likely to take out loans to finance higher education; are likely to pay higher interest on those loans; and are more likely to attend for-profit colleges, which cost more and have a significantly lower graduation rate than nonprofit four-year colleges.

Based on data from 2016, 85 percent of Black students graduate college carrying loans, compared to 69 percent of white students. Black students owed, on average, $34,000, compared to $30,100 owed by white students. Nearly half of Black students default on their loans; the default rate for white students is 21 percent. Two-thirds of Black students who take out loans to pay for education at for-profit colleges default on their student loans.[59]

Some of these students end up filing bankruptcy, such as this single Black 27-year-old who filed chapter 13: "I'm currently a nursing student at [a for-profit college]. I am a black male, not a thug, not a gangsta. I am a nursing student. I lost my job. I've been without lights, gas and money. I filed bankruptcy not out of pity but because I had no other road to go down." He owed $44,000 on student loans, similar to the median amount owed by Black chapter 13 filers who carry student loans. He indicated that food was the single most important thing that he went without in the year before his filing and wrote that he sold his clothes, shoes, and schoolbooks to make ends meet.

The racial disparities in the student loan market are discernible in the bankruptcy system. Black filers are more likely to enter bankruptcy with student loan debt, and those Black filers with student loans owe more on the loans than other filers, as detailed in table 6.2. Black filers also have lower overall educational attainment than other filers because more have attended some college, meaning they graduated from a two-year institution, earning an associate's degree, or they dropped out of a four-year institution. This matches the racial gap in college completion. Seventy percent of white students complete a college degree within six years, compared to forty-five percent of Black students.[60]

Consistent with more having attended some college, Black filers indicated more often than other filers that they went without education to make ends meet in the years leading up to their bankruptcies. Earning associate's degrees or dropping out of college often creates educational debt but seldom yields the same income bump as earning a four-year college degree. Although there may not have been money or time to continue their education, over the long term student loans often add pressure to a financial situation that reflects and exacerbates other discrimination and racial barriers. Indeed, Black filers were more likely than others to agree that unmanageable student loan payments contributed to their bankruptcies. As with home loans, auto loans, and unsecured debts, disparities and predation in the marketing and funding of higher education stymy savings and ultimately transfer wealth away from the Black community, contributing to the perpetuation of the racial wealth gap.[61]

## Taking Care of Family and Community

That Black filers set aside their educational goals in times of financial stress connects with the handful of characteristics that set them apart from other filers, which fall into the broad category of family and community dynamics. As we explore in the next chapter, Black filers, and particularly Black women, are more likely to have dependents in their households. They are less likely to be married. They are more likely to indicate that helping others contributed to their bankruptcies. And they are more likely to look to friends and family, government assistance, and charity for help. For example, the Black nursing student also wrote about how he approached his church for assistance before turning to the bankruptcy system.

Focusing on Black filers' prebankruptcy actions again reflects the racial wealth gap and speaks to the lack of a social safety net in the United States, as well as the Black community's attempts to support each other. That Black households look to family and friends for help suggests a lack of resources and a lack of adequate support when they seek assistance from the government. The lack of support offered in times of need matches the current expectation that people will personally shoulder the costs associated with many of life's expenses and risks: owning homes and cars, dealing with fluctuations in the employment market and stagnant wages, paying for their educations, and recovering from health scares. Past and continued denial of civil and economic rights and opportunities leaves the Black community less able to shoulder these costs, which almost necessarily sets them up to struggle more financially. Because they have few, if any, other places to turn, more Black households file bankruptcy than one would predict given their share of the population.

## BANKRUPTCY LAW'S LIMITATIONS

For some Black households, the bankruptcy system has become the leading solution to their financial problems. Once they decide to file, however, they will find a system that, like many institutions in the United States, is stacked against them. Some Black filers will end up in chapter 13 not for its financial or legal benefits, but seemingly solely because of their race. They will pay more to file chapter 13, and because they are less likely to get a discharge, they will receive fewer benefits.

More subtly, in both chapters 7 and 13, bankruptcy law can remedy fewer of Black filers' financial problems. As detailed by legal scholar Mechele Dickerson, bankruptcy law, while facially neutral, systemically favors people with certain asset and debt profiles. Bankruptcy law imagines a debtor with a home and some equity in that home, who is married, has a retirement account, is employed, provides financial support only to legal dependents, and has little if any student loan debt.[62] Black filers meet two of these assumptions, one of which they only meet sometimes: they are as likely to be employed as other filers, and those Black households that file chapter 13 while owning a home have a similar amount of home equity, at the median, as other chapter 13 filers with homes. Other households are more likely to meet every other criterion.

Because bankruptcy law presupposes the finances and life situation of a non-Black household, other households, and specifically white households, experience more benefits. They can retain their home and home equity; among all people who file bankruptcy, white households are more likely to have both. They are more likely to be married, and as married couples, they can shield more property via exemptions. They can take advantage of exemptions to keep the retirement accounts they are more likely to have. They can take advantage of bankruptcy law provisions that allow them to craft repayment plans that include expenses for their legal dependents, who are likely to be all their dependents. Because they are less likely to owe student loan debt, or if they have student loan debt, they owe less of it, they exit bankruptcy with a greater percentage of their unsecured debt discharged. They retain more property, and their fresh start is fresher.

In contrast, Black filers enter with less property, exit with less property, and discharge a lesser percentage of their unsecured debt. Their relative lack of property connects with the racial wealth gap. But what they receive from bankruptcy law is the debt discharge. If they owe loans on their homes and cars, their homes and cars are more likely to be underwater; if so, bankruptcy law does not allow them to walk away from these loans if they want to keep their house or car. Their student loans are unlikely to be discharged. Bankruptcy law does not fully recognize their household structure and does not allow them to include expenses in repayment plans for assistance they provide for other people they consider family, making it harder to fulfill plan payments and decreasing their chances of obtaining a discharge through chapter 13.

Black filers' fresh start is less fresh—tarnished and scuffed compared to that of other filers. Bankruptcy law, of course, cannot fix wealth and income inequalities. It does not provide a job. It does not put money in the bank. It does not buy a house. Rather, bankruptcy law provides tools to help people deal with their obligations to others. Although facially neutral, key portions of bankruptcy law do not work well for Black filers. Bankruptcy law does not address the obligations Black filers are likely to have, and the tools it gives to filers assume household resources Black filers are less likely to have. Sometimes it gives Black filers less access to the most effective tools. The accumulation of discrimination across the economy and society directs Black households toward the bankruptcy system, where they face more inequality.

Although filing bankruptcy will help some Black households, bankruptcy law, as currently enacted and practiced, exacerbates racial economic disparity. Although bankruptcy law cannot solve disparities in the broader economy and across society, it should not add to those disparities. In this book's conclusion, we propose discrete changes to bankruptcy law to make its provisions a more equitable lifeline of last resort.

# 7  All the Single Ladies (with Children) in Bankruptcy

> After my divorce I found it really hard to just maintain a
> household. Paying for the necessities and paying rent and
> trying to pay a car payment all became much too much.
> My health started to take a turn for the worse and in comes
> medical bills. I took out payday loans, pawned title to my
> car and borrowed money from friends and family just to
> make ends meet. The wage garnishment was like a punch
> in my gut. I was scared, depressed, and really didn't know
> what else to do. I prayed about it and decided after a long
> debate with myself that bankruptcy may be my only option.
>
> —Thirty-eight-year-old single Black woman with
> a twenty-year-old dependent daughter

Women are the largest demographic group in bankruptcy. Fifty-eight percent of bankruptcy filers are women. Some women file jointly with their spouses. Some women have significant others in the household but file bankruptcy alone, without their spouse or partner. And some women are single, meaning that there is no other adult in the household.

Single women stand out among bankruptcy filers, especially when their frequency of filing is juxtaposed against that of single men.[1] As detailed in table 7.1, twice as many single women as single men file bankruptcy. Single Black women in bankruptcy outnumber single Black men more than three to one.

Women were not always the majority of bankruptcy filers. Based on CBP data, in 1981 men constituted 54 percent of the people who filed bankruptcy. Twenty years later, in 2001, the percentages had flipped, and

Table 7.1.  Percentage of Bankruptcy Filers, by Relationship Status
and Race

|  | All Filers | Black Filers | White Filers |
|---|---|---|---|
| Single woman | 37% | 51% | 30% |
| Single man | 16% | 15% | 16% |
| Married or partnered | 47% | 34% | 53% |

NOTE: The bankruptcy data are by household. For two-person households, race is
counted if either person identified with that race. N for all filers is 2,292. N for
Black filers is 615; N for white filers is 1,455.

women's share of bankruptcy filers had increased to 54 percent.[2] Since
then, women's filing numbers compared to men's have remained steady.

The roots of the increase in women filing bankruptcy trace back to the
1970s, which marked the beginnings of what would become a profound
shift in the economics of households in the United States. This shift dis-
rupted traditional employment models, elevated the importance of pursuing higher education, and changed marriage patterns. Combined, these
shifts have led more women to go it alone, either never marrying or di-
vorcing, including when raising children.

But women face barriers to financial stability: pay inequality, relatively
larger amounts of student loan debt, childcare expenses, housing costs,
and particularly the lack of stable housing situations in which parents
hope to raise their children. Women who divorce or separate from partners must figure out how to provide for their kids, who are more likely to
remain in their homes, sometimes without the help of child support. And
some women find themselves drowning in debt that their former partners
put in their names.

The financial effects of raising children are noticeable among the single
women who file bankruptcy. When they file, single women are more likely
to be responsible for dependents, which we define as those listed in the
bankruptcy court records as dependents and who are twenty-two years
old or younger. Our definition of a dependent thus includes college-age
members of the household but only if the filer identifies them as financially dependent.

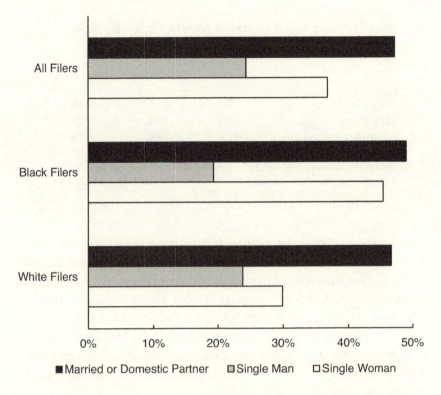

*Figure 7.1.* Percentage of bankruptcy filers with dependents in their households, by household type and race

As figure 7.1 depicts, single women are 50 percent more likely to have dependents than single men.[3] The disparity becomes especially pronounced along racial lines, with single Black women who file bankruptcy being almost more than twice as likely to have dependents as single Black men who file. Among white filers, single women are 25 percent more likely to have dependents than single men.

How women have experienced the shifting economics of family life divides along socioeconomic and racial lines. Economic class, education, and race are among the key characteristics that have shaped the overall dramatic shifts in family life. Understanding these broader trends is crucial to understanding why women turn to bankruptcy for help. This chapter draws from the 841 bankruptcy cases in our dataset filed by single women to describe the financial concerns that define single women's lives.

The single women who file bankruptcy display the effects of the shift in household economics. What single women do to try to stay financially afloat prior to filing reflects the struggles of single women across the United States. And single women's skepticism about bankruptcy's ability to improve their situations further points to systemic problems that make financial security elusive for women.

## FAMILY LIFE IN THE UNITED STATES

### More Work, More Education

The largest contributor to the shift in household economics and family life in the United States since the 1970s is women's increased participation in the workforce. Women now rival men in the total number of jobs held across the United States.[4] Women's integration into the workforce encouraged them to invest in higher education, and women now are more educated than men. For instance, there are 40 percent more women in two-year colleges and 30 percent more in four-year colleges.[5]

Single women who file bankruptcy both do and do not reflect these broader trends. At the time they file, two-thirds of single women are employed, the same percentage as single men. Single women filers are as likely to have completed college as single men, at about 23 percent, but they are more likely to report only some college or an associate's degree than are single men, 42 percent compared to 30 percent. Single women filers also are less likely to complete college than the general population. But they are more likely to have student debt and to owe more on those loans than other filers, as detailed later.

Women's entry into the workforce and increased education vary across demographic groups. Notably, Black women are more likely than white women to hold jobs.[6] Black women likewise differ from white women in their educational experiences and are less likely to pursue an associate's or a bachelor's degree. Like white women, Black women are more educated than their male counterparts both at the college and graduate levels. Black women also are more likely to enroll in for-profit institutions, particularly for graduate education.[7] For-profit institutions generally cost more to attend than other schools.[8]

Again, bankruptcy filers do and do not reflect these broader trends. Single Black women who file bankruptcy are more likely to have a job than single white women who file—72 versus 64 percent. Black women filers, however, have similar educational levels to white women filers but are more educated than Black men. Almost three-quarters of the single Black women who file have completed some college, have a bachelor's degree, or have an advanced degree, compared to about half of the single Black men who file bankruptcy.

## Less Marriage, More Single-Parent Households

At the same time that women working became the norm, marriage trends started to shift. Since the 1970s, marriage rates in the United States have fallen by almost 50 percent.[9] This decrease appears among the people who file bankruptcy, as evident in the 50 percent decline in joint petitions, which only married couples can file, over the past forty years.[10] As with women's employment and education, marriage, divorce, and childrearing trends differ based on socioeconomic status and across racial lines. These demographic differences also align with the demographics of people who file bankruptcy.

Norms about pursuing higher education and working outside the home, combined with widening income inequality, drive the demographic differences in marriage, divorce, and child-rearing trends in the United States. As detailed by legal scholars June Carbone and Naomi Cahn in *Marriage Markets*, economic inequality has shaped these trends, leading to disparities between working-class, middle-class, and more educated, elite women.[11]

Perhaps counterintuitively given that they are also most likely to have resources that would allow them to live independently, the most educated women are those most likely to get married and to stay married, typically to equally educated, elite men. In contrast, as argued by Carbone and Cahn, because of rising income inequality, working-class women face difficulties finding men who they think will contribute to the household and are worthy of a long-term relationship. These changes have altered the "gender bargain" such that "the top and the bottom of the socioeconomic system [are pushed] in different directions."[12] Marriage has become the norm at the top, and divorce or never marrying has become the norm at the bottom.

In the middle are more educated working-class women, most of whom graduated from high school and started a four-year degree but then transferred to a community college, earned a vocational degree, or dropped out of college. These women are less likely to get married and stay married. Instead, they cohabitate with a partner; maybe get married, then get divorced; and then perhaps live with a different partner without marrying again.[13] Based on their educational attainment, these women make up many of the single women who file bankruptcy.

The decline in marriage over the past several decades has coincided with a change in the share of children living in single-parent households. In 2023, one-quarter of children lived in single-parent households, compared to one-fifth in 1980. At present, a mother heads 83 percent of single-parent households. Eighteen million children live in single-parent households.[14]

Marriage, divorce, and child-rearing trends among Black households differ from households generally. Black adults marry less.[15] Fifty-one percent of Black men and forty-eight percent of Black women never marry.[16] Scholars have attributed lower marriage rates among Black adults to the unavailability of well-paying jobs and to financial instability resulting from centuries of racism, economic mobility experienced by more educated Black women, and mass incarceration among Black men, which further separates Black women and Black men.[17]

Black women have the same number of children on average as other women.[18] More Black children, however, grow up in single-parent households. Forty-six percent of births to Black women are to "solo" mothers, meaning women who are neither married nor cohabitating. In contrast, 9 percent of births to white women are to solo mothers.[19] Overall, in 2020, 18 percent of children from white households lived in a single-parent household, compared to 50 percent of children from Black households who lived in single-parent households.[20] Again, the bankruptcy data reflect these broader societal patterns. Single Black women are over 40 percent more likely to file bankruptcy with a dependent in their household than single white women.

The shifts in family life would not be problematic for single women if they made enough money to cover their expenses, including those of their children. But despite their educational achievements, women still lag behind men in pay. They also carry more debt, particularly student loans. Facing these two factors combined, some women will fail financially, prompting some to turn to bankruptcy for help.

## FEMALE FINANCES: MORE LOANS, STILL LESS INCOME

The finances of single women in bankruptcy show major fault lines in women's lives that lead them to struggle. Tables 7.2, 7.3, and 7.4 summarize key financial information about single women who file bankruptcy, single men who file bankruptcy, and married or partnered bankruptcy filers, respectively, disaggregated by relationship status. Each table reports student loans only for those filers with student loans.

*Table 7.2.* Finances of Single Women Bankruptcy Filers, by Race (Medians)

|  | All Women | Black Women | White Women |
|---|---|---|---|
| Total assets | $25,232 | $21,654 | $28,368 |
| Homeowners | 34% | 31% | 37% |
| Total debts | $82,548 | $79,381 | $87,334 |
| With student loans | 31% | 42% | 25% |
| Student loans | $40,767 | $50,713 | $30,544 |
| Annual income | $39,504 | $42,000 | $38,388 |

*Table 7.3.* Finances of Single Men Bankruptcy Filers, by Race (Medians)

|  | All Men | Black Men | White Men |
|---|---|---|---|
| Total assets | $20,958 | $13,464 | $21,047 |
| Homeowners | 29% | 27% | 28% |
| Total debts | $69,332 | $65,267 | $67,918 |
| With student loans | 20% | 28% | 17% |
| Student loans | $31,274 | $28,874 | $33,855 |
| Annual income | $37,836 | $32,892 | $39,060 |

*Table 7.4.*   Finances of Married or Partnered Bankruptcy Filers, by Race (Medians)

|  | *All Filers* | *Black Filers* | *White Filers* |
|---|---|---|---|
| Total assets | $66,739 | $68,277 | $69,622 |
| Homeowners | 50% | 51% | 50% |
| Total debts | $140,431 | $139,460 | $149,938 |
| With student loans | 27% | 33% | 28% |
| Student loans | $33,112 | $46,238 | $32,974 |
| Annual income | $60,342 | $61,848 | $60,786 |

NOTE: The bankruptcy data are by household.

Notably, single women are more likely to have student loans and owe more in student loans when they file bankruptcy than single men, with single Black women owing the most. Single women also are more likely to own their homes than single men, which increases the value of their assets but also increases their total amount of debt. In our survey, the single women filers wrote about difficulties with student loans and mortgages and with stretching income to meet expenses, particularly when their income had to cover their and their children's needs.

## Contending with Student Loans

### STUDENT LOANS AMONG WOMEN GENERALLY

The federal government's support of people pursuing higher education by guaranteeing student loans has led to a dramatic increase in borrowing over the past fifty years.[21] Now less than half of students graduate from four-year institutions without any student loan debt.[22] That single women who file bankruptcy are more likely to have student loans and owe more in student loan debt than men (and married or partnered couples) tracks with overall disparities in the United States in how women and men finance their educations.

Women are both more likely to take out student loans and to borrow more when they do so than men, regardless of when they start their degrees, when they graduate, or whether they pursue a two-year or four-year degree. Black women take out even more student loans than white women and Black men. Black women's higher rate of attendance at costlier for-profit institutions accounts for some of the increase in loan amounts.[23]

Increased education and an established place in the workforce have not equated to women earning as much as men, which affects their ability to pay back student loans and makes it difficult for them to keep their families financially afloat, particularly if they are single and have children. More than five decades after the passage of the Equal Pay Act, women continue to fight for pay equity. In 2022 women earned 83 percent of what men earned.[24]

Partly as a result of women's lower incomes, it takes two years longer for them to pay off student loans, and women default on their student loans at higher rates than men.[25] Black women face even greater difficulties in paying their larger student loans.[26] Their heightened struggles relate, in part, to their higher rate of attendance at for-profit institutions, which besides costing more have lower graduation rates and worse career outcomes than other schools. Black women's lower incomes further contribute to their struggles paying student loans.[27] Regardless of educational attainment, Black women make less than white men.[28]

## STUDENT LOANS AMONG SINGLE WOMEN IN BANKRUPTCY

The single women who filed bankruptcy discussed student loans and how they break their already tenuous budgets. For instance, a thirty-year-old Black woman who completed some college and who worked as a police officer wrote: "Trying to make the best financial decisions but always seem to be so far behind. Student loans were overwhelming, medical bills unrealistic. Taking care of needs was all I could manage. Living paycheck to paycheck, borrowing from one family member to pay another."

Similarly, a single fifty-year-old white mother of three (now adult) boys recounted struggling for years to make ends meet despite going back to school. In line with research about how it takes women longer to pay back student loans, she described her student loans ballooning as interest accrued.

> I went back to college to finish what I started when my children were very
> young to better myself and in hopes to have a good career and to make more

money, to hopefully save. I did eventually graduate with an associates degree and I did have to take out additional money from my student loans to help take care of my family. I'm still struggling to pay off my student loans, which originally were $[24,000] or so, and due to interest over the years, it jumped up to $[67,000]. It's shocking to say the least.

Some single women wrote about the challenges of managing student loans with insufficient income. A divorced licensed practical nurse, which is an associate's degree known for being offered by for-profit colleges, stated: "Student loans issued at a pay rate above market rate." Likewise, a twenty-four-year-old Black woman with over $106,000 in student loans discussed how her graduate degree did not pay off as she had expected: "After college, the pay was nowhere near what I thought so I kept sinking into more debt. . . . I still make nowhere near enough money as I thought I would with an MBA."

## Keeping Up with the Mortgage

### HOMEOWNERSHIP AMONG WOMEN GENERALLY

In addition to managing student loans, many women also must budget to keep up with home loans. The finances of single women who file bankruptcy reflect the wider trend in the United States of women owning homes more frequently than men, either when they live alone or when they cohabitate with men.[29] Part of women's higher homeownership stems from their increased likelihood of keeping the family house when they divorce or separate.

Women also purchase homes by themselves. In 2021 single women accounted for 19 percent of home purchases, compared to single men's 9 percent.[30] The single women who take out mortgages to fund their home purchases have distinctive characteristics. Compared to single men and couples who borrow, single women have lower incomes, are more likely to be minorities, and are more likely to live in lower-income areas. They also pay more for mortgages than single men and couples, in part because they have lower credit scores and in part because they are more likely to be sold subprime loans. Lower credit scores and taking out subprime mortgages result in higher interest rates and fees.

Overall, single women's mortgages, though smaller than single men's and couple's mortgages, consume more of single women's income.[31] As with student loans, women's lower incomes combined with more expensive mortgages make homeownership financially tenuous.

## HOMEOWNERSHIP AMONG SINGLE WOMEN IN BANKRUPTCY

In line with these national trends, single women who file bankruptcy own homes more often than the single men who file. Single women's homes are worth less at the median than single men's homes, $133,000 versus $155,000. Both are lower than the median worth of a couple's home, $170,000.

Single women's homeownership may be more precarious than single men's, however, because single women are more likely to have dependents in their homes. Their incomes must stretch to cover more expenses. In their narratives about why they turned to bankruptcy, single women noted falling behind on mortgage payments and facing foreclosure.

Consistent with women keeping homes when they split from their partners, divorced women identified homeownership as the impetus for their bankruptcies, such as this recently divorced mother of one who said that high mortgage payments were the main contributor to her filing: "My spouse left me and my family behind on the mortgage and I could not pay the late payments alone with my income. Was behind 3 months when [he] left. Tried to get a modification loan on the mortgage. They said I could for as long as 6 months, then said that I could not when it was close to time for foreclosure on the house."

When she filed, her house was worth $146,000 and her mortgage balance was $174,000. With a gross income of $34,500, she faced significant barriers to meeting her chapter 13 repayment plan. She fell behind on the plan soon after its confirmation but successfully requested a plan modification and subsequently received a debt discharge. Nonbankruptcy public records indicate that she held onto the house and remains in it ten years post-filing.

Single women also wrote about the financial consequences of selling their homes. Their concerns included that they were having trouble selling in tough markets and that they would owe their mortgage lender money if they sold because their homes were underwater, meaning that they owed more money on the home than its market value.

## KEEPING HOMES FOR CHILDREN

Along with the financial ramifications, some single women stated that they wanted to keep their homes for their children's benefit. Their desire to ensure that their children stayed in their homes tracks with parents purchasing houses based on the reputation of zoned public-school districts. The push for parents to choose where they live based on school district has shaped housing decisions for decades, leading to increased housing costs in certain neighborhoods across the United States.[32] Single women with children may worry about losing their homes and thereby being forced to change school districts. More simply, they may want to keep their children in a familiar place.

For example, a woman with two dependent older children—eighteen and twenty-one—kept the house when her partner left. When she filed bankruptcy, besides her ex-partner owing $42,500 in overdue child support, the mortgage was her primary problem. "My second mortgage fell behind. I had a modification but fell behind again. They were foreclosing soon. Also a credit card company put a lien against my house." But she did not want to give up the house and did not think doing so was financially savvy. "My house needs many repairs and upgrades so even if I sold, I would not make ends meet. Now I have bad credit and would not be able to rent or buy a less expensive or smaller place, but I still have a son at home and a daughter in college, so we still need a home for all of us."

Her chapter 13 repayment plan required payments of approximately $780 per month, $300 of which went toward the second mortgage. Separate from the plan, she had to maintain the $900 per month payment on the first mortgage on her house. She successfully completed her plan and obtained a discharge. Based on nonbankruptcy public records, as of this writing, she continues to own her house, more than five years after the bankruptcy filing.

Like many of the single women who file bankruptcy, this mother had completed some college and had a stable job with the same employer for fourteen years. She even made more than the median single female filer—$68,000 before taxes per year. And yet with two children, she wrote that she had to put mortgage payments on a credit card to avoid defaulting.

*Stretching Income to Meet Expenses*

Single women have incomes comparable to single men when they file bankruptcy. Still, the comparison can be inapt because job loss and reduction in income is a leading reason people file, but people often file after they secure new employment. As part of their bankruptcy paperwork, people must report their income for the two calendar years prior to the filing. In the years leading up to their bankruptcies, single women made less than single men. In the calendar year prior to their filings, single women made a median of $29,417, compared to single men's median of $30,000. Two calendar years prior to their filings, single women made a median of $28,280, compared to single men's median of $32,898. In addition, for single women, their incomes more often had to sustain themselves and their children in their homes.

SUPPORTING CHILDREN

Single men wrote about troubles with child support payments more frequently than about struggles supporting children in their homes. A thirty-nine-year-old father who listed two elementary school–aged children as dependents focused on paying child support after his divorce: "I got myself into credit card trouble before my divorce. I was always trying to keep up with the Jones as they say. . . . Now after the divorce I have to pay a lot of child support, and I just couldn't keep up any longer." Although some single men wrote about child support payments, only 6 percent of single men entered bankruptcy owing domestic support obligations.

In contrast, single women wrote about not receiving child support, such as this divorced mother of a seven-year-old: "With child support and him making half the house and boat payment as agreed in divorce decree, I could manage [with a low paying job] but still had to use my [credit cards] for other things/necessities. After about a year, he totally stopped paying me child support and half the house and boat payment." She summarized the main contributor to her bankruptcy filing as "Divorce—ex wasn't paying his part of divorce."

Single women also detailed childcare expenses. A thirty-four-year-old paralegal with a college degree wrote: "My ex-husband and I bought a house and had three small boys. He worked nights, I work[ed] days. We split. . . . I was then forced to pay high mortgage alone as well as forced to put kids (2, 3, 4) in daycare because he wasn't at home to watch them anymore." She turned to credit cards to pay for necessities, such as fuel and groceries. "[The credit cards] were all maxed out. I would pay the minimum every month just to have that much available for the next month. It was a vicious cycle of debt and no solution." On her bankruptcy schedules, she listed $74,000 in unsecured debts, the vast majority of which she owed to credit card companies.

Another single mother, of a two-year-old and a fourteen-year-old, who worked as a certified nursing assistant told of the tragic and disastrous financial effects of divorce combined with domestic abuse.

> I divorced my first husband and received full custody of our two children. . . . I made a quarter of what my then-husband did. I fell behind on mortgage, car payments, insurance, utilities progressively through the following months. I lost my job because I found myself in a domestically violent relationship that wouldn't allow me to work. I had many cars repo'd and utilities shut off. . . . I became homeless and pregnant and not able to find a place because of my credit and debts as well as my income.

When she filed, she listed $15,000 of property, including a car worth $5,300, which she owned free and clear. She had total debts of $50,000, including over $43,000 for three separate car repossession deficiencies. She owed much of her remaining debt to utility providers.

In what she wrote, she also expressed the devastation she felt and explained why she turned to bankruptcy for help: "Long story short, I lost everything I'd worked for 15 years including my credit and monetary things. . . . Claiming bankruptcy and employment will allow me to take the steps I need to get back on my feet with my own home." But with only $2,850 in income per month, after tax and including child support, she faces an uphill battle to make ends meet.

RECOVERING FROM DOMESTIC ABUSE

As illustrated by the previous two stories, besides taking care of children and meeting everyday expenses, single women filers highlighted the effects of their divorces and splits with partners on their debts. Conceptually, when people divorce or split, their debts are divided between both adults. For example, if the mother gets the house, she assumes the mortgage, which she can pay, in part, from child support. But legally, the person whose name is on the debt is responsible for it.

Research suggests that upon divorce or separation, women become saddled with debts taken out in their name, even though these debts benefited the entire family. Some of these debts originate from financial abuse, an aspect of the domestic abuse that women suffer more often than men.[33] Financial abuse is coercive control by an intimate partner in the form of misusing money, such as opening or using credit cards without permission. It occurs in most abusive relationships, and survivors cite it as a main reason that they stay in or return to abusive relationships.[34]

Single women's comments confirmed financial abuse. One woman summed it up: "Divorce—he had put stuff in my name while married." Another woman linked financial abuse with domestic abuse.

> Got separated from an abusive husband. He was the one that had a steady income. With all of my stress, my bipolar Type II flared up and I got really unstable disallowing me to work. I'm living with my parents and my two kids, getting no child support or alimony. Had no income whatsoever to continue to pay all me and my husbands bills. Everything was in my name cause he did not have good credit so had no choice but to file. My aunt gave me the money to pay for a lawyer.

On our survey, she indicated that during the years she struggled to pay her debts prior to filing bankruptcy, she went without dental care, put off car maintenance, pawned her property, took out payday loans, and like the other single women quoted earlier, put expenses on credit cards. What she tried to do to avoid filing matches the experiences of other single women who file bankruptcy.

## STRUGGLING TO PAY DEBTS (WHILE CARING FOR CHILDREN)

A consistent theme in women's stories is their efforts to manage their finances prior to filing bankruptcy. Sixty-four percent of single women indicated that they seriously struggled with their debts for two years or more before they filed; that is, they were what we term long strugglers. As discussed in chapter 2 of this book, a key aspect of people's use of bankruptcy is addressing their financial situations *after* they have tried multiple ways to tackle their financial problems. Single women's struggles manifest in what they reported doing to try to make ends meet (coping mechanisms) and what they reported going without (privations) to stave off having to file. More than 50 percent of single women indicated that they tried five (of fourteen) tactics to make ends meet and went without four (of fourteen) common expenses.

Although all women who file bankruptcy struggle in the face of inadequate incomes and high expenses, single women with children struggle longer, employ more coping mechanisms, and cut more expenses from their budgets prior to filing. More single women with children were long strugglers. Sixty-nine percent of single women with children—again, defined here as dependents twenty-two years old or younger—indicated that they seriously struggled for two or more years before they turned to bankruptcy for help. Single women with children went without more and did more to address their financial problems in the years leading up to their filings. More than half of them tried six coping mechanisms and cut six common expenses.

Figures 7.2 and 7.3 (discussed in following sections) detail the coping mechanisms used and privations endured most often, respectively, by single women, comparing single women with or without children. Each figure includes the coping mechanisms or privations that at least 40 percent of single women with or without children experienced.

### Robbing Peter to Pay Paul

Of the coping mechanisms that single women filers used (see figure 7.2), taking on more debt appeared often, both in frequency across filers and in women's discussions of their bankruptcy filings. The effects of caring for children on women's decisions about how to try to make ends meet are displayed across the actions they took to find money to pay for necessities. Nonetheless, discussions of incurring debt to pay for expenses, including other debts, ran throughout the accounts of all single women, with or without children, about their prebankruptcy struggles.

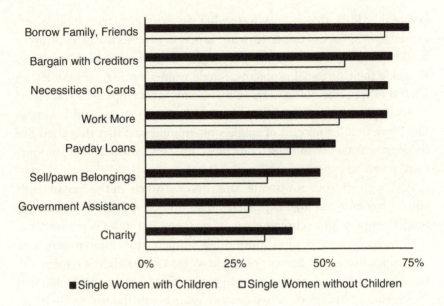

*Figure 7.2.* Coping strategies of single women bankruptcy filers during the two years before bankruptcy, by presence of children

In particular, versions of "robbing Peter to pay Paul" appeared in a noticeable handful of women's narratives. This took several forms: putting expenses on credit cards, taking out payday loans, pawning property, and borrowing from family and friends. Like the story of the thirty-eight-year-old single woman quoted at the start of the chapter, many single women took out multiple types of debt.

Single women turned to taking on more debt after they tried to work with their creditors, which also stands out among women's coping mechanisms. For instance, a sixty-three-year-old Black woman purchased a house shortly before the Great Recession. She financed the house with an adjustable-rate mortgage (ARM). She "[t]ried three times, within the five year period prior to [when the interest rate would adjust], to refinance or get modification. Denied all three times due to appraisals not being high enough. Had five credit cards. Paid off three but two creditors would not negotiate sufficiently enough to bring down monthly payments." She turned to taking on more debt, in the form of letting the two remaining credit card balances increase, "in order to pay mortgage." When she filed bankruptcy, the house, which she listed as worth $253,000, was $18,500 underwater.

Coupled with taking on more debt, single women also tried to find more work or to find new work after being laid off. For example, a thirty-four-year-old administrative assistant who made $30,000 per year before taxes when she filed told of job loss followed by troubles finding a new, comparable job: "The plant I was working at for seven years shut down. I had perfect credit til that point. Because I filled out the unemployment form wrong, my benefits were delayed by a few months. During that time, I used my credit cards to pay rent, buy food, gas, clothes, school supplies, etc." Before she was laid off, she was paying down some medical bills, which she described as "manageable while I was working. I still had some that was left over though." She closed her story with: "Now I have been working full time for over three years, but I got paid less than I did on unemployment. For six years, tried to avoid bankruptcy, but I can't avoid it anymore."

That single women's most-used coping mechanisms hinged on taking on more debt is remarkable given women's historical exclusion from credit markets. Prior to when the Equal Credit Opportunity Act took effect in 1975, banks sometimes required that single or divorced women have men cosign their credit applications, discounted women's income in deciding how much credit to grant, and forced women to reapply for credit under their husbands' names upon marrying.[35] Now many households, including those led by single women, use credit to balance their budgets.[36]

Although credit flows freely, women do not borrow the same as men. In addition to the "pinklining" that includes women receiving more expensive subprime mortgages, women are more likely than men to turn to high-cost lending in times of need, partly because payday lenders focus on marketing to women.[37] One study found that women make up about 60 percent of payday loan customers and that payday loan usage is even higher among single mothers.[38]

Among those who filed bankruptcy, single women reported a higher usage of payday loans than single men or couples. Forty-five percent of single women indicated they turned to payday lenders as a coping mechanism. In comparison, 39 percent of single men and 41 percent of couples indicated that they did so.

Single women emphasized the pernicious effects of trying to balance their budgets by taking on high-cost debt. After incurring medical bills because of hospitalizations, a forty-five-year-old single woman "took out one payday loan to help and then ended up taking more and more payday loans to cover everything. Everything snowballed in my life. . . . I was getting behind on my bills and the payday loans. The payday loans were harassing me and I could not keep up." She listed getting "in trouble with payday loans" as the main contributor to her bankruptcy.

Other women framed taking out payday loans and incurring other debt as both needed and futile. One woman chastised herself for incurring more debt. "I got payday loan after payday loan. I was borrowing one to pay off the other, and then I'd borrow again on the one I just paid off!! Stupid!!" A single mother wrote: "In order for me to keep up living as a four family household I would seek out payday loans, title loans, and personal loans which caused my financial situation to be worse."

Women also turned to family and friends for help, which included borrowing from them, and which was part of their stories of incurring debt to pay debt. "In order to get my car out of the shop, I had to use my bill money for the repairs. It was down hill from there. I was robbing Peter to pay Paul to pay electric, car insurance, water, gas, and phone. I had to borrow from others to get by on." In her bankruptcy schedules, she listed among her assets one car, model year 1989, worth $1,500.

## Sacrificing for Children

The sacrifices single women make for their children appear in their decisions about what to cut from their budgets. They wrote about their struggles with how best to care for their children while still trying to pay their debts. Figure 7.3 shows which privations single women turned to most often, again comparing single women with or without children.

Children are expensive. Having children in the home increases single women's risks of incurring medical expenses, of having to take off work to care for sick children, and of losing jobs because they must miss work to care for children. Children require more expensive housing, which increases utility costs. They must be fed and looked after in daycare or after-school care. And they must be transported to and from appointments and daycare. Some parents may choose to supplement public

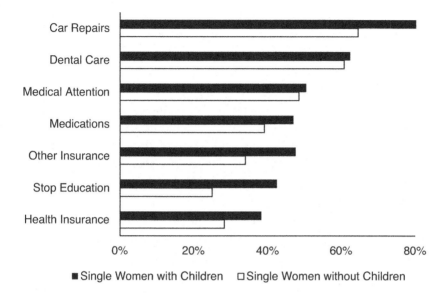

*Figure 7.3.* Privations reported by single women in the two years before bankruptcy, by presence of children

school education with extracurricular activities, such as sports, or to help with college expenses. Still others will continue to house their now-adult children.

The increased struggles of single women with children who file bankruptcy convey the reality that the United States places the financial burden of rearing children almost exclusively on parents. Single parents, especially those with children in their homes, who are more likely to be women, bear the brunt of that burden. Based on CBP data from 2001, single women with children were more likely to file bankruptcy than couples with children, and couples with children were more likely to file bankruptcy than couples without.[39] The same is true now. Higher numbers of bankruptcy filings among parents suggest that having children in the home increases economic precarity.

## COMPROMISING HEALTH

Going without health care—medical care, dental care, medications, and health insurance—stands out among single mothers' descriptions of their time before filing bankruptcy. For a variety of reasons, women are susceptible to incurring medical bills, which means they may decide to cut health care when money is tight. Because women are more likely to work part time, they are less likely to be eligible for health insurance through their employers. Pregnancy typically requires doctors' visits and hospitalization. And parents are responsible for children's medical care.

For most people who file bankruptcy, including single women, going without health care often meant sacrificing more than one aspect of their well-being. For single women with children, it also meant considering how best to provide for their kids. When asked what was the most important thing that they or a family member went without in the two years before bankruptcy, a single mother who had struggled for five years or more wrote: "Couldn't pay for my kids orthodontist, and college, and my co-pay for hospitals and doctors."

Another single mother compromised her health to ensure that her children were taken care of. "I went without medication for my seizures because I had to feed the kids or make sure we had a roof over our head." Other single mothers similarly listed medicine, such as for depression, allergies, and asthma, as the most important thing they went without. Their comments mentioned protecting their children's well-being. "Life goes on. Kids are 13, 11, and 10 and are healthy."

## TRANSPORTING CHILDREN

Most single women who went without some aspect of health care also sacrificed in other areas of their lives. For single women with children, transportation loomed heavy. A single woman with one child wrote that the most important thing that she went without was a vehicle, despite also struggling to pay $900 in monthly rent and to afford medications: "I was overwhelmed with debt. Not being able to pay rent. Then deciding, do you buy food or put gas in the car or pay the light bill. Nobody has health or dental insurance at all. Teeth are bad. Take anxiety medicine but can't get prescription cause can't afford the doctor bill."

She filed chapter 13 bankruptcy while owning a car worth $14,000, on which she owed $14,000. Besides paying the trustee and her attorney, almost all chapter 13 plan payments were to go to her auto lender. She filed to keep her car. However, she defaulted on the plan after a year and a half, and her case was dismissed soon after. What became of her car post-dismissal is a mystery.

Although it may seem sensible to give up the car and not to have to worry about maintenance and insurance, transporting children via public transit is difficult in most places in the United States and impossible in smaller cities or rural areas where public transit simply does not exist. Women with children still prioritized maintaining transportation, such as the mother of four children with a vehicle listed as worth $16,000 and on which she owed $25,000. "My truck broke down and with small children, I was unable to ride the bus. I had to spend $[1,300] on fixing my auto. Things got out of hand and I was working to not even pay all my bills. My hours were reduced due to health issues (mostly stress) and here I am today, starting over." She listed car repairs as the most important expense that she went without prior to filing.

This single mother also filed chapter 13 to keep her car. Her chapter 13 repayment plan required her to pay the entire amount she owed her auto lender, with 5 percent interest, over three years, plus her attorney's and trustee's fees. She defaulted on the plan less than two years after its confirmation. What became of her car likewise is a mystery.

Other single women with children listed not qualifying for a car loan, not fully fixing vehicles in need of repairs, foregoing oil changes, or temporarily giving up car insurance as the most important expense that they went without.

## STOPPING EDUCATION

Besides sacrificing health and dealing with challenging transportation situations, most noticeable among the privations experienced by single women with children was to stop their education. A forty-year-old single mother wrote.

> For me, I was underpaid. I have worked for the same company for over 10 years. I recently earned a pay increase over two years ago. However it is still not enough. My rent is over a thousand dollars, I'm a single parent whose daughter just completed high school. Car note, insurance, medical, and sorts of other things in life. There has been times where I could not buy food for myself and child. There has been plenty of times where I did not pay my lights or gas, therefore they were shut off due to nonpayment. Working

over time is not always a for sure thing. I had to stop school in order to work secondary work.

When she filed bankruptcy, she owed $27,000 in student loans and had completed some college.

Similarly, a forty-five-year-old secretary who made about $40,000 per year indicated that she went without education. When she filed bankruptcy, she owed $164,000 in student loans. She lamented that she had "no support system, no family" to help with her child. She "[worked] 2 jobs to try and make ends meet. My credit was not good. When I try to improve it, if one thing goes wrong, like a major repair on a car or something needs repaired on my house, it spins my finances out of control." She concluded her story: "I have to rob Peter to pay Paul as the old adage goes."

### Surrendering to Accepting Help

Returning to robbing Peter to pay Paul, borrowing money from family and friends, though technically loans, more often amounted to receiving help from family and friends, without their having an expectation of receiving anything in return. Single women's stories confirmed that they turned to family and friends for true help. For instance, a forty-year-old nursing assistant who made $37,000 a year before taxes, and who had two older children, wrote: "Sometime[s] we have had to eat at other people's house because there was no money to buy food. I borrowed money to pay bills and couldn't pay the money back."

Women also hinted at the embarrassment that they felt in having to rely on others, including turning to the government or a charity for assistance. They wrote about first employing a host of other coping mechanisms. A thirty-year-old single woman lost her job and ended up living with her parents. Soon after, her father lost his job. She used credit cards to help pay their mortgage and buy food, and they sold "a lot of things" before finally applying for food stamps.

Likewise, a single mother struggled to "continue paying the minimum payments on my credit card debts and loans. I tried unsuccessfully for a long time. Lack of income and not being able to find a job made it very difficult, [e]mbarrassing, stressful and shameful." She ended by confessing:

"I even had to apply for food stamps and that was the most painful aside from dealing with all the phone calls of my debtors. I could not deal with the situation any more so I made the decision and filed."

She reported seriously struggling to pay her debts for at least two years before she filed. Her emotions about the time leading up to bankruptcy reflected the feelings of many of the single women who filed. Their feelings overall bring out bankruptcy's limited ability to address the broader economic realities that single women continue to face.

## REALIZING IT MAY NOT GET BETTER

Single women's stories suggest that their financial circumstances weighed on their minds when seeking bankruptcy's proverbial fresh start. We asked the people who filed about their feelings and provided them with a list of emotions that might be associated with filing bankruptcy. Along with the shame and guilt that people historically have reported feeling, we included emotions that indicate hopefulness—optimism, confidence, and happiness—and emotions that point toward uncertainty and despair—hopelessness, depression, and fear. Single women's collective responses to the questions about emotions matched the feelings expressed in what they shared about their financial troubles, such as the fear and depression about which the thirty-eight-year-old quoted at the start of the chapter wrote.

As summarized in figure 7.4, single women tipped noticeably toward uncertainty and despair, particularly when compared to single men and couples. Thirty-five percent of single women reported feeling depressed "a great deal," and a third reported feeling fear "a great deal."

The positive emotions of optimism and confidence were more of a mixed bag. Single women were both more likely to feel both emotions a "great deal" and "not at all" than were single men and couples, with a visibly larger subset of single women feeling "not at all" confident upon filing. To understand the overall pattern, we constructed an Emotion Index, summing answers across all four emotions. We scored the emotions of confidence and optimism as positives and the emotions of depression and fear as negatives. Single women were the only group with a negative

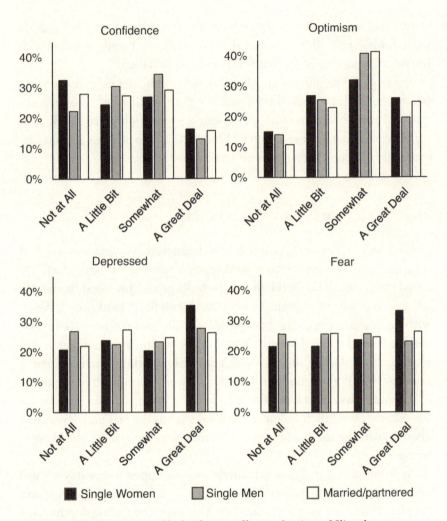

*Figure 7.4.* Emotions reported by bankruptcy filers at the time of filing, by household type

score, indicating more negative emotions than positive, whereas positive emotions dominated for single men.[40] If these emotions stand in for hope about the future, then single women seem to view their prospects post-bankruptcy as less encouraging. What some women wrote, combined with their reported emotions upon filing, emphasized this downheartedness.

For women, their depression and fear also were wrapped up in shame. "Was very skeptical about the filing for bankruptcy as I felt I was letting down my creditors that I owed money to. Made me sad, depressed, and fearful. I just kept putting it off as I didn't want to do it." Forty-five percent of single women reported feeling shame "a great deal" when filing, compared to 37 percent of married or partnered couples and 31 percent of single men who filed bankruptcy.

A thirty-year-old police officer with an elementary school–aged child reported feeling "a great deal" of shame, guilt, depression, fear, and hopeless at the time she filed, which came through in what she wrote: "After having my wages garnished, I felt as if I had failed both myself and my child. Me and friend discussed bankruptcy. I felt sick. I felt less and didn't want go to through with it but I had no other choice!" Although she also wrote—"After talking with my mother, she advised me to look at it as a new beginning and not the end!"—those thoughts did not translate to optimism or confidence.

The comments of a single mother of a young child who lost her job less than two weeks after she filed chapter 13 expressed the anxiety that many women may feel about their future financial prospects. She explained: "[N]ow I don't know what is going to happen with my case. I went from feeling so relieved and safe to frightened and scared again. God, help me. My doctor has now referred me to a specialist due to anxiety and not being able to sleep."

She was among the 55 percent of women who indicated that they felt "a great deal" of relief when they filed. Yet she also wrote about still having nondischargeable student loans and debt from "overpayment of state benefits which I never understood." She filed chapter 13 first and foremost to remove the boot from her car so that she could drive her daughter to school and to see her father.

Bankruptcy supposedly brings a fresh start. But bankruptcy and its discharge cannot solve continuing financial issues, such as not making enough money to cover daily expenses and to save for emergencies. The shifts in family life in the United States over the past fifty years have in many ways benefited women. Women have wider career prospects; they have more educational opportunities; and they have made strides in accessing credit and, somewhat less, in pay equity. But women continue to occupy a place within the economy that brings unique financial problems—problems that may continue to haunt them postbankruptcy.

Filing bankruptcy may get the boot off a car, may wipe away payday loans and credit card debt, may save the house from foreclosure, or may repair some of the consequences of financial abuse. But it will not solve women's pay inequity or provide reasonably priced childcare. It will not ensure that mothers will not lose their jobs, see their working hours cut, or incur unmanageable medical bills when their kids get sick. It will not resolve the budget shortfalls that led women to fall behind on student loans and mortgages. And it will not prevent single mothers from being unable to collect child support.

When asked about the reasons that contributed to their need to file bankruptcy, single women disproportionately (compared to other filers) pointed to family size and helping others. Websites and blog posts, passed around by influencers, tell women to have a growth mindset and invest in themselves and in their kids. But the economic realities of being a single woman in the United States mean it is not that simple. The prospect of failing shows up in women's reactions to the period before bankruptcy and about what is to come.

# 8  The Riskiest Years— Bankrupt Seniors

So, at sixty-five years old, we are starting over. We will declare bankruptcy and hope there is some chance we will do something again. My husband and I have worked since we were fourteen years old. Now, we are in a system we hate being in. Unemployed, taking Social Security earlier than we wanted, renting a home, getting help with propane, help with food allowance, filling out a form for a university project for what feels like a sad-assed loser story, now that I reread it. . . . So, there you go.

—Sixty-five-year-old white woman

The ideal and appeal of individualism runs deep in the United States.[1] Americans cling tightly to "the cult of the individual, the self-made myth, the will to power."[2] Those who seemingly have pulled themselves up by their proverbial bootstraps are revered. The successful have forged their own paths to prosperity, while those who flounder have brought their situations upon themselves.

In accordance with "the cult of the individual," seniors (people aged sixty-five or older) are presumed to have adequate retirement savings, supplemented by Social Security, to see them through their final years. If they do not, surely they have brought their financial insecurity upon themselves.

At present, many older Americans do not look forward to their retirement years with visions of stability and security. At the same time that they lose their independence and ability to work and to care for themselves, their financial futures become quite risky. This later-in-life precarity is a result of policy shifts over the past four decades or so that have left people financially adrift during their final years.

In the first half of the twentieth century, to lessen old-age insecurity among seniors, government programs, such as Social Security and Medicare, and employer-sponsored, defined-benefit pensions were woven into the US social safety net. With these programs in place, many older Americans could live out their final years in relative comfort and security. Consequently, people who retired during the last half of the twentieth century experienced the "golden age" of retirement.[3]

Today these benefits are rare, as in the case of pensions, or are often inadequate, as in the case of Social Security and Medicare. These changes did not happen by chance. Beginning in the 1980s, policies encouraged the government and employers to off-load onto individuals the costs and responsibilities of financial security during their senior years.[4] For instance, health-care costs shifted increasingly to individuals, an especially consequential development for older Americans, and 401(k) plans replaced the more stable traditional pension. These transitions have been cloaked in the terminology, and justified by the ideology, of individual responsibility and personal choice. But the accumulation of these changes has resulted in many seniors struggling, if not collapsing, under the substantial risks that are intimately associated with aging.

If the golden years of retirement began to wane at the end of the twentieth century, as some social scientists have suggested, then by now there should be evidence among older Americans of the increasing risks and associated struggles. Bankruptcy filings provide some confirmation of those risks and struggles. Persons aged sixty-five and over—seniors—are the fastest growing demographic group of bankruptcy filers. In 2001 seniors comprised 5 percent of the bankrupt population. Now they are 18 percent of all filers.

Like many people aged sixty-five and over, most seniors who file bankruptcy are no longer in the workforce. They are transitioning into the final chapter of their lives—ideally a time of relative financial stability. Their debts and expenses should be minimal, and their Social Security income and retirement savings should be adequate to meet their needs. Instead, most bankrupt seniors experience financial chaos. Most have nothing in savings, in part because some emptied their retirement accounts to pay debts prior to filing bankruptcy. Yet almost all who file have sizable debt, which despite Medicare frequently comes from medical bills that they cannot afford to pay.

## INCREASED BANKRUPTCY FILINGS AMONG OLDER AMERICANS

Bankruptcy has historically been, and continues to be, filed most often by people who are middle-aged, between thirty-five and fifty-five years old. Given the many costs and risks associated with this time of life—children, divorces, mortgages, multiple car payments, and possibly caring for one's elderly parents—increased frequency of filing bankruptcy during these years is predictable.

Historically, younger and older people were less likely to resort to bankruptcy. These patterns made sense. Younger individuals have had less time to accumulate debt, such as home mortgages, and are less likely to face the financial consequences of children or divorce. If they do have debt, such as student loans, they have years of employment and income ahead of them, and even if they are struggling now, they may trust that their financial situations will improve.

Older individuals also should be transitioning into a time of financial stability. They should no longer be responsible for children. They should have paid off mortgages and student loans. Their retirement savings, when combined with Social Security, should meet their monthly expenses. Their credit card or medical debt should be easily paid month to month. Stated differently, seniors should move into retirement with a balanced budget.

This historical distribution of age-determinant bankruptcy filings, however, no longer holds. It has dramatically shifted over the past thirty years, as shown in table 8.1 and figure 8.1. The percentage of younger filers has dropped steadily, while the percentage of older filers has increased substantially.

The changes within the population of bankruptcy filers are magnitudes beyond the graying demographics of the overall population. The US Census estimated over 12 percent of the population was sixty-five years or older in 2000.[5] That figure increased to 17 percent by 2020— a 42 percent increase over twenty years.[6] In comparison, between 2001 and 2021, bankruptcy cases involving seniors increased more than threefold.

*Table 8.1.*   Percent of Bankruptcy Filers, by Age Group

| Age Group | 1991 | 2001 | 2007 | 2013–18 | 2019–23 |
|-----------|------|------|------|---------|---------|
| 18–24 | 9 | 5 | 4 | 2 | 1 |
| 25–34 | 37 | 26 | 22 | 15 | 16 |
| 35–44 | 31 | 34 | 28 | 23 | 21 |
| 45–54 | 16 | 23 | 24 | 26 | 23 |
| 55–64 | 6 | 7 | 15 | 22 | 21 |
| 65+ | 2 | 5 | 8 | 12 | 18 |

## OLDER AMERICANS WHO FILE BANKRUPTCY: OUR SAMPLE

We coded a bankruptcy case as a "senior bankruptcy" if the person who completed the survey indicated that they or their spouse or partner were sixty-five or older. Using this definition, our sample had 387 senior bankruptcy cases. Of those, 99 were filed jointly, meaning that both spouses of a married couple were listed on the petition.[7] Among the 288 single filer (solo) cases, men filed one-third and women filed the remaining two-thirds. The oldest person in the senior sample was 92.

As summarized in table 8.2, bankrupt seniors differ, demographically, from nonbankrupt seniors in a few important ways. Bankrupt seniors are considerably less likely to be married than the senior population generally and are more likely to be separated or divorced than their nonbankrupt counterparts. Bankrupt and nonbankrupt seniors also differ on racial demographics. Compared to the nonbankrupt senior population, white seniors are underrepresented and Black seniors are overrepresented in bankruptcy.

## DRIVERS BEHIND SENIORS' BANKRUPTCIES

Bankruptcies are messy and complex, regardless of the filer's age. Rarely does a single incident push someone to file. More often, the combination of a series of events leads a debtor to toss in the towel and seek the advice

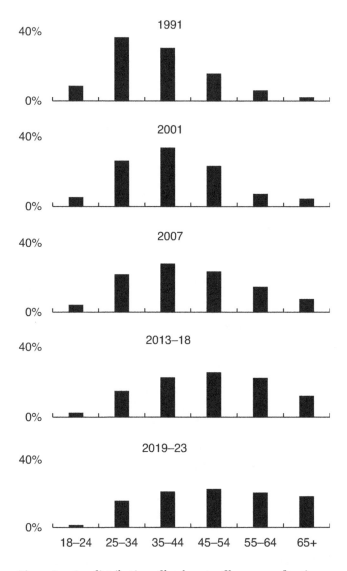

*Figure 8.1.* Age distribution of bankruptcy filers across five time periods of the CBP

*Table 8.2.* Demographic Characteristics of Bankruptcy Filers
Compared to US Population, 65 Years and Older

|  | Bankruptcy Sample (%) | United States (%) |
|---|---|---|
| **Marital status** | | |
| Married | 41 | 56.0 |
| Divorced or separated | 31 | 16.0 |
| Widowed | 24 | 21.0 |
| **Race** | | |
| White | 71 | 75.0 |
| Black or African American | 21 | 9.0 |
| Hispanic | 7 | 9.0 |
| Asian | 2 | 5.0 |
| American Indian/Alaska Native | 3 | 0.5 |

NOTE: The bankruptcy data are by household. For two-person households, race is counted if either person identified with that race. Because respondents in the bankruptcy data could choose more than one racial or ethnic category, the total percent is greater than 100%. US figures on marital status and race are from American Community Survey, ACS 1-Year Estimates, 2022, US Census Bureau, "S0103 Population 65 Years and Over in the United States."

of a bankruptcy attorney. Insufficient income, unmanageable debt, and health-care costs most typically prompt seniors to file bankruptcy.

*Small Incomes, Large Debts*

Indebtedness is not unique to seniors who file bankruptcy. Older Americans, overall, carry increasingly large debt loads. The total debt burden among people at least seventy years old, which includes credit card debt, mortgage debt, and auto loan debt, increased more than fivefold over the twenty years between 1999 and 2019.[8] According to a 2019 report from the Congressional Research Service, between 1989 and 2016, the percentage of persons aged sixty-five and over with any type of debt climbed from 38 to 61 percent, and the average amount they owed increased from $7,500 to $31,000 (measured in 2016 dollars).[9]

*Table 8.3.* Finances of Bankruptcy Filers, 65 Years and Older and under 65 (Medians)

|  | *65 Years and Older* | *Under 65 Years* |
|---|---|---|
| Total debt | $100,475 | $104,361 |
| Total secured debt | $31,620 | $20,810 |
| Total unsecured debt | $37,655 | $49,916 |
| Annual income | $39,126 | $48,696 |
| Debt-to-income ratio | 2.3 | 2.2 |

Not surprisingly, seniors who file bankruptcy have considerably more debt than older Americans generally. As detailed in table 8.3, their median total debt surpasses $100,000. Secured debt, typically home mortgages and auto loans, accounts for about one-third of their total debt. Their unsecured debt is more than $37,000, which is most likely credit card debt and medical bills.[10]

The median annual income of bankrupt seniors is quite modest and is more than $9,000 less than their nonbankrupt senior counterparts. That extra income could be the difference between paying for needed prescriptions and the mortgage, rather than forgoing medicine or falling behind on the mortgage and losing the place where they live.

Bankrupt seniors' total debt load of more than two times their median annual income exposes the magnitude of their financial insecurity. Drilling down on their unsecured debt, this debt is almost equal to their annual income. This means that if seniors could somehow transfer all their pretax income for an entire year to their unsecured creditors, then those creditors, and only those creditors, would be paid. Of course, that is not possible. Without the debt discharge, seniors will likely spend the rest of their lives trying to pay only their unsecured debt and, depending on interest rates, might never even reduce the principal.

*Postponing the Inevitable while Increasing Their Debts*

The years before bankruptcy can be extraordinarily stressful. More than four out of ten seniors indicated that they filed bankruptcy, in part, because of pressure from debt collectors. Collection attempts are often relentless and intrusive, with collectors calling numerous times a day and sometimes contacting neighbors, family members, and employers in hopes of shaming people into paying. Creditors also resort to filing lawsuits, garnishing wages, foreclosing homes, and repossessing cars.[11] During this time, marriages are damaged beyond repair; relationships between parents and children become strained; and depression, insomnia, and even thoughts of suicide take hold.[12]

Given this situation, we might assume that seniors would rush to bankruptcy courts, desperate for relief from creditors and debt collectors and eager to protect their few remaining assets to cover their expenses during the coming years, when they will be even less able to earn additional income. That, however, does not appear to be the case. Most bankrupt seniors indicated that they struggled for years trying to pay their debts. Six out of ten seniors reported that they seriously struggled to pay their debts for two years or more. Only 10 percent reported struggling for fewer than six months. The remainder persisted for between six months and two years before filing bankruptcy.

Although it is commendable that people who find themselves struggling with debt work to pay what they owe—and doing so certainly aligns with America's emphasis on personal responsibility—seniors are in a different stage of financial life than people generally. Most seniors live on fixed incomes and will need what money and assets they have saved and can continue to save to make it through the end of their lives, especially since their prospects of earning more money diminish every year. For many older Americans, filing bankruptcy to preserve most of their assets, particularly retirement savings, makes financial sense. Although our data do not show how much money bankrupt seniors transferred to their creditors and debt collectors during their years of struggling, they do show that some of their fixed income and savings were used to pay debts. Every dollar that went toward a debt was one less dollar that could be used later to pay for ongoing living expenses.

Even though seniors postponed filing for years, they did not sit idly by during that time. Instead, as reflected in figure 8.2, they employed a range of strategies to try to make ends meet and thereby avoid bankruptcy altogether. Unfortunately, while most of these tactics may have made sense at

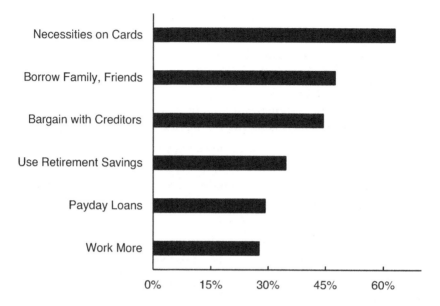

*Figure 8.2.* Six most common coping strategies reported by senior bankruptcy filers during the two years before bankruptcy

the time, they ultimately resulted in increased debt and financial precarity. For example, over six out of ten seniors put necessities on credit cards. This was done to help them make ends meet, but ultimately this strategy only increased their total amount of debt.

Almost half of seniors borrowed money from family or friends. Not only does this increase debt, but it may also be emotionally taxing. Borrowing from their adult children may evoke shame or cause tension within the family.

Over four out of ten seniors asked their creditors to "work with them," which most likely means they requested lower monthly payments, which in turn usually results in increased interest payments over the life of a loan. Although this tactic eases some of the immediate financial burden, the total amount the borrower will owe increases. And more than one-quarter of seniors relied on payday or car title loans, both of which come with hefty annual interest rates of around 400 percent.[13] Charging necessities to credit cards, borrowing from friends and family, taking out payday loans, and asking creditors for help all increase seniors' debt loads.

Seniors also looked to their savings and their earning potential to make ends meet. One-third of seniors extracted money from their retirement savings to pay down debts. Again, in the short term, this may resolve some financial distress, but ultimately it undermines their financial security in their final years. Depending on the timing of withdrawal and the type of retirement account, the early withdrawal may trigger taxes and penalties.

Finally, about one-quarter of seniors reported working more hours, which is an effective way to make ends meet without taking on more debt or depleting resources. However, many seniors may not physically be able to work, while others, though willing and able to work, may be unable to find employment due, in part, to age discrimination.[14]

Without adequate resources to make ends meet, people will necessarily take on more debt. Bankruptcy likely will erase the debts, but it cannot replace retirement savings. That fewer seniors made ends meet by working more and instead drew on retirement accounts and fell further into debt suggests that they lacked sufficient income prebankruptcy, which is likely to continue postbankruptcy. Lacking retirement money, life after bankruptcy may continue to be financially precarious.

*Life on a Fixed Income*

INCOME ON THE DECLINE

For many Americans, turning sixty-five coincides with retirement. Ideally, this shift from wages to retirement savings and Social Security is relatively seamless. However, for those who have been unable to grow adequate retirement savings and who are otherwise primarily dependent on Social Security, the lost earnings may result in financial insecurity. Even if people enter retirement with enough income to break even every month, their expenses may increase as their health and ability to live independently decline.

In line with the typical retirement age in the United States, most seniors who file bankruptcy have left the workforce and are no longer employed. More than three-quarters of seniors who lived alone at the time of filing were out of the workforce. Eighty-four percent of senior men who lived alone, compared to seventy-five percent of senior women who lived alone, entered bankruptcy not employed. Among seniors who lived with a spouse or partner at the time of the bankruptcy, 60 percent indicated that *neither* adult was employed, while only 12 percent reported that *both* people were employed.

Considering that a decrease in income often accompanies retirement, understandably, when asked about changes in income two years before their bankruptcies, 46 percent of bankrupt seniors reported a significant decrease, a little over half said that their income had held constant, and only 2 percent indicated that their income had significantly increased. If retirement savings are adequate, retirees presumptively should have enough money to meet expenses. Instead, seven out of ten seniors "very much" or "somewhat" agreed that a decline in income contributed to their bankruptcy. Their incomes declined such that they struggled to survive financially.

Bankrupt seniors' stories depict several of the reasons for the income decline. In some instances, older filers could not physically continue working. They described career-ending illnesses or injuries that forced them from the workforce permanently, such as this seventy-one-year-old man: "Had heart attack and had to retire. No retirement, only S.S. [Social Security]. If I had not had the attack I would have been OK. Sometimes things happen beyond your control. Thank you. God protected me or I would not be here." Based on what he wrote, it is probable that his only income for the rest of his life will be Social Security. He has no other retirement savings and will likely never work again.

In other situations, the death of a spouse led to the decline in income. A seventy-three-year-old woman shared: "[M]y husband of 36+ years passed away after an 8 year illness with complications. When he died his pension went from 'almost' $1800 to $159.02. I hung on as long as I could. . . . Please send the Walmart Card ASAP as I will use it for Pet (cat) food. Thank You." Her story illustrates an unfortunate fact about survivor's pension benefits: the surviving spouse does not always continue to receive the full benefit.

Illness and death did not precipitate all retirements. Some seniors, who were able and willing to work, described being fired from good jobs and then struggling to find subsequent, adequate, and dependable employment. For example, a sixty-five-year-old filer lost her job after twelve years.

This person's story is described in chapter 5 of the book. She was not able to find new full-time employment. Trying to make ends meet, she tapped out her retirement savings in both an IRA and a 403(b) plan. After an extended period of unemployment, she found a much lower paying job. Although of retirement age, her financial circumstances suggest she will need to continue to work until she is not able to do so. The one resource she has—her ability and willingness to work well into her golden years—will be gone just like her retirement savings.

Ideally, people retire by choice and with adequate savings. Seniors who filed bankruptcy seemingly did not. Instead, they experienced unmanageable income declines. When they could no longer stretch what little they did have to meet their expenses, they turned to bankruptcy.

## SOCIAL SECURITY INCOME

For older Americans generally, "the value of expected future Social Security retirement benefits represents the largest single source of wealth."[15] Most seniors can depend on Social Security to provide them with some income during their retirement years. However, it was never intended to be the primary source of retirement income. Instead, Social Security was conceptualized as a *supplement* to more substantial retirement savings and pensions.[16] For instance, in 2024 the Social Security Administration estimated that average payments would be $1,907 a month, or $22,884 a year, before deducting taxes and Medicare premiums.[17] Despite this modest amount, almost three out of ten households headed by someone approaching retirement age have no retirement savings or access to a defined-benefit plan, such as a pension plan.[18] Half of seniors rely on Social Security for at least half of their income.[19]

In the past, Social Security payments were more substantial. Beginning in the 1980s, policy changes diminished the worth of benefits. After peaking at approximately 50 percent of preretirement income for most workers in the late 1970s, payments declined and remain at about 40 percent of preretirement income for most workers.[20] In 1983, amendments to the Social Security Act increased the age to claim full benefits from sixty-five to sixty-seven. This increase was phased in gradually. At present, everyone who is approaching retirement age will be eligible for full benefits when they are sixty-seven. Americans receive increased benefits if they postpone retirement until age seventy. In contrast, those who retire early and draw benefits are penalized. Prior to 1983, the early retirement penalty was a 20 percent reduction in monthly benefits. After 1983, the penalty increased to 30 percent.[21]

In their stories, bankrupt seniors provided some insight into the inadequacies of Social Security, and their difficulties in maintaining a minimal standard of living on the benefits, let alone paying debts. A sixty-five-year-old woman appeared to be completely dependent on Social Security income. "I live on S.S. [Social Security] check of $793 a month. I pay rent, car payment, insurance, utilities, food. It's hard. I can't work and making extra money is NOT an option." Prior to filing, she went without food, prescriptions, and medical and dental care. At time of filing, she owed more than $37,000 in unsecured debt. Given her circumstances, the debt discharge should provide immediate financial relief. However, with her total reliance on Social Security, her future appears difficult.

Even dual-retired households, in which both individuals receive Social Security, can find it challenging to make ends meet. The words of a seventy-nine-year-old man, with an eighty-three-year-old wife, were laced with hopelessness: "Social Security only $1500 per month for us (together). Need to live off credit cards to be able to survive. New health issues and lots of doctor bills. We can't keep up and it's slowly killing us." They filed owing almost $34,000 in unsecured debt. Prior to filing, they went without medical care, dental care, and food. Bankruptcy will alleviate the debt payments, but again, their futures are precarious, at best.

Those seniors who enter bankruptcy exclusively dependent on Social Security simply do not have adequate incomes. Regardless of whether they file bankruptcy, they will continue to live in exceptionally risky situations. Those who do file may get temporary relief, but postbankruptcy they eventually will have little choice but to resume putting daily expenses on credit cards because their monthly expenses still exceed their incomes.

## WHAT RETIREMENT SAVINGS?

Because Social Security is only intended as supplemental income, people need retirement savings to meet their financial obligations after retiring. Conventional wisdom teaches that, by age sixty-seven, people should have retirement savings of at least ten times their annual income.[22] If they do, the decline in income that typically accompanies retirement need not spell financial distress. Bankrupt seniors' median annual income at the time of their filing of approximately $39,000 would translate to approximately $390,000 in retirement savings.

Seniors who file bankruptcy have saved nowhere near that sum. To be blunt, their retirement savings are abysmal. The mean amount in their 401(k)-type plans and Roth IRA accounts, Keogh plans, and pension plans is a mere $6,533. This average amount is skewed by a few filers who manage to save higher sums. The median amount of savings in seniors' retirement accounts is *zero*. Seventy-two percent of seniors reported that they had nothing at all set aside for retirement income—no pension, no 401(k) or IRA, no other retirement savings.[23]

Older Americans in general fare better than their bankrupt counterparts. At the end of 2022, Americans sixty-five and over had a median balance in their 401(k)s of $70,620.[24] This amount, while certainly more than zero, still is deficient. Likewise, as of 2022, one in nine Americans sixty years and older had nothing in retirement savings—no pension, no 401(k) or IRA, no other savings.[25] Again, though better off than bankrupt seniors, this portends serious financial struggles for many during their final years.

Contrasting bankrupt seniors' retirement savings with those of their junior counterparts also raises concerns. The comparison suggests that older Americans come to bankruptcy with so little savings in part because they have spent some or all the money in their retirement accounts to pay their debts. Like older filers, younger filers, those under sixty-five, also have a median of zero dollars in their retirement savings when they enter bankruptcy, but their mean amount is $9,822. Senior filers enter bankruptcy with approximately $3,250 less on average in retirement savings than younger filers.

RETIREMENT STRIPPING

Were the seniors who filed bankruptcy simply unable to delay gratification during their working years, and rather than saving money for retirement, spent frivolously? Maybe. But when more than one hundred thousand seniors file bankruptcy every year, individual-level justifications ring hollow.

Other explanations point to systemic issues that prevent people from building and maintaining adequate savings for their retirement. In the last forty years, the US retirement system has changed radically. Up until the 1990s, many employees received pensions, often referred to as defined-benefit plans, as part of their income and benefit packages. Employers invested and managed these pensions, and employees could not access the funds until they retired. Upon retirement, recipients received a regular monthly check until their deaths. This ensured that they did not outlive their retirement income.

Starting in the 1990s, 401(k)-type retirement savings plans replaced many defined-benefit plans. Employees must initiate these plans and decide how much money to contribute. Employees also are responsible for investing and managing the funds, and they have relatively unfettered access to the money in the funds. They can make withdrawals at any time, for any amount, even before they retire—something that is not allowed with pension plans. This system aligns with America's notions of individualism. Employees have control over their savings, free from the guiding hand of their employers.

Although creditors and debt collectors cannot attach funds in retirement accounts, they can cajole people into draining those accounts. In some instances, creditors may not even need to coax people to look to their retirement accounts as a means to pay. People may shame themselves out of a sense of moral obligation into withdrawing retirement money to pay for health care, prescriptions, and other critical expenses.

These withdrawals are ill-advised. Preretirement withdrawals come with penalties and taxes and cannibalize the principal that is meant to grow during the years leading up to retirement. The accumulated money, post-retirement, likely is allocated to necessary expenses for many years. Any withdrawal means there will be less money to cover expenses in the future.

Nonetheless, many senior filers made this choice. As noted, slightly over one-third of them cashed out or borrowed from their retirement accounts to help make ends meet. A similar percentage stopped making contributions to their retirement accounts prior to filing. The current retirement system presumes that people will build their savings until they retire so that they can sustain themselves, without outside assistance, during their final years. Seniors almost certainly understood what stopping contributions or pulling significant sums from their retirement accounts would mean for their futures, but when faced with a mortgage payment or a hospital invoice, taking care of the bills became the more immediate and pressing concern.

A sixty-eight-year-old man described how he and his wife used retirement savings to manage an income deficit. Upon retirement, their income was reduced by half, but their bills remained constant. Because Social Security was inadequate, they had to use retirement money to make up the difference. When large and unexpected medical bills came, they turned to retirement savings to pay them, then had to take stock of the reality of their financial situation.

> I retired . . . resulting in some drop in income. Continued with same life-style. My wife was fired from her job [two years later]. She was forced to retire and draw SS [Social Security] at sixty-two. Our income was reduced by 50%. Tried to maintain mortgage payments and credit payments on time. Began to use our savings and retirement accounts. My wife had special back surgery [three years later]. This was a bill over $33,000 plus travel and hotel expenses. This was the last of our savings and retirement. We began to borrow money to maintain our home and credit payments. Sold our second car to daughter who needed a car. Used this money [for four months] to live and pay bills and expenses. We hit bottom . . . when we realized that no more money was coming anytime in the future.

This couple's story illustrates the detrimental effects of using a large portion of retirement savings to pay for unexpected expenses. It also points to two other systemic issues. The first is health insurance and health care. The wife lost her job, and presumably her health insurance, at age sixty-two, when she was ineligible for Medicare coverage for three more years. This likely explains the couple's large medical bill.

The second systemic issue is the paucity of retirement savings generally. The couple exited the workforce around the expected age of retirement. They started their retirement with at least $33,000 in savings and funds in retirement accounts, which is about half the median balance of all people's retirement accounts at age sixty-five. By the time they filed, the couple had a bit over $5,000 in retirement savings. If one surgery plunged them into bankruptcy, the same likely can spell financial disaster for a sizable portion of all senior households in the United States.

The paucity of seniors' retirement savings links directly with income inequality and the adequacy of income. For the past several decades, wage growth for most Americans has been minimal at best, as detailed in chapter 5. If incomes barely allow people to keep up with expenses, they likely save only a very small portion of their incomes in 401(k)-type retirement plans. Instead, people allocate most or all of their earnings to paying bills. Because it is their "choice" whether to contribute to their retirement savings plans, most people retire with a small fraction of what they will need to pay expenses for the remainder of their lives. As a result, many seniors will live their final years on a shoestring budget, and many will eventually rely entirely on Social Security.

A sixty-six-year-old man was forced into retirement when his employer terminated him. He withdrew his retirement savings for two reasons: a sense of responsibility to help his mother keep her home, and to keep up with everyday expenses.

> [M]y brother took a loan on Mom's house. A few months in, he decided not to pay it so I assumed it. I was making $4000 a month and it was no problem. Later, he decided to end his life, and I was terminated from [my job]. I drew my retirement, 401K out to help with this. Then I retired, went from $4000 a month to 1000. He [his brother] borrowed $15,000 [against Mom's house]. I've paid $42,000 and still owe another $30,000. So you tell me. Then my mother passed away and I assumed all those bills so I'm just stuck. I guess a bullet would be the way out.

These two stories further illustrate one of the shortcomings of 401(k)-type retirement plans: people can extract funds for any reason. In these examples, seniors used the money to pay for large medical bills and for family members' mortgages. In the case of the medical debt, the couple could have left the bills unpaid because state and bankruptcy laws exempt retirement accounts from creditors' collection efforts. For this couple, an earlier consultation with an attorney would have freed them from medical debts and left their retirement savings intact.

The man in the last story had no legal obligation to withdraw his retirement savings to protect his mother's house. He could have chosen to let her lose it in foreclosure. She would have had to move, and that would have been difficult for them both, but his savings would have been preserved, and he may have been able to scrape by for decades. In both situations, if they instead had pensions, their retirement savings would not have been available to them, and they would have been forced to make different choices.

## DECLINING HEALTH AND RISING HEALTH-CARE COSTS

### The Costs of Declining Health

Bodies and minds eventually falter. Consequently, most people will confront substantial medical problems as they age. Health care is one of the largest expenses for seniors. The National Council on Aging characterizes medical debt as "the most significant barrier to economic well-being" among older adults.[26] Even when covered by Medicare, the average couple retiring in 2023, both sixty-five years old, can expect to spend approximately $315,000 out-of-pocket on medical expenses between the time they retire and when they pass away.[27] The expenses include Medicare and supplemental insurance premiums, deductibles, and copays. If the couple lives to their mideighties, their out-of-pocket medical expenses will be approximately $15,000 a year. Fidelity Investments, a financial services corporation that provides retirement advice, tells people to expect to spend about 15 percent of their retirement income to pay for health care.[28]

Those who file bankruptcy reflect these larger national trends. As summarized in table 8.4, more than four out of ten seniors reported that they filed because of either direct medical expenses or the indirect costs associated with lost wages when they missed work to care for themselves or others.

Bankrupt seniors' stories illustrate their struggles with some of the direct costs of health care. For example, a seventy-eight-year-old man described how, despite Medicare, he and his sixty-nine-year-old wife faced large medical debts. She had several surgeries that insurance did not cover, which resulted in approximately $70,000 in medical bills over a five-year period.

An eighty-year-old man shared a similar experience. Even though he and his wife had "good health insurance," the cost of their medical care, much of which they charged on credit cards or paid for by taking out

*Table 8.4.*   Medical Contributors to Bankruptcy and Prebankruptcy Deprivations, 65 Years or Older (%)

| Do you very much or somewhat agree that the following things contributed to your bankruptcy? | |
| --- | --- |
| Either missed work for medical problems or medical expenses | 43 |
| Medical expenses, doctor and hospital bills, prescriptions | 35 |
| Missed work because of medical problems | 26 |
| During the 2 years before your bankruptcy, did you do without because you could not afford it? | |
| Medical privation index—at least one of the following: | 65 |
| Dental care | 58 |
| Medical attention | 35 |
| Prescriptions | 29 |
| Mental health care | 12 |

payday loans, drove them into bankruptcy. "The biggest factor was medical debts, prescriptions, had 2 major back surgeries, 2 hip replacements. Although I had good health insurance, I had to miss car payments, daughter had to help, things just got very stressful, with late fees and interest on credit debts and payday loans. Was not able to meet all." This story includes both the source of the problem and the consequence: incurrence of debt that led to bankruptcy. With comprehensive health care, this couple might have avoided these struggles and avoided bankruptcy altogether.

Chronic health issues likely exacerbate the financial struggles of seniors. Nine out of ten Americans over the age of sixty suffer from at least one chronic health condition, such as high blood pressure, high cholesterol, arthritis, heart disease, diabetes, depression, and dementia. Almost eight out of ten older adults live with two or more chronic conditions.[29]

Several bankrupt seniors shared stories of their struggles with persistent illnesses. A seventy-three-year-old senior with recurring heart problems wrote: "I had carotid artery surgery. [A month later], I had open heart surgery . . . and two bypasses. Could not work. [A year later], I had a second [heart] surgery with critical complications." A seventy-four-year-old veteran described numerous chronic medical conditions, including heart problems, that had marked his life for many years: "pulmonary embolism, angioplasty, open heart/4 bypass, congestive heart failure, sleep apnea, depression, anxiety, etc. etc. etc."

Chronic illnesses likely are more costly and affect seniors' ability to work more permanently than one-time illnesses. Filing bankruptcy will wipe away their medical debts, but it will not address the future medical bills and employment challenges they undoubtedly will face.

Of course, both the body and the mind can require care. And mental health issues can also undermine financial stability. In the general population, mental health struggles among seniors are well documented. In 2020, between 25 and 30 percent of older adults reported struggling with anxiety and depression.[30] A seventy-four-year-old debtor described the effects of his wife's mental health struggles, which, given that she could not work, appeared to be chronic.

> My wife is bipolar and is not able to work any longer. All of the responsibility of paying our bills rested with her. I declared bankruptcy if only to stop paying down my credit cards and direct that income to expenses, like utilities, that had previously been paid by my wife when she still had an income.

With age, staying alive and healthy becomes increasingly expensive, possibly prohibitively expensive. Whether the illness or injury is short-term or chronic, physical or mental, the costs associated with treatment contribute to many seniors' bankruptcies.

## Medicare Deficiencies

Medicare is complicated. Original Medicare has two components: Part A and Part B. Original Medicare Part A provides coverage for hospital care. Most seniors do not have to pay a monthly premium for Part A, but they remain responsible for deductibles and coinsurance costs. Original Medicare Part B provides medical insurance. It covers doctors' services and preventative care—the day-to-day portion of health care that people do to minimize getting sick. Seniors must pay a monthly premium for Part B coverage, which averaged $165 a month in 2023, as well as deductibles, copays, and coinsurance.[31] Original Medicare has no out-of-pocket limits for either Part A or Part B.[32] The more medical services seniors need, the higher their medical costs.

Because Original Medicare coverage is not comprehensive—for instance, it does not cover dental care, eye care, or the cost of hearing aids—and comes with the potential for large out-of-pocket costs, it is recommended that seniors purchase supplemental insurance plans from private companies. For example, Medigap supplemental insurance covers the out-of-pocket copays and deductibles not covered by Original Medicare. Medicare Part D covers the cost of most prescription drugs. Seniors wholly dissatisfied with Original Medicare can turn to Medicare Advantage, an alternative to Medicare provided through private insurers. It offers the same coverage as Parts A and B, plus prescription drug, vision, hearing, and dental coverage.[33]

More than one-quarter of Medicare recipients spend at least 20 percent of their annual income on supplemental insurance premiums and out-of-pocket medical costs.[34] Lower-income recipients and those with chronic illnesses spend an even greater percentage of their income on care. Comments from a seventy-year-old widow, whose husband died from ALS, illustrate how difficult it can be to pay for supplemental insurance. "[I] lost his income and had to get a job. I had to get SS [Social Security] Supplemental that is now $213 a month. The supplemental [insurance] takes a load of money so it makes bills a lot harder to pay. Old people should not have to pay so much for health insurance. I have no family to help me."

Many bankrupt seniors also reported that they went without various types of medical attention because they could not afford it, even though they had Medicare. Since Original Medicare does not cover most dental care and dental procedures, including cleanings, fillings, crowns, and dentures, it comes as no surprise that the majority of seniors indicated that they went without dental care. A woman in her mid-seventies wrote about the consequences of this lack of affordable health insurance and health care: "I went without medical and dental. Even with Medicare and supplemental dental insurance, the co-pays were more than we could afford. I still need dental work. It will have to wait until I can save up the money."

In addition to being unable to afford dental care, more than one-third of bankrupt seniors reported skipping doctor visits and surgeries because of the cost. And three out of ten reported that they went without medications or prescriptions, again because of the cost. Original Medicare's coverage limitations seem to result in seniors bearing those costs, often to the detriment of their health.

## AGING INTO RISK

Social scientists who study seniors write about "the two worlds of aging."[35] As people transition from childhood to adulthood, they generally start off on somewhat equal footing, but as they age, the amount of inequality among them increases. As a result, there is more financial disparity among individuals when they reach their retirement years than during their prime working years.[36] Over the past several decades, the inequality within aging cohorts of people has grown.[37]

An exclusive group of seniors enjoys financially sound retirements. Glossy retirement advertisements feature them. They experience the golden years of their retirement. These people largely matured into the economic privilege of high-status careers with significant salaries and ability to save, with top-notch health insurance, and sometimes with pensions. The people who live in this world of aging will experience little risk when they retire.

For most seniors, the seniors without these privileges, the path to and through retirement is much more precarious. Wages are probably more common than salaries, and salaries are low relative to everyday expenses. They have little opportunity to save. They may have to privately purchase health insurance because their employers do not provide it. Any retirement savings are in 401(k)-type plans rather than pensions. People must manage these plans independently and may deplete them to pay for emergencies during their working years. For them, Social Security will be more than supplemental. These individuals are not necessarily poor. Like the rest of the people who file bankruptcy, they were probably middle class when they were employed. However, they will not have the resources to move into and through their retirement years with financial security. They will face significant barriers to successfully negotiating the transition from employment to retirement, from independent to dependent.

The United States often marginalizes discussions of the vulnerabilities and dependency of our seniors because they expose the unpleasant fact that most people will reach a point when they can no longer work. Unless seniors have accrued substantial retirement savings, they will be dependent on others or the government. This age-based dependency explicitly challenges the American reverence for individualism. But despite the discomfort, the fact remains that the proportion of older Americans filing bankruptcy has grown rapidly over the past twenty years. Absent significant policy changes to cushion seniors from financial blows, they will continue to seek protection in bankruptcy courts. The population of seniors will increase nearly 50 percent, to eighty-two million, by 2050. In thirty years, seniors will comprise almost one-quarter of the population, a considerable increase from the current 17 percent.[38] Given this, the proportion of seniors in bankruptcy likewise will continue to increase.

The data from bankrupt seniors expose the required changes that could stem the tide of increased senior filings in the future. The national transition to privatization and individual responsibility has taken a heavy toll on older Americans. Where once defined-benefit pension plans guaranteed an income for the life of the retiree, now privatized retirement saving accounts can be cannibalized in response to bills and debt collectors. Instead of a health-care system that fully covers the costs associated with aging, seniors must purchase expensive supplemental coverage to meet their needs. Social Security benefits come later and provide a smaller percentage of preretirement income.

The couple whose story opened this chapter had known financial independence since they began working when they were teenagers. On the cusp of their retirement years, they stumbled. Unable to recover, they filed bankruptcy. And while she hopes they can "do something again," which certainly means return to the workforce, they are already dependent on Social Security and charity. They rail against this dependence. She desperately wants to reclaim that time when they could pull themselves up by their bootstraps and make their own way. Odds are that those days are well behind them.

Bankruptcy does not feel like an appropriate place for this country's oldest citizens. After decades in the workforce, raising families, and contributing to communities, people should have stability during their final years. Instead, our data suggest that absent policy changes, seniors across the United States will continue to face economic risks that will push them toward financial collapse. In the coming years, an even greater percentage of seniors may file bankruptcy as a last resort and in hopes of getting some relief.

# 9  Lawsuits and Debt Collectors

> I was so overwhelmed with all the debt collectors that kept
> calling me, so I decided to do something about it. I had
> some pretty good sized bills I couldn't afford and it was too
> much stress on my shoulders. As soon as I started to file
> bankruptcy, putting every single last bill I had owed in
> there, I felt immediately relieved of my debt. I don't want
> to go down this road again, so I know I will take better care
> financially.
>
> —Twenty-four-year-old, single white man
> with medical expenses

Living on the financial margin often means living with debt collectors. The nightly routine might entail a dinnertime dunning call. Daily reality includes the constant threat of asset or income seizure. In 2017 the Consumer Financial Protection Bureau (CFPB) found that, in a random sample of *anyone* with a credit report, 32 percent reported contact from a debt collector in the previous year.[1] About 80 percent of bankruptcy filers have faced debt collectors in the years before filing.

In chapter 2 of this book we discussed how many filers suffer privations for years before turning to bankruptcy. People often cite debt collection as the motivating factor that finally led them to seek bankruptcy relief. This chapter expands on that finding, as well as looking more broadly at debt collections and prebankruptcy lawsuits. After explaining who tries to collect debt and how informal and formal debt collection procedures work, we turn to what our data show about how the financially precarious interact with these debt collection systems.

## PLAYERS IN THE DEBT COLLECTION INDUSTRY

Broadly, two batches of creditors may be attempting to collect on a debt. First, the original creditor who made the loan or extended the credit may be doing the debt collection. The original creditor is more likely to do its own debt collection for debts that have only recently gone into default. For example, financial institutions like credit card lenders tend to collect the debt until the end of the 180-day period after which they must formally show the debt as uncollectible on their financial statements.[2] This "charge off" rule for bookkeeping purposes is sometimes misunderstood. It has no bearing on the borrower's legal obligation to pay the amount owed. But it often does prompt the original creditor to think about getting help in collecting the debt.

Second, and more often, the company collecting the debt is a third party who has become involved with the debt in a few ways. The original creditor may have hired a third party to collect the debt for a share of the amount collected. Or the original creditor may have sold the debt to a debt buyer for a fraction of the face amount of the debt. In this scenario, the debt buyer's profit is the difference between what it pays for the debt and whatever it manages to collect. Sometimes the debt buyer collects on its own behalf. Other times, a debt buyer might hire a third-party collector who receives a share of the amount recovered. Many debt buyers who use third-party collectors are investors who have purchased the debt for pennies on the dollar.[3]

The debt collection industry is stratified depending on the nature of the debt and its collectability. For example, a debt collector might specialize in certain types of debt—credit card or medical—or in debts that are particularly difficult to collect. Using data from credit reports, the CFPB found that 57 percent of the debt in collection is medical debt, but this medical debt is more likely to be in the hands of a debt collector rather than a debt buyer.[4] Online marketplaces also exist where debt buyers can bid for portfolios of debt. The consumer debts in these online marketplaces tend to be of low quality, from the buyers' perspective, and most sell for less than 1 percent of the face amount of the debt.[5]

There are more than six thousand debt collection companies in the United States.[6] Almost all are small businesses with few employees.

Nonetheless, there is substantial industry concentration. In 2018, of delinquent accounts reported to credit reporting agencies by debt buyers, over 90 percent came from four debt buyers.[7]

The debt collection industry has changed dramatically over the past fifty years. Sociologist David Caplovitz's classic study of debt collection lawsuits in 1967 told a story of merchants, car dealers, and small loan companies suing the consumers with whom they had dealt for payment on past due loans. Tellingly, his book's index does not include the concept of a "debt buyer" and includes only a few, scattered references to debt collection agencies.[8] The Federal Trade Commission puts the dawn of the debt-buying industry in the late 1980s and early 1990s, when investors who had purchased debts from failed savings and loans looked for new opportunities to make money.[9] Legal scholar Daniel Wilf-Townsend picks up the story from there, describing a transition in the civil litigation system such that contract claims—claims for payment on past due debt—now dominate state courts. Since 2004 there has been a steady increase in the number of lawsuits filed by debt collectors and an increasing concentration of those lawsuits into fewer debt-buying firms.[10] Today's bankruptcy filers are likely to have had a different debt collection experience than those people who filed bankruptcy twenty years ago.

For simplicity's sake, we use the terms *debt collection* and *debt collectors* to refer to the collection activity of original creditors, debt buyers, and debt collectors. To someone on the receiving end of debt collection, the industry dynamics matter, not these fine distinctions. From chapter 2 of this book, we know that most bankruptcy filers struggle for at least two years before filing, and almost all struggle for at least six months. They owe debts that will have moved well into the machinery of the debt collection industry. Some of these debts may even have changed hands several times among different parties. The lender or merchant or service provider with whom they originally dealt is long out of the picture. Their pursuer is not someone who needs their goodwill for continued business but whose business model depends on squeezing out as much money as possible. Indeed, their debt collector is likely to be a well-resourced and experienced adversary who collects from hundreds of thousands of people each year.

## HOW DEBT COLLECTION WORKS

As well-resourced and experienced players in the system, debt collectors will engage in a layered approach to collect on a debt, beginning with informal efforts, moving to formal legal action, and returning to court to access a person's property or wages. Depending on their leverage at the beginning of the relationship, the original creditor may already have the right to access a person's property, which will significantly aid their ability to collect.

### Informal Efforts

Debt collectors typically begin their collection efforts informally, outside the legal system. This is the most economical approach. They try to persuade the person to pay voluntarily. In a previous era, debt collectors would send a letter in the mail or use the phone, unless the debt collector wanted to make an in-person visit. Today, they can email, text, or even direct message on a social media app. The federal Fair Debt Collection Practices Act and various state laws limit the nature and timing of the communications that debt collectors can make. Consumers report widespread violations of these laws. We discuss these laws further later.

Although informal debt collection efforts are widely used, it is not immediately clear why they should be effective. The person is already delinquent on the account. Why would further communications change the situation? The delinquency rarely stems from an outright refusal to pay. For some, contact from a debt collector may serve as notice of an overlooked bill that is easily remedied. For others, the debt collector may change the cost-benefit calculus of not paying, either because the presence of a debt collector signals that more serious consequences, such as formal collection efforts, are imminent, or because they do not want to deal with the increased annoyance and mental stress of persistent communications. For those reasons to work, the person must have the money to pay. Many people likely do not, and for some of them, bankruptcy offers a way out. Our data, detailed later, reaffirm previous studies finding that escaping debt collection remains an important reason that people file bankruptcy.

While these informal debt collection efforts continue, the amount the borrower owes is almost certainly increasing. If the contract provides, the borrower can be charged interest and the costs of collection, including attorney's fees. Almost every contract includes this provision. The amount a debt collector is pursuing often greatly exceeds the original amount owed by the borrower, possibly multiples of the original amount. The borrower is mostly powerless to contest the amount the debt collector claims. Although federal and state laws provide some protections against false or excessive claims, these protections are generally not very effective.

### Formal Efforts

If informal efforts do not produce payment, the debt collector can pursue formal legal action. Absent a question of federal law, only cases involving more than $75,000 can be brought in federal court. As a result, consumer debt collection exclusively occurs in state court. The debt collector alleges essentially a breach of contract: the person promised to pay and did not. The legal technicalities from state to state need not concern us. The case formally looks like what we think of as a lawsuit. It incudes a plaintiff (the debt collector), a defendant (the person who promised to pay and did not), motions, discovery, and potentially even a trial.

The reality is very different. Exceedingly few people sued by a debt collector have an attorney. Studies across jurisdictions find that consumers only file any sort of response in approximately 15 to 20 percent of cases.[11] Courts generally, by far, award a default judgment to the debt collector because the consumer has failed to appear.[12] Rather than an adversarial process in which the judge hears from both sides, consumer debt collection bears a closer resemblance to an administrative process for the creditor to get the imprimatur of the state to collect the amount owed.

The industry concentration among debt collection firms shows up in court. Several studies document the high percentage of cases filed by a handful of debt collection companies. One study found the top ten filers in twenty jurisdictions in 2019 accounted for 22 percent of *all* civil cases, debt collection and otherwise. In New Jersey, ten debt collection plaintiffs alone were responsible for 281,000 cases by themselves, which was 42 percent of the entire civil caseload across the state.[13] The typical civil lawsuit in the United States today is a debt collection case against an un-represented individual.

High volumes allow economies of scale in litigation that in turn lower costs for debt collectors.[14] To get a sense of how low, consider that one study found that a traditional contract lawsuit would require 165 hours of attorney time for pretrial matters only, implying a cost of $41,250 at a rate of $250 per hour.[15] Yet multiple studies have found debt collection lawsuits involve low sums of money, as low as $700 or $800.[16] Even al-lowing that the debt collector might expect to shift the costs of the law-suit onto the consumer, the numbers convey how efficiently large debt collectors can litigate a claim. Wilf-Townsend described them perfectly, as "assembly-line plaintiffs."[17] Debt collectors rely on high rates of default judgments to keep costs low. When people resist, lawsuits quickly become too expensive to justify the cost. Debt collectors often dismiss suits when consumers show up in court.

## After the Judgment

Winning a court judgment, such as a default judgment, does not put any money in the debt collector's pocket. The court judgment is simply a piece of paper recognizing that the consumer owes the money. The real value of that piece of paper is that it gives the debt collector access to the power of the state to coerce payment. Lawyers refer to this part of the process as postjudgment remedies. Although the details vary in each state, the laws follow the same general pattern.

The debt collector can use the judgment to coerce payment in a couple of ways. They can obtain a lien against the person's property, such as a house, car, or other valuable property. In theory, the court will sell this property and turn over the sale proceeds to the debt collector to satisfy the debt. In practice, such sales are uncommon. The most valuable assets that people have are homes and cars, and their mortgage lender or car lender will come ahead of this lien. Also, the same types of assets exempt from the bankruptcy process described in chapter 1 of this book are exempt from sale to satisfy a debt collector's court judgment.

More commonly, the debt collector will use the judgment to obtain a writ of garnishment that will be directed to a third party who owes the consumer money. The third parties most often subject to garnishment are banks and employers. Banks owe their customers for the money deposited in bank accounts, and employers owe their employees for earned but unpaid wages. A business that receives a writ of garnishment must comply. There are some protections for the consumer. Debt collectors cannot reach Social Security funds in a bank account. Generally speaking, federal law prevents garnishing more than 25 percent of a paycheck. Some state laws provide greater protection, and four states—North Carolina, Pennsylvania, South Carolina, and Texas—prohibit wage garnishment against consumers altogether.

Research finds garnishment is related to bankruptcy filings.[18] States with greater garnishment restrictions tend to have fewer bankruptcy filings. From 2018 to 2023, for example, the bankruptcy filing rate per person was 42 percent lower in the four states that prohibit wage garnishment.[19] Evidence on the relationship with exemptions for personal property, in contrast, tends to find no relationship with bankruptcy filing rates, which is not surprising given that exemptions protect assets. For most people, losing their income flow is a more serious threat to their financial well-being. Exemptions protect the person's important assets, often in full. It is not surprising that people use bankruptcy to stop garnishment and protect their income.

*Collecting on Secured Debts*

The classic concept of a debt collector is someone collecting an unsecured debt such as a credit card or hospital bill. Creditors with a security interest in property, such as a home or a car—holders of mortgages and car loans—also engage in prebankruptcy collection efforts.

As explained in chapter 3 of this book, creditors with a security interest in personal property—everything that is not real estate—can seize the property on their own if they can do so without committing a "breach of the peace." This is called repossessing the property. Although in theory creditors can repossess any personal property in which they have a security interest, for what everyday people own, that property in which the creditor has a security interest almost always will be a car. New technologies such as license plate scanners and quick-acting tow trucks that can drive away with a car within seconds have made it cheaper and easier for car lenders to find and then haul away cars. Within a few weeks, the repossessed car will be sold at auction, with the proceeds applied to the amount the borrower owes. If after applying the proceeds the borrower still owes money, called a deficiency, the lender can continue to pursue the borrower for that amount. Indeed, the original creditor often will sell the deficiency claim into the same debt collection system discussed earlier. Car repossessions thus may end up being a "double whammy" for people. Not only do they no longer have the cars that might have provided transportation to jobs or schools, but also they now have debt collectors pursuing them.

In contrast, enforcement of a defaulted home mortgage requires a very formal process. The laws vary not insignificantly between the states and are highly technical. We can only give them a broad brush. Twenty-one states require the creditor to bring a lawsuit, known as *judicial foreclosure*. The other states allow the creditor to create the loan using a *deed of trust* that permits a third party to sell the property when the consumer misses a certain number of payments. When we discuss *foreclosure* or *mortgages* we mean those terms to include deeds of trust. Either a judicial or deed-of-trust process terminates a person's interest in their home, hence the term foreclosure. The deed-of-trust process is quicker than judicial foreclosure. Procedures vary so widely between states that it is most accurate to say that the process may take anywhere from a matter of months to a year or more. Federal and state laws heavily regulate both. Foreclosure itself is a long process. The period of informal debt collection that typically precedes it begins what could be years and years of worry, stress, and sleepless nights.

*Regulation of Debt Collection*

Given the scope of debt collection, there exists a potential for abuse. In 1977 Congress passed the Fair Debt Collection Practices Act (FDCPA) to regulate debt collectors. It only applies to someone collecting the debts of another or whose principal business is debt collection. The FDCPA does not apply to financial institutions, merchants, and others collecting their own debt. Many states have their own debt collection laws, and a few of those—notably California—extend those laws to original creditors collecting their own debts.

The FDCPA includes protections for people from debt collectors' harassment and collection of debts not owed. It requires debt collectors to notify consumers of their right to contest the debt. If the consumer contests the debt, the debt collector must pause its activity until it verifies the debt. The FDCPA also makes it illegal to repetitively call people, call people's employer, or continue to communicate with people after being told by the consumer to stop. A debt collector cannot threaten to sue unless it intends to do so or imply that nonpayment will result in arrest or imprisonment. In 2021 the CFPB enacted new regulations to bring the FDCPA into the modern era. For example, CFPB regulations added specific rules about contacts through social media.

The CFPB and the Federal Trade Commission bring FDCPA enforcement actions against debt collectors. FDCPA violations, however, remain common. In 2022 the CFPB reported receiving nearly 116,000 complaints about debt collectors, with the most common complaint being that the debt collector was pursuing a debt that was not owed.[20] A consumer can bring a lawsuit for a FDCPA violation, but in many instances the consumer's recovery will only be statutory damages of $1,000, an amount that has not changed since the FDCPA's 1977 enactment. In addition, the US Supreme Court has cut back the FDCPA as a remedy, both through interpretations of the FDCPA itself and jurisdictional requirements it has put in the way of consumers more broadly. Although debt collectors do not operate in a regulatory vacuum, people facing aggressive debt collectors, especially ones not inclined to follow the FDCPA, do not have practical legal relief available to make them stop. For some people, bankruptcy may become a leading option to deal with debt collection.

DEBT COLLECTION BEFORE BANKRUPTCY

To assess prebankruptcy debt collection activity, we combined data from our surveys and bankruptcy court records. The bankruptcy schedules do not ask about informal collection activity prebankruptcy. We asked bankruptcy filers on our survey, "What went wrong?" and provided them with a list of fourteen items that may have "contributed" to their bankruptcy.[21] Two of these items directly asked about out-of-court collection activities: "a car was repossessed" or "pressure from debt collectors." Another item asked whether home foreclosure contributed to the filing. These three questions thus identified prebankruptcy debt collection activity. A limitation is that we have only four years of data during which car repossession was a response option on our survey.

For formal lawsuits, bankruptcy court documents require people to disclose if, within one year before they filed bankruptcy, they were "a party in any lawsuit, court action, or administrative proceeding." If so, the filer must provide a short description about the "nature of the case." We use this description to divide the lawsuits into three mutually exclusive categories. First are home mortgage foreclosures. Second are actions against the filer's property other than the home, such as a foreclosure against other real estate or seizure of the filer's car. Third are "nonproperty actions," which are mostly collection lawsuits, but also include divorce proceedings. We combine these categories to create a variable that captures whether the filer reported any prebankruptcy lawsuit.

As described in table 9.1, debt collection activity is prevalent among people who file bankruptcy. Our data about debt collection activity align with what previous studies have reported for bankruptcy filers, suggesting an enduring fact that about four out of every five filers will come to bankruptcy after experiencing debt collection.[22] The survey responses substantially overlap, with almost as many persons reporting pressure from debt collectors as a contributor to their bankruptcy as reported any of the three reasons (foreclosure, repossession, or debt collection) combined. Although the classic definition of a "debt collector" is someone collecting an unsecured debt, the overlap suggests people do not make these fine distinctions.

Filers reported a higher incidence of debt collection activity on the surveys than lawsuits in the court records. A contributing factor is undoubtedly that the court records ask about lawsuits within the year before bankruptcy, while the survey response was not time limited. More importantly, the survey did not ask about formal lawsuits specifically. Again, filers were not making the sorts of fine distinctions about debt collection that legal or financial professionals might make. A homeowner who has

*Table 9.1.* Level of Debt Collection Activity among Bankruptcy Filers

| | Entire Database (2013–2023) (%) | COVID Rounds (Q2 of 2020–2022) (%) |
|---|---|---|
| Bankruptcy contributor on survey | | |
| House was in foreclosure | 18 | 13 |
| A car was repossessed | 30 | — |
| Pressure from debt collectors | 77 | 78 |
| Any of the above | 81 | 82 |
| Lawsuits disclosed in bankruptcy records | | |
| Foreclosure involving home | 5 | 3 |
| Lawsuits on other property | 12 | 11 |
| All other lawsuits | 40 | 43 |
| Any of the above | 49 | 50 |

received a notice of default on the mortgage and is getting notices from the lender about next steps likely perceives the foreclosure process as having begun, even if the mortgage lender has not initiated the formal legal proceeding. We cannot rule out overreporting on the survey, and we suspect underreporting on the court records. Our survey responses correspond with the court records, bolstering the reliability of both. For example, filers who reported that foreclosure was a contributor to bankruptcy were more likely to list a foreclosure in the court records. Filers who reported debt collection on the survey were more likely to list "other lawsuits" in the court records.

Table 9.1 also considers the possible effects from the COVID-era federal and state moratoria on foreclosures, car repossessions, and debt collection.[23] Foreclosure activity decreased after the pandemic. Debt collections remained the same before and after the pandemic. The likely reason is that states universally adopted foreclosure moratoria, and foreclosure moratoria were federally imposed for many mortgages. In comparison, moratoria on debt collection varied substantially by state and were in place for shorter periods. Another study similarly found that, if anything, debt collection activity only grew during the pandemic.[24] (We omit car repossessions for the COVID era because we only have four years of responses for that datapoint, and most of those responses are from the COVID era.)

Bankruptcy filings plummeted in the wake of the pandemic, mysteriously so. Many experts cited the COVID-era moratoria, but those moratoria were not likely to have slowed bankruptcy filings, for two reasons. First, as discussed in chapter 2 of this book, most bankruptcy filings are not the result of a sudden crisis but are the culmination of at least two years of financial distress. Second, bankruptcy filings plummeted practically overnight, before the moratoria came into full effect. Our findings reinforce the view that other factors were more likely the explanation.[25]

### Whose Debts Go to Collection

To ask who is more likely to experience debt collection activity among bankruptcy filers can misleadingly imply that some groups experience low levels of debt collection. That is not true. Debt collection is a predominant experience of bankruptcy filers generally. With that caveat, we assessed many of the demographics explored in other chapters of this book. Debt collection falls equally across almost all types of bankruptcy filers. However, debt collection's burdens fall disparately on a couple of groups of people who file bankruptcy.

The largest differences are age related. Auto repossessions and debt collection tend to be a younger person's problem. In the survey, filers who are age sixty-five or over are 15 percent less likely to cite pressure from debt collectors as a contributor to bankruptcy and 61 percent less likely to cite a car repossession. The same results occurred in the bankruptcy court records. Filers who are age sixty-five or over are 36 percent less likely to list a lawsuit involving property other than a home, such as a car repossession, and 47 percent less likely to list other lawsuits, such as a debt collection action. Foreclosures, in contrast, are equally likely to fall across all age groups.

The reasons for the age differences are not apparent. Car repossessions cannot be explained by car ownership rates, because those sixty-five or over are slightly more likely to own a car. Filers who are sixty-five or over are less likely to have a regular paycheck that may be an attractive target for garnishment. Across our various measurements of debt collection lawsuits, older ages remain a significant and negative predictor for such lawsuits even after controlling for the presence or amount of a regular paycheck. Additionally, the relationship of age to debt collection's burdens runs consistently throughout the entire range of ages of bankruptcy filers. The younger a filer is, the more likely they are to have experienced debt collection prior to filing. It is not merely an effect for those 65 or over. The relationship between age with car repossessions and debt collection lawsuits are topics asking for further study.

As mentioned in chapter 6 of this book, Black people are often targeted for debt collection.[26] Black households that file bankruptcy were 8 percent more likely to report pressure from debt collectors as a contributor to their filing than other households. They were also more likely to report a car repossession or home foreclosure. Again, financial situations inside of bankruptcy seem to reflect what happens outside of bankruptcy. In their bankruptcy court records, however, Black debtors were 10 percent *less likely* to list a prebankruptcy debt collection lawsuit and 5 percent *less likely* to list any type of lawsuit.

We suspect these diverging findings from the survey and the court records may be rooted in bankruptcy chapter choice. As detailed in chapter 6 of this book and many other studies, Black filers disproportionately file chapter 13. To the extent this steering of Black filers to chapter 13 reflects lower-quality lawyering, the lower numbers of listed prebankruptcy lawsuits in the court records may reflect attorneys' underreporting of these lawsuits. The existence of a prebankruptcy lawsuit will have no effect on the outcome of the bankruptcy case, and no one is likely to check or notice if a lawsuit is omitted. An attorney working quickly to save time may skip that portion of the bankruptcy paperwork entirely.

### Debt Collection and the Sweatbox

Debt collection contributes meaningfully to the financial sweatbox detailed in chapter 2 of this book. Debt collection activities correlate with more reported privations from filers. Filers who agreed that pressure from debt collectors contributed to their bankruptcy were more likely to report privations across all categories. These filers reported an average of six privations, compared to four privations for all other filers.

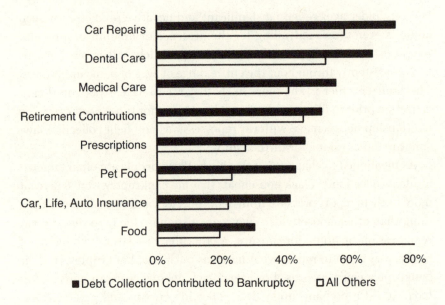

*Figure 9.1.* Percentage of bankruptcy filers who reported "going without" during the two years before bankruptcy, based on whether pressure from debt collectors contributed to the bankruptcy

Figure 9.1 shows how debt collection especially exacerbates the privations people experience before bankruptcy. Some of the differences in individual categories are dramatic. People who cited debt collection as a contributor to their bankruptcy were almost twice as likely to report going without food for their pets or other animal care or foregoing car or homeowner's insurance. Thirty percent reported going without food for themselves versus nineteen percent for other filers. The absolute numbers are also high. Three out of four reported going without car repairs. More than half reported foregoing medical care or dental care, and a little under 50 percent reported going without prescription medications.

The same pattern occurs among filers who indicated that a car repossession contributed to the bankruptcy. These filers reported an average of more than one and one-half more privations than all other filers. Those who cited a car repossession as a contributor to bankruptcy were more likely, across every category, to have said they suffered any particular privation. On the whole, the differences are not as dramatic but are still large in many categories. More than half reported going without medical or dental care, and almost half reported going without prescription drugs. Thirty-seven percent reported going without food.

Yet again, the same pattern occurs with filers who cited a foreclosure as a contributor to bankruptcy. These filers reported an average of six privations, compared to five privations for all other filers. They also were more likely, across every category, to say they suffered any particular privation. The differences with those who do not cite a foreclosure shrink even further, with many not being significant. There is one exception. Not surprisingly, those who reported a foreclosure are 50 percent more likely to report that they made a rent or mortgage payment late.

Using variables from the court records about whether the filer reported a prebankruptcy lawsuit, we get the same pattern for foreclosure lawsuits, lawsuits against "other property," and debt collection lawsuits. A filer with these lawsuits, either considered alone or in combination, is more likely to have reported a privation across every category. On average, filers with any prebankruptcy lawsuit reported more privations than those without prebankruptcy lawsuits. The differences are strongest for general debt collection lawsuits and weakest (although still present) for foreclosure lawsuits, with lawsuits against "other property" falling somewhere in the middle.

How debt collection interacts with the prebankruptcy sweatbox also affects what people do to make ends meet. One of these relationships is mechanical. Someone who cites a foreclosure as a contributor to bankruptcy is six times more likely to say they sold a house.

More troubling, prebankruptcy pressure from creditors leads to more borrowing as a way to make ends meet, but the type of borrowing varies depending on the nature of the underlying obligation. As table 9.2 details, those who reported car repossessions were more likely to use expensive fringe lending than those who were subjected to general debt collection, who in turn were more likely to use fringe lending than those with foreclosures. Again, the results hold whether using the survey response or the court records. The absolute levels vary on car repossessions and lawsuits about other property, probably because the categories are not perfectly overlapping, but the same patterns remain.

The levels of borrowing are also high compared to those who do not have any prebankruptcy creditor actions. For example, those who reported any prebankruptcy collection activity on their surveys were 47 percent

*Table 9.2.*   Prebankruptcy Borrowing and Prebankruptcy Actions from Creditors

|  | Credit Cards (%) | Payday Loans (%) | Pawn Loans (%) | Family/Friends Loans (%) |
|---|---|---|---|---|
| Bankruptcy contributor on survey | | | | |
| House was in foreclosure | 51 | 45 | 44 | 65 |
| A car was repossessed | 67 | 62 | 56 | 78 |
| Debt collector pressure | 66 | 48 | 45 | 71 |
| Any of the above | 65 | 47 | 45 | 70 |
| Lawsuits disclosed in bankruptcy records | | | | |
| Foreclosure involving home | 49 | 39 | 39 | 53 |
| Lawsuits on other property | 61 | 52 | 49 | 64 |
| All other lawsuits | 62 | 46 | 46 | 71 |
| Any of the above | 62 | 46 | 45 | 69 |

more likely to have used a pawn loan. Those with any prebankruptcy lawsuit were 21 percent more likely to have used a payday lender.

Prebankruptcy collection efforts affect how people think about their bankruptcy case. Generally speaking, filers who went through prebankruptcy collection activities of all types reported being angrier at the time of their bankruptcy filing. They were also more likely to say they deserved a fresh start and did the responsible thing by filing bankruptcy. It seems likely that filers feel they have "paid" for their second chance by living through the misery that debt collection creates. It is that feeling that may lead to the capitulation we discussed in chapter 2 of this book, when even people who seriously struggle to pay their debts for two or more years finally give up and file bankruptcy. Those struggles, however, may take a toll.

## Health Effects

We asked filers about their physical and mental health at the time of filing and about whether they had "physical, mental, or emotional health problems that were caused or made worse by the stress of the debts?" We asked the same questions about the filer's spouse or partner, regardless of whether that person joined the bankruptcy.

There were no relationships between any types of debt collection activities and self-reported physical or mental health at the time of filing. There was, however, a meaningful difference in the filer's self-reported perception that health problems were worsened, but only for general debt collections. Those who reported pressures from debt collectors as a bankruptcy contributor on the survey were 11 percent more likely to say their health had worsened. Those with general debt collection lawsuits on their bankruptcy court records were 20 percent more likely to say so. Foreclosures or car repossessions had no effects.

For these self-reported observations to be an accurate assessment of one's health, those who have debt collectors haranguing them must have started out as systematically healthier than those who do not. Otherwise, we would expect self-reported health at filing to be lower by those with debt collectors on their doorsteps. It seems unlikely to be true that those with debt collectors pressuring them were systematically healthier. At the same time, we do not want to make the mistake of dismissing these self-reported effects. The effect is not small and is consistent across both identifiers of debt collection in the survey and the court records. There is a perception that debt collection has taken a prebankruptcy toll. Intriguingly, there is no greater likelihood of reporting feeling "relief" at the time of bankruptcy. The link between indebtedness and mental health is only beginning to be understood. Debt collection activity may be an important window into the dynamic.

### Foreclosure Is Different

Among prebankruptcy debt collection activities, foreclosure stands out. Far fewer filers come to bankruptcy in the wake of foreclosures than of other debt collection proceedings. As noted in chapter 3 of this book, only 10 percent of bankrupt homeowners file following a foreclosure action. Foreclosure prompts privations, but those who experienced foreclosure reported smaller differences in what they went without prior to filing than those who were not subject to foreclosure.

Those who experienced foreclosure also reported different reactions to bankruptcy and emotions about filing. Someone who experienced a foreclosure was less likely to report that the bankruptcy filing brought them a sense of relief. This tracks with bankrupt homeowners' heightened feelings of fear upon filing as compared to other filers.

In addition, foreclosure results in people borrowing less often from fringe lenders prebankruptcy. As mentioned in chapter 3 of this book, the resources it takes to be able to purchase a home or other real property may have pushed these filers into a socioeconomic position that they were unwilling to abandon, at least psychologically. Turning to fringe lending networks would be an admission to themselves and a public signal that they had slipped down society's socioeconomic rungs, and thus they turned to other coping mechanisms to make ends meet.

Foreclosure also lasts longer and has procedural antecedents to formal legal action. Filers may become accustomed to living in constant crisis from the threat to their housing. The consequences can have a longer tail. Bankruptcy can pause a foreclosure and restructure a debt. But the filer still faces years of mortgage payments on a fragile budget. It is little wonder they felt less relief from the filing. Instead, the foreclosure that led them to bankruptcy likely will continue to loom large, signaling to them how far they have fallen and, more broadly, showing one place where household financial precarity manifests uniquely.

## What Bankruptcy Filers Tell Us about Debt Collection

Debt collection efforts are not monolithic. The institutional details matter both for policymakers to understand how debt collection affects people and for people in the outcomes they obtain. Industry and technological changes have turbocharged debt collection efforts, even to the point where collectors can justify lawsuits over a few hundred dollars.

Those dynamics show up in bankruptcy court, where the vast majority of filers have experienced some type of debt collection. These filers reported privations that demonstrate how debt collection worsens the sweatbox of financial distress. Dealing with debt collection means more borrowing and often with high-cost credit that was unlikely to improve the filer's financial prospects.

Those who have experienced extensive debt collection efforts turn to bankruptcy because they have run out of options. The next chapter uses our data to try to find bankruptcy filers who do not exhaust their options and file bankruptcy while they still "can pay." We will give away the ending: we do not find many.

# 10 "Resourced" Bankruptcy Filers

> Mortgage company unwilling to work with us to adjust
> payments or refinance with terms we could afford after
> both myself and spouse experienced periods of loss of
> income. We became too far behind in payments to be able
> to ever catch up even after using all the savings, retirement
> and educational funds to try to keep the house.
>
> —White couple in their late fifties who owned a home
> and had five dependents

Some people file bankruptcy utterly broke—they owe hundreds of thousands in debts and have virtually no assets. Other people file bankruptcy also owing considerable debts, but they have considerable assets. These people may be in financial distress, but they may not have lived in deep financial precarity. This chapter considers bankruptcy filers who had more than other bankruptcy filers, yet noticeably less than most households outside of bankruptcy.

Popular media and some legislators may disparage these people by calling them "cheaters," people who take advantage of and abuse the bankruptcy system. Judges, when writing cases, may refer to these people as "can pay debtors." To say someone "cheats" implies an agreed-upon set of rules or norms that the person has transgressed. Everyone who files bankruptcy breaks promises they made to others. An old saying goes, "Bankruptcy is the land of broken promises." Under that reasoning, all bankruptcy filers are "cheats." Societies across the world have bankruptcy systems, such that some level of promise breaking must be tolerable. Our data can help assess when promise breaking crosses boundaries, when someone who invokes the protection of bankruptcy law perhaps truly "can pay" and should pay.

In a world without bankruptcy, creditors would race to the courthouse to act in their own financial interest to collect what they were owed from the debtor before other creditors. Depending on the debtor's financial circumstances, this race could waste time and destroy value. In 1800, the US Congress first created the bankruptcy discharge as an incentive. Only those debtors who cooperated with the bankruptcy process received a discharge. The discharge was a quid pro quo bargain for the debtor's cooperation that in theory maximized the return to creditors.[1]

Maximizing creditor recovery remains a reason for bankruptcy today. For those filers who have assets or income to repay, creditors as a group fare better than they would individually pursuing the filer in state court. It hardly can be said, however, that the discharge remains a quid pro quo for the debtor's cooperation. Nowadays, only filers who do something that rises to the level of fraud or who obstruct the bankruptcy proceeding can lose their discharge.

A capitalist system necessarily produces financial winners and losers. The aphorism attributed to Frank Borman, "Capitalism without bankruptcy is like Christianity without hell," captures that essential truth.[2] We do not condemn the financially distressed in perpetuity. In its current incarnation, bankruptcy primarily exists to provide a second chance for overburdened, "honest but unfortunate" debtors. The discharge is the manifestation of that second chance. Why should it be so? The most persuasive answers are instrumental.

First, many people could never pay a significant portion of the debt that a bankruptcy has discharged, especially considering the interest and costs that continue to accrue on the underlying obligation. In these instances, the bankruptcy discharge is no more the cause of the debt not being repaid than a medicine is a cause of the illness it treats. The bankruptcy discharge merely recognizes the reality of nonpayment. The filer benefits from the peace of mind, to the detriment of no one.[3]

The bankruptcy discharge also restores the filer back to economic life. Persons who use their current income to pay down past debt necessarily consume less today. Studies have linked high indebtedness to lower rates of business formation, homeownership, marriage, and family creation.[4] Reduced spending means others will not benefit from creating the goods and services that otherwise these persons would have purchased. The economic term for the effect is *debt overhang*, which the bankruptcy discharge works to alleviate.

Even so, some debtors could repay something on even their largest debts, even if it is mere pennies on the dollar. This chapter's goal is not to measure how many more pennies they might pay. Rather, we analyze the situations of the "wealthy" and "high-income" debtors in our dataset to determine if they might reasonably be characterized as trying to work the bankruptcy system to their advantage. Is there more we can expect of people before seeking bankruptcy relief? How many people who file bankruptcy, in the words of some judges, are "can pay" debtors who could satisfy a significant portion of their debt obligations? To spoil the surprise, the answers are "not much" and "not many."

Even for the "can pay" debtors identified, it is difficult to say they are taking advantage or unfairly filing bankruptcy. They do not appear to be the "cheaters" called out by popular media and some legislators. They use the bankruptcy system as Congress designed it. Many apply the tools of the bankruptcy system to solve a specific financial problem in their lives. For these filers, turning to bankruptcy when they are in comparatively less disastrous financial circumstances allows them to make the most of bankruptcy's promised fresh start.

## IN SEARCH OF THE "CAN PAY" DEBTOR

Broadly speaking, there are two ways to pay debts. You can pay from what you have, or you can pay from what you will have. That is, you can use assets on hand or future income. To find people who most likely had the capacity to pay, we studied the filers with the most assets and highest incomes. We created a subset of the 315 filers who were in the top 10 percent in both income and assets. As a shorthand reference, we call these persons resourced filers.

We also considered an alternative definition based on the filer's equity in their assets. A filer who owns a $250,000 home free and clear of mortgages may have more resources than a filer with a $750,000 home encumbered by a $740,000 mortgage. As compared to other filers, resourced filers tend to have more equity in their assets but not in amounts likely to make a difference. Nonetheless, we checked and found it made no difference to our conclusions which definition of a resourced filer was used and thus kept the more understandable definition based on asset value combined with income.

We supplemented this quantitative analysis with a more qualitative review, in which we read each of the bankruptcy court files for resourced filers between 2019 and 2022. This qualitative review allowed us to appreciate the circumstances of each case in a way that the aggregate analyses can obscure. We share descriptions from the qualitative review later.

Other chapters in this book lay out how little bankruptcy filers generally have. Only 9 percent of filers have an income above the state median for a household of their size. Forty percent of filers own homes, compared to the national average of about sixty-five percent. Bankruptcy filers with homes have less valuable homes. The median filer's home is worth about half the value of the median home value nationally. More than 90 percent of filers have less than $25,000 in retirement savings—67 percent report no retirement savings at all. The median value of a bankruptcy filer's *most valuable* car is $9,100.

Resourced filers have resources only compared to other bankruptcy filers. They are not wealthy. They are also not impoverished. Their financial profiles are not dissimilar to typical American households. If there are "can pay" debtors in bankruptcy, they are most likely to be among our resourced filers.

## WHAT DOES IT MEAN TO BE A RESOURCED FILER?

### Finances and Demographics

Table 10.1 details differences between resourced filers and all other bankruptcy filers. The key characteristic of a resourced filer is homeownership. Almost every resourced filer—97 percent—owns a home. Because a home is usually someone's most valuable asset, it is not surprising that homeownership sets resourced filers apart from other filers. As homeowners, resourced filers deal with twice as many foreclosure actions prior to bankruptcy than other filers—9 percent versus 4 percent.

Because we define resourced filers as in the top decile of income, their income is about three times higher than that of other bankruptcy filers. Their annual income of almost $140,000 compares favorably even to

*Table 10.1.* Financial and Demographic Characteristics of Resourced
and All Other Filers

| | *Resourced Filers* | *All Other Filers* |
|---|---|---|
| Assets (medians) | | |
| Total assets | $530,959 | $32,444 |
| Home value (homeowners only) | $421,400 | $154,953 |
| Home equity | $41,727 | $15,832 |
| Homeowners | 97% | 38% |
| Number of cars | 2 | 1 |
| Value of most valuable car | $19,046 | $8,929 |
| Retirement assets | $4,719 | $0 |
| Debts (medians) | | |
| Secured debts | $555,827 | $21,625 |
| Unsecured debts | $81,530 | $44,000 |
| Income (medians) | | |
| Annual income | $138,444 | $48,564 |
| Debt-to-income ratio | 3.8 | 2.0 |
| Above state median income | 51% | 8% |
| Case & demographic information | | |
| Chapter 13 | 63% | 34% |
| White | 76% | 64% |
| College degree or higher | 55% | 21% |
| Married or partnered | 85% | 45% |
| Has dependents | 69% | 49% |

the general population. The US Census reported a median income for a
married couple—another dominant characteristic of resourced filers—of
$119,400 in 2023. Although above the national median and in the top
decile of bankruptcy filers, resourced filers are far from the top national
income decile of $234,900.[5]

As discussed in chapter 6 of this book, general social and economic
dynamics show up in bankruptcy. Resourced filers demonstrate these

dynamics again. They are about twice as likely as other filers to be coupled households—have a spouse or domestic partner—and are more likely to have children. Their larger households give them both more resources and more obligations. Resourced filers are more likely to be white and have a college degree. Outside of bankruptcy, these demographic characteristics likewise make one more likely to be "resourced" than other people.

### Prebankruptcy Experiences

Resourced filers stand apart from other filers in the precipitators that they indicated led them to bankruptcy. Divorce, debt collection, and missing work for medical problems are not prevalent contributors to their bankruptcies. Recall that these are among the typical reasons people cite for turning to the bankruptcy system for help. Resourced filers instead indicated that unaffordable mortgage payments prompted their filings more often than they did other people. Given that almost all resourced filers own homes, it is expected that troubles with keeping up with the mortgage would push them to file.

Chapter 2 of this book considered the prebankruptcy "sweatbox" that filers experienced before seeking relief through bankruptcy. Resourced filers reported struggling similar amounts of time as other bankruptcy filers did, both averaging around three years. Resourced filers, however, seem to have had a less difficult time in the sweatbox. They went without fewer things in the prebankruptcy period. Resourced filers reported an average of three privations, compared to five for all other filers. Still, it was not an easy time even for resourced filers. Thirty-four percent said they went without medical care. Forty-seven percent reported they went without a car. Fifty-nine percent indicated they stopped saving for retirement.

## ARE RESOURCED FILERS TAKING
## ADVANTAGE OF THE SYSTEM?

The financial and demographic profiles of resourced filers show that they are advantaged compared to other bankruptcy filers. That they are not particularly advantaged compared to the general population suggests that they are not elites cheating the system. The question remains, however, whether they are largely "can pay" debtors using bankruptcy to unfairly walk away from their debts.

Any measure of who is a "can pay" debtor will be subjective. The bankruptcy schedules lack an obvious place to look, but our survey data provide clues. That resourced filers struggled for an average of three years before bankruptcy suggests few ran to the bankruptcy courthouse at the first sign of trouble. In addition, before they filed, they tried several tactics to make ends meet. Seventy-five percent specified they charged necessities to credit cards. Seventy-two percent reported making a late mortgage or rental payment. Sixty-one percent noted that they cashed out or borrowed from retirement savings. Fifty-five percent reported trying to negotiate with creditors. Fifty-three percent indicated that they borrowed money from family or friends.

Resourced filers resemble business debtors in many ways. Eighteen percent of resourced filers reported self-employment, twice the rate among other bankruptcy filers. As discussed in chapter 5 of this book, they used bankruptcy to leave behind the financial problems of the business that spilled into their personal lives. Almost every small business owner has personal responsibility for their business's debts in some way or another, and these filers were no different.[6] As one filer put it: "We personally guaranteed everything in our business." These filers cited the sort of problems that could plague almost any business: a line of credit that evaporated, sales that declined, a business expansion that failed, and especially COVID-era shutdowns. With the business out of operation, they had small prospect of paying back the hundreds of thousands of dollars in the business's unsecured debt on which they had personally guaranteed repayment. The debt overhang prevented them from starting a new business or from productively reentering the mainstream workforce. The bankruptcy system offered them a chance to move forward.

Resourced filers, as a group, based on their collective statistics, do not look as if they are taking advantage of the system. Still, some individual resourced filers may be the elusive "can pay" debtors. But diving more deeply into individual cases qualitatively, it remains difficult to find them.

Consider a married couple with two children who had an expensive house with substantial equity. Both professionals, their household income placed them in the top 20 percent of earners nationally. They stand out among our bankruptcy court records so much that to give more details risks their anonymity. Their credit card debts equaled only 2 percent of their annual income, compared to the median filer, who owed about one year of income just on unsecured debts. They should have had no problem paying their debts. They reported none of the many hardships that other bankruptcy filers suffered. They indicated they did not struggle at all before bankruptcy. At first, they look like hard-core bankruptcy abusers.

This couple's path to filing distinguishes them in one particular way: their home had been in a natural disaster. They had tried to negotiate with the mortgage lender simply to take the house. Under their state's law, the couple would not have been liable for any deficiency if the house had been damaged so badly that it was worth less than what they owed to the mortgage lender. The best outcome for the lender was to have the house, and the couple was offering to save the lender the cost of a foreclosure by handing it over. Still, for unclear reasons, the lender refused. The couple filed bankruptcy to surrender the house to the mortgage lender. They paid their other creditors in full in under one year.

One could characterize this couple as "can pay" because they had the resources to pay the mortgage lender all the money owed. In most other states, they would have been responsible for the full amount of the mortgage, regardless of the value of the house. Their state's law, however, capped their responsibility at the value of the house. They used bankruptcy to vindicate their rights under the state law that applied to them, extricating themselves from the stress and uncertainty caused by the natural disaster that had befallen them. They should not be faulted for voluntarily paying no more than what they were legally obligated to pay to the bank, which obviously was in a position to fully appreciate the deal it had made.

Now consider a different couple who had over $170,000 in annual income and a home worth over $700,000 at the time of filing. With only $10,000 in unsecured debts, at first blush they appear to be a classic case of a "can pay" debtor couple abusing the system. Filling in details suggests otherwise. The home was eighty years old and a modest thirteen hundred square feet in size. The eye-popping home value was only about half the median value of other homes in the county, one of the most expensive in the United States. With two children, the household income only put the family at the county median.

Two mortgages against the home totaled $300,000 more than the current value of the home. That the couple had received a second mortgage suggested that the lender believed the home was once worth more than its current value. Indeed, court documents stated the current value reflected the costs of mold and asbestos remediation needed to make the home safe. The second mortgage lender had not sent a statement in ten years and never appeared in the bankruptcy case. The couple used bankruptcy to eliminate the second mortgage, as bankruptcy law allowed under the circumstances of the case.[7] With the second mortgage gone, they had the resources to catch up on twelve months of arrearages on the first mortgage and prevent a foreclosure. As of this writing, the case was four and a half years into a five-year chapter 13 plan and appeared on its way to successful completion. Although not without means, the couple had modest resources for the area where they lived. They used the tools in the bankruptcy law to save their home.

As a final example, consider another couple, with a $410,000 house and $138,000 in income at the time of filing. They filed chapter 13 less than three years after a previous chapter 7 filing. That meant they no longer had personal liability on either the first or second mortgages against their home, although they needed to pay those mortgages if they wanted to stay in the home. The first mortgage exceeded the value of the house. Using the mortgage modification programs created in the wake of the Great Recession, they had attempted to negotiate with both lenders. Although there was no value in the home to support the second mortgage, the lender would not cooperate. Like the previous couple, they filed bankruptcy to eliminate the second mortgage, a prerequisite to renegotiating the first mortgage.

This couple's story presents yet another example in which bankruptcy court records hide the complete picture. A respectable income, a decent home, and only $5,000 in unsecured debt do not indicate the financial precarity that runs through the rest of this book. Their low unsecured debt likely resulted from the fresh start they received in their recent, prior chapter 7 filing. But even after that bankruptcy case, they still had one financial problem: not enough income to service their mortgage debt. They had tried unsuccessfully outside of bankruptcy to renegotiate the debt. Bankruptcy gave them a tool to bring the creditors back to the bargaining table. Their story differs from the previous ones in an important way. Their attempt to deal with their mortgage creditors failed. Unable to confirm a chapter 13 plan, the court dismissed their case. According to state court records, a little over a year later, they lost the home in foreclosure. This final example shows how difficult it can be to dig out of financial distress, even with resources. Bankruptcy offers tools to help but does not guarantee recovery.

Even after pinpointing resourced filers, looking at data either in the aggregate or cases individually, it is difficult to find "can pay" debtors who are abusing the bankruptcy system. There remain other ways to find filers whom we might characterize as inappropriately using bankruptcy, which we turn to next. They are rare, but in a system with hundreds of thousands of cases each year, they are not nonexistent. When they do file, the system often flushes them out.

## IN SEARCH OF OTHER "CAN PAY" DEBTORS

There could be many definitions of a resourced filer other than our definition of filers in the top decile of income and assets. In addition to the inherent subjectiveness of the inquiry, there are two other challenges in thinking about who might be a "can pay" debtor making questionable use of the bankruptcy system. First, dollar amounts are relative to the person's situation. For example, knowing that a person discharged $30,000 of debt and has $100,000 of income does not tell us much without knowing the other demands on that income. Second, we are limited by our methodology. Bankruptcy court files can tell one story on their face, but, as shown by the three cases detailed earlier, a deeper dive often tells a very different story. We gathered more detailed information by asking bankruptcy filers to fill out a survey. Many of the more useful details about filers come from that survey. Some people are unlikely to admit to socially undesirable conduct in a survey, although some of the people who returned our survey did.

With those caveats, another way that someone might misuse bankruptcy is to walk away from large amounts of unsecured debt with an income that would allow meaningful repayment. Filing chapter 7 will allow that, and we now only consider chapter 7 filers to try to find "can pay" debtors based on this measure. As explained in chapter 1 of this book, chapter 13 filers must devote all their disposable income to repayment. The chapter 13 process thus screens filers for devoting an appropriate amount of their income to repayment, albeit not perfectly. Chapter 7 filers generally cannot walk away from student loans or tax debts, and we ignore those debts. We also do not count small business owners who listed predominantly business debt.

Measures of a "large" amount of debt and an income that allows meaningful repayment are, naturally, subjective. We looked for filers with at least $100,000 unsecured debt totaling less than one year's worth of income. Out of the eighty-eight hundred cases in the database, there are sixteen chapter 7 cases fitting that description.[8] Four of those cases involve married couples with children with a household income below the state median for a household of their size. Five cases list predominantly medical bills as their unsecured debts. For example, a military veteran wrote about his wife dying from cancer and how his own health problems forced him to quit his job as well as shut down a company he had started. The medical problems suggest diminished earning capacity going forward. Medical bills also do not imply freewheeling prebankruptcy spending.

The remaining seven cases do not seem to have any ameliorating factors. As chapter 7 cases, all had to pass the "means test" described in chapter 1 of this book that Congress enacted to screen abusive cases. The means test is highly technical, and six of the cases simply followed the rules. One filer had a higher income at the time of filing but filed at a time when the six-month lookback period made them eligible for chapter 7. Congress also allows filers to deduct mortgage and auto loan payments. Two of the filers had high monthly mortgage payments ($2,300 and $2,600) that brought them within the means test. All these filers look like the filers outlined previously, using the rules as Congress wrote them.

The remaining case is more problematic. A single filer earning $190,000 annually sought to discharge $103,000 in unsecured debt, almost all of which was credit card debt, through chapter 7. The filer's only other significant obligation was a $27,000 car loan, about which the filer stated an intention to redeem, meaning the filer believed they could come up with that amount in cash. This person did not live in financial precarity like so many others in this book. But this filer also did not get a discharge. The Office of the United States Trustee, the component of the US Department of Justice that monitors the integrity of the bankruptcy system, filed a motion to dismiss the case as an abuse of the bankruptcy process. The filer initially voluntarily converted the case to chapter 13, and the court dismissed the case when the filer could not put together a chapter 13 plan. The bankruptcy system thus screened out this problematic case. The system worked.

Using dismissed cases to identify "can pay" debtors or at least problematic cases has a contradiction at its center. That someone might attempt to use a system inappropriately is not surprising, especially in a country as large as the United States. That the system can screen out these cases is a strength, not a weakness.

Also, the fact of dismissal alone does not disclose much. For example, 47 percent of chapter 13 cases for which the court has approved a plan result in dismissal because the filer missed plan payments. These dismissals suggest continued, postbankruptcy financial struggles rather than abuse. A dismissal also does not inform about what happened before bankruptcy. Someone who struggles for years and goes without necessities such as medical care or food before they file almost certainly is not someone who uses bankruptcy to escape debts they could pay.

Again with those caveats, we also looked for dismissed cases that might bear the hallmarks of a "can pay" debtor seeking to use bankruptcy to avoid their obligations. Specifically, we searched for filers who had chapter 7 dismissals or preconfirmation dismissals in chapter 13, reported struggling for less than a year before filing bankruptcy, and reported no more than one privation in the two years before bankruptcy. There are four such cases in the dataset.

None of the four cases presents particularly problematic bankruptcy filings. The bankruptcy courts dismissed three of the cases for failing to file all the paperwork required of a debtor. One filer did not have an attorney and joined the legions of pro se chapter 13 debtors whose cases are dismissed. Another case was that of a chapter 7 debtor with $43,000 in annual income. This individual was represented by an attorney, and on the face of the court file itself, the attorney should have been able to file all the required paperwork. Perhaps the filer had not provided it to the attorney, but then the attorney should not have filed the case. In the third of the four cases, the chapter 13 debtor spent over seven months in bankruptcy negotiating with the home mortgage holder. Those negotiations proved futile or resulted in an out-of-court workout. The bankruptcy court record does not say. Either way, it appears to have been a good faith attempt to deal with a home mortgage by a filer making $43,000 per year. Those figures do not suggest a "can pay" debtor.

The final case is a married couple, represented by an attorney, who filed chapter 13 but did not file the necessary paperwork. The court dismissed the case after only eighteen days. The filing appears to have been a "skeleton filing," taking advantage of the fourteen-day grace period the bankruptcy procedural rules allow to file all the paperwork. On our survey, they indicated a pending foreclosure prompted their filing. A "skeleton filing" would have immediately halted the foreclosure and bought them some time. There are hints in the record that they had attempted to work out a mortgage modification with the lender.

The bankruptcy court file does not provide the exact details of what happened with this couple, but public land records show that the filers remained owners of their home six years later. Lawyers may not take actions that have "no substantial purpose other than to . . . delay."[9] Their chapter 13 filing certainly caused delay, but it had aims beyond that. The purpose of the filing was not only to buy a few more weeks in the house. Instead, it appears to have allowed a renegotiation satisfactory to all parties to keep the homeowners in the house long term. This couple used the legal tools available to them.

## SAVVY FILERS

This chapter serves somewhat as a "robustness check" on our data. The rest of the book relies on bankruptcy filers to describe what it means to live on the financial edge. Every year, hundreds of thousands of people file bankruptcy, adding up to millions of people across the timeframe for our dataset. It is a mathematical certainty that at least some of those people did not merit bankruptcy relief. We have used our data to try to understand how many bankruptcy filers can pay. We looked at different slices of the data, including focusing on filers with high incomes and valuable assets, although as it turns out, "high" and "valuable" are only relative to other bankruptcy filers. We employed qualitative approaches as well as alternative ways to think about who might be labeled as abusing the system.

No matter how one slices the data, the answer to how many "can pay" debtors exist is "exceedingly few." Those cases that, at first blush, appeared to have substantial resources for repayment turned out to be more complicated upon more detailed examination. Often this means an attempt was made to save a home using the legal tools that the bankruptcy system offers. Even then, these filers used these legal tools because they lacked the financial resources to deal with the problem outside of bankruptcy. The worse that can be said of them is that they were "savvy."

The bankruptcy system often does not work as well as it could because of its many rules, complexities, and documentation requirements designed to stop abusive filings. Yet abusive filings are rare, and we are hardly the first to make that point.[10] Instead, the system's rules, complexities, and requirements become hurdles that keep deserving people out of bankruptcy altogether, delay when people file because they need to raise significant funds to do so, and prevent people from getting effective relief once they do file. Throughout the book, we have documented how financially strapped most filers are and how desperately they need a bankruptcy system to help them. Although we have repeatedly noted that the bankruptcy system cannot fix the systemic issues that cause so many people in the United States to live in a constant state of financial precarity, people will continue to turn to bankruptcy for help. The book concludes with our data's lessons for broader reforms and for targeted changes to the bankruptcy system.

# Conclusion

REFORMING BANKRUPTCY'S INJUSTICES

Over the past forty years, life in the United States has changed. In some ways, perhaps many ways, life has improved. People live longer. Cars are safer. Houses have more features and are less expensive to heat and cool. Educational attainment across the population has increased. Electronics, such as televisions, computers, and microwaves, cost considerably less. Technology has transformed how people interact, and it has allowed people to get the goods they want delivered to them quickly, sometimes the same day.

People's financial lives have changed also, although not necessarily for the better. Between 1980 and 2023, household debt more than doubled, even after adjusting for inflation and population growth.[1] Defined-benefit retirement plans have decreased to about one-third of the total number at their peak in the early 1980s.[2] More older Americans transition into their retirement years dependent on personal retirement savings rather than secure and predictable pensions. Over the same time, student loan debt has ballooned from nearly nonexistent to outpacing car loans and credit card debts.

In this book, we have leveraged data about bankrupt households to draw out the individual changes in the financial risks that many people experience over the course of their lives. The changes flow from decisions that leaders and policymakers in the United States have made that transfer risk onto individuals. The accumulation of these risks causes many individuals and families to struggle under a state of constant precarity. This precarity has become so pervasive that most Americans are pessimistic about future standards of living, their financial futures, and the ability of leaders to reduce levels of income and wealth inequality.[3]

Taken separately, each decision that has shaped people's pessimism might go unnoticed for its effect on households' finances. Some changes may be subtle. Some changes may originate from policy decisions. And some changes are part of the perpetuation of discrimination that has been woven into the United States for centuries.

Nonetheless, these changes have reshaped some of our most powerful social institutions and have become systemic components of these institutions. This book showed these systemic issues through the experiences of the people who file bankruptcy. Almost every family is vulnerable to financial collapse. The leading solution to financial downfall for many families will be to take on debt to pay other debts, while cutting necessities, such as health care and food, from their budgets. For some people, the initiation of lawsuits; the threat of home foreclosure or car repossession; or realizing that regardless of personal and family sacrifice, they will never climb out of the financial hole, will push them to consider filing bankruptcy.

The data about bankruptcy filers and the stories that they write demonstrate that bankruptcy law cannot address the core economic and social structural problems that leave many people perpetually worried about their finances and some struggling to survive. Bankruptcy may be where households turn now, but it is not designed to be the catchall safety net that it has become. The findings presented in this book pinpoint where broader reforms are needed. Still, even with these reforms, and definitely without, people will continue to file bankruptcy. A robust bankruptcy system is a key feature of a capitalist economy, and it is an important part of the social safety net. Bankruptcy law can and should better address the problems that households will continue to bring with them when they file. At the very least, the bankruptcy system should not add to people's financial battles.

TACKLING SYSTEMIC ISSUES

A handful of themes emerges from people's bankruptcy court records, combined with the details about their lives that they disclose in the survey. They file bankruptcy to save their homes and cars, because of medical bills and lost income when dealing with health issues, and in the wake of job loss or chronic underemployment that leaves them with insufficient income. They also file to get out from under failed small business ventures; to clear other debt so they can pay student loans; and to recover from divorce, death of a spouse or partner, or another change in household structure. Across these reasons, people's race, gender, and age make them more susceptible to the financial precarity that develops into financial problems that subsume their lives.

Of the leading contributors to people's bankruptcy filings, health problems have grabbed the attention of popular media.[4] For the past forty years, scholars on the CBP have documented the relationship between medical debts and bankruptcy. Each decade, the relationship between medical bills, income loss from health issues, and bankruptcy has tightened. Health and bankruptcy now are so entwined that two-thirds of the people who file bankruptcy do so following health issues.

That Congress enacted the Affordable Care Act during the years that we and other scholars tracked what is colloquially termed *medical bankruptcy* was momentous, but it did not alter the incidence of medical contributors to bankruptcy. The stickiness of health's connection to bankruptcy is an indictment of the US health-care system. Calls to eliminate current medical debt or to ignore medical debt when calculating credit scores will amount to trying to treat a massive heart attack with a few aspirin.[5] For decades, the United States has needed a health-care overhaul.

Part of that overhaul should focus on employment in the United States. That medical bankruptcy includes people losing income or their jobs while recovering from illness or to care for loved ones is a symptom of failures of the employment system. That our laws do not mandate adequate paid time off, including pregnancy and maternity leave, is a systemic issue that leads to precarity. In part, it is an inability to see women as economic actors, despite women's labor force participation rate trending steadily upward since the 1970s and more women being considered heads of households. It may be labeled as a health-care system issue or an employment system issue, or a combination of both. Regardless, the finances and stories of bankruptcy filers show that people have trouble financially surviving a medical crisis, a pregnancy, or a chronic health problem beyond paying their medical expenses.

These bankruptcy filings also illustrate how a lack of savings creates financial precarity. Bankruptcy filers' dearth of savings reflects how difficult it is for many people across the country to save. The finances of bankrupt seniors, in particular, point to how shifts in the employment system can drive that lack of savings. Fewer and fewer people enter their retirement years with economic security, as evidenced by the increasing percentage of seniors among the bankrupt population.

Seniors' economic insecurity manifests from persistent wage inequality, the shift from pensions to self-funded retirement plans, and changes in the nature of work. Employment once was a core part of the social safety net, and there were workplace laws and regulations, plus implicit agreements that made it so. Now employers effectively may more freely take from employees, which has been made possible by a slow creep away from a structure whereby employers supported employees. Although seniors' finances emphasize these changes, everyone suffers under current labor market realities. These structural changes require systemic solutions: increased empowerment of workers in the businesses where they work, greater access to employer-provided benefits, comprehensive worker security, and strengthened assistance during unemployment and for those who cannot work.

Solutions also must address the long-standing racial and gender disparities in the employment market such that Black persons and single women are more likely to file bankruptcy. When people emerge from bankruptcy, the systemic disparities in the employment market will remain. They will return to the same wage gaps, occupational segregation, unequal bargaining power, and disproportionate burden of costs of caregiving. Increased enforcement of existing discrimination laws will help, but it is unlikely to be a solution by itself.

The same goes for the education system that both leaves Black students behind and convinces Black and women students to take on burdensome loans with the hope of improving their social class and economic security.[6]

These loans feed their disproportionate use of bankruptcy. The solution lies in overhauling the broader education system, including primary education, and transcends forgiving currently outstanding student loans. As to postsecondary education, attention should be directed to enhanced regulation of for-profit institutions and reforms to the funding of higher education.[7]

Bankruptcy filers' financial situations show two other significant fault lines from the loading of financial precarity onto individuals. They accompany the dramatic increase in consumer debt over the past forty years along the axes of the two items that people need most: housing and transportation. In the United States affordable housing is more a dream than a reality for too many people. It also has crafted a transportation system that requires people to have cars and take on the associated debt of purchasing them. As with home mortgages, in recent decades car loans have become riskier, threatening people's access to reliable transportation. Underlying disparities in the consumer credit markets make those debts more costly for Black borrowers, again funneling more Black persons into the bankruptcy system.

That people struggle to afford homes and cars does not come from a national endemic moral failing but instead reflects housing and transportation policy choices. These struggles are a testament to how resilient and innovative Americans have become to survive financial precarity. The things people do to make ends meet in the years before their bankruptcies, however, are often stories of sacrifice. A just society would not require its citizenry to forego food, medical care, or other privations to survive financially.

Tackling these systems—health care, employment, education, housing, and transportation—would overhaul how people use consumer credit. People would likely still have debt, but they would have less of it. And they would have less to fear from the consequences of not being able to pay back that debt despite their good-faith best efforts.

To borrow a word from a former colleague, consumer credit also needs to be safer.[8] High interest rates and default fees and penalties can make loans profitable for lenders even when borrowers do not repay in full. For the borrower, these loans still pile on misery. All lenders should have a legal obligation to ensure the borrower can repay before extending credit to consumers. (That the government needs to impose an "ability to repay" requirement says a lot about the state of consumer lending.) Such rules already exist in mortgage lending, imposed in the wake of the Great Recession by the Dodd-Frank Act. Exotic home mortgages with risky terms are now only a small fraction of all home mortgages. The Credit CARD Act of 2009 imposed ability-to-repay requirements on credit card lenders, but these rules have been less successful because they are not as strict. Ability-to-repay should apply to any consumer lender, enforced either through new legislation or existing concepts of unfair trade practices. We are not naïve enough to think that these rules would have no effect on the availability of credit, but consumers should not have to borrow to put food on the table or to keep the heat on in the winter.

People's struggles with debt also should change. At present, bankruptcy filers' leading privations—going without health care, food, and utilities—are obviously detrimental. Feelings of guilt and shame push them to sacrifice. Another driver is fear. They suffer physically and emotionally under the weight of debt.

None of this is to say that we believe people should be able to walk away from their debts at the first sign of trouble. Borrowing is a prediction about the future—that the money will be there to repay. Inevitably, things sometimes will go wrong. When they do, people may need to sacrifice and turn to some of the same coping mechanisms that bankruptcy filers do now. They may look for more work. They may negotiate with creditors. They may ask friends and family for help. They may feel guilt and shame for not being able to live up to their contractual obligations. They may wonder when the debt collector will call.

The idea of debt collection also needs to change. Embedded in how we conceptualize debt collection is the assumption that many people can pay if they simply try. That is usually not true. The reality is that a foreclosure, eviction, car repossession, or wage garnishment is the start of a financial spiral. In extreme situations, this spiral can put the borrower out on the streets.[9] The creditor goes unpaid, and the borrower remains in a dire situation. If the United States provided the basics for its citizens, debt collection should be less catastrophic. A repossession would still mean loss of a car, and a foreclosure might mean loss of a house. A strong social safety net, however, would provide alternatives for transportation, housing, and other necessities of life. All would benefit.

One of the most transformative shifts in reforming the US core systems is the potential to alter women's economic position. The narratives of women who file bankruptcy show the relationship between debt and domestic abuse. That women report staying longer in relationships because of economic abuse is a symptom of the US economic and social structures that create precarity in people's lives.[10] Only with broader reforms will women have fewer reasons to be trapped in abusive and violent situations by credit and debt concerns. Proposals such as legislation that allow women to remove themselves from liability for coerced debt—debt incurred by an abuser in the name of a victim of domestic abuse—are needed, but they are most helpful once women leave abusive situations.[11]

Because people will still take on debt, some will need to file bankruptcy. The bankruptcy system is an economic and social institution. It is a well-established part of the economy and social safety net. People will file bankruptcy, regardless of reforms, bringing the same basic household finance issues with them. Although we have focused primarily on the systemic problems that affect people, the analysis in this book shows ways in which to improve bankruptcy law and process.

## IMPROVING THE BANKRUPTCY SYSTEM

Reforms to the bankruptcy system fall into three categories: bankruptcy law itself, debt collection in bankruptcy, and access to and the structure of the bankruptcy system. We propose improvements with the goal of making bankruptcy a more equitable lifeline of last resort. Like all discussions in this book, the proposals draw from our data about the people who file bankruptcy, including what they tell us about their prebankruptcy lives.

### Bankruptcy Law

The federal bankruptcy law is incredibly complex and overdetermined. Its rules often make unjustified assumptions about who files bankruptcy. It builds on the ideal of a white middle class couple: married, employed, with certain assets of a particular value, and with or without certain problems, such as not having student loan debt.[12] But that is not the typical person who files bankruptcy. And it does not consider demographic skews of bankruptcy filers, much of which result from the unequal systematic loading of financial precarity onto people. The law can account for the range of bankruptcy filers and their assets and debt problems. Notably, the Consumer Bankruptcy Reform Act of 2024—introduced by Senator Elizabeth Warren and Congressman Jerry Nadler, which seeks to "simplify and modernize the consumer bankruptcy system"—proposes broader rules for many aspects of bankruptcy law that our data demonstrate will benefit from broader rules.[13]

To assist people's struggles associated with homeownership, bankruptcy law should include an exemption for equity in houses that accounts for regional variation in the cost of houses. It also should permit homeowners to modify mortgages based on the market value of houses, thereby allowing homeowners to deal with underwater mortgages in the same way that big corporations can restructure their debts. To address the rental market, bankruptcy law should give renters fresh starts with their landlords. Unpaid rent that is discharged in bankruptcy should not be grounds for an eviction.

These changes will particularly help Black persons, who face barriers to homeownership and thus are more likely to rent, and who are more likely to be shunted to expensive home loans and live in areas where homes appreciate slowly, and thus are more likely to have underwater mortgages. These changes also should be economically neutral, if not beneficial. If people lose their housing, either outside of bankruptcy or because they cannot meet bankruptcy law's requirements, they will have difficulty paying their debts to landlords, mortgage lenders, and other creditors. It is also not fair to borrowers and lenders alike that a federal bankruptcy law allows a borrower to keep vastly different amounts in home equity depending on the state where the borrower lives.

To assist with people's struggles to purchase and hold onto their cars, bankruptcy law should allow debtors to modify car loans based on the current value of their cars. The only exception would be for cars very recently purchased, in the weeks prior to bankruptcy, instead of the current two-and-one-half-year limit. Such a change would allow car owners to address underwater car loans. As with home loans, this change will particularly help Black persons, who face barriers in the car loan market such that they are more likely to enter bankruptcy with underwater car loans.

This should allow people to be more successful in paying their modified car loans postbankruptcy and may incentivize car lenders to work with people before bankruptcy.

Somewhat related to people's use of cars is penal debt—debt from criminal penalties and fines, court fees, usage fees, and interest—which includes fines for traffic violations and parking tickets.[14] Among the penal debts that bankruptcy law currently does not discharge are fines and fees for low-level offenses, such as parking tickets, and costs incurred as a direct result of being tried in the criminal justice system, such as prosecution costs, court fees, incarceration charges, and fees for postrelease supervision. Penal debt can create downward financial spirals, particularly for Black persons and low-income individuals, who are more likely to be involved in the criminal justice system. Debt-based driver's license suspensions can cause people to lose their jobs, making it even more difficult to pay the underlying debt.[15] Many inmates leave prison owing money, debt that can come with hefty interest charges and late fees.[16] This debt often haunts them, making reentry into society more difficult and creating barriers to financial security and economic mobility.[17]

The law should change. Penal debts should be divided into dischargeable and nondischargeable categories. Among dischargeable debts should be those that arise from operating in the criminal justice system; those which amount to civil fines, such as parking tickets and traffic violations; and those that relate to the collection of penal debt, such as interest and fees. Among nondischargeable debts should be those related to the outcome of a criminal proceeding, such as those designated as a fine or those that are for restitution—that is, traditional criminal fines.

Besides home mortgages and car loans, student loans stand out among consumer debt, having grown considerably over recent decades. At the same time, Congress made student loan discharge difficult to attain by repeatedly amending bankruptcy law, first by increasing the time during which student loans were presumptively not dischargeable after first coming due and then by expanding the types of student loans presumptively not dischargeable regardless of when they first came due.[18] Providing that student loans are dischargeable like other unsecured debts, such as credit card debt, or that student loans are dischargeable without showing undue hardship after a period of years once they become due, will give people struggling with student loans the ability to get relief and move on with their lives.

This change to bankruptcy law particularly will help Black and women borrowers, who are more likely to have higher amounts of student loans, who spend longer trying to pay back student loans, and who are more likely to default on student loans. It too should be economically neutral, if not beneficial. Many people will be unable to pay burdensome student loans, and those loans hold people back from getting married, having children, buying homes, and contributing to the economy.

Two final reforms focus on people's assets and ensuring equity in the bankruptcy system, even if that means that some people must give up more property than they currently would in their case. The first deals with *exemptions*, which is the legal term for the property bankruptcy filers can keep even after filing bankruptcy. As we explained in chapter 1, that property includes equity in a home or a car. The exemptions filers receive depend on where they live. Currently, states can opt out of the exemptions in the federal bankruptcy law and require filers to follow a state-prescribed list of exemptions.

State exemption law varies widely in the dollar value allowed and property that people may keep, often containing detailed lists of property, such as wedding rings, bibles, and guns. Even if a filer lives in a state that allows use of the federal exemption law, that law similarly contains a detailed list of property. These lists are outdated, reflect arbitrary value judgments about what property people should be allowed to keep, and envision a filer who lives a certain life that does not necessarily reflect who uses the bankruptcy system. They also result in pointless litigation over categorization—such as, is a tractor-lawnmower "furniture"—raising costs to bankruptcy filers and creditors alike.[19]

Decisions about what property to keep are best left to individuals and families. They are the people who will use that property going forward and who may have special attachment to specific items. States should not be allowed to opt out of the federal exemptions in bankruptcy law. Bankruptcy law should provide full protection to retirement savings and other necessary items such as wheelchairs and other health aids. After that, bankruptcy law's exemptions should be revised to provide a lump-sum amount depending on household size, such as $30,000 or $40,000, that filers can apply to property that they want to exempt.

The second reform deals with how people pay their creditors. Bankruptcy law presently allows people to file chapter 7, whereby they devote their assets to repayment, or chapter 13, whereby they devote their income to repayment. This allows people to shield their assets in exchange for giving up their non-necessary income for three to five years. The trade-off may be quite beneficial to a debtor and thus disadvantageous to creditors. The Consumer Bankruptcy Reform Act proposes the creation of a "minimum payment obligation" measured by both assets and future income. This obligation would require wealthy (in bankruptcy filer terms) debtors to give up assets and income if they want bankruptcy's benefits. It will compel some people to hand over property that they would keep under current bankruptcy law, which is a more equitable and distributive outcome.

### Debt Collection Tactics

The past thirty years have seen a dramatic shift in the way that creditors collect debts, including the use of the state court system. Debt collection cases now are by far the predominant civil suit in the United States. Because of the way debts are bought and sold, these lawsuits may involve the collection of debt barred by the statute of limitations.[20] These debts and these lawsuits become part of people's cases when they file bankruptcy. In bankruptcy, creditors and debt buyers can continue collection of debts despite collection being barred by the statute of limitations, creditors may misrepresent amounts that they are owed, and creditors can try to collect on debts even though doing so violates consumer protection laws.

Bankruptcy law can address these creditor and debt collector practices through an amendment that provides for the disallowance of a creditor's claim if the underlying debt violates consumer financial protection laws. Correspondingly, the Fair Debt Collection Practices Act should prohibit filing a bankruptcy claim without a good faith belief that the debt is still within the statute of limitations.

### Bankruptcy System Access and Structure

Racial, gender, and age disparities in who files bankruptcy reflect discrimination and disparities that people face outside of bankruptcy, as well as the broad shifting of financial precarity onto people. The bankruptcy system also erects barriers to access, particularly the cost of filing, and is structured in a way that has produced racial disparities in chapter choice. As detailed in chapter 6 of this book, the evidence is overwhelming that Black households' disproportionate use of chapter 13 is due to their race and not other factors, such as their financial profiles or legal situations. How attorneys collect their fees in chapter 13 during the case, versus up-front in chapter 7, accounts for at least some of the racial disparity in the use of chapters 7 and 13. The racial disparity in the use of bankruptcy is an indictment of the bankruptcy system. Importantly, the bankruptcy system should be fixable.

The most readily apparent solution is to remove chapter choice. A single entry point to bankruptcy, as the Consumer Bankruptcy Reform Act pro-poses, would accomplish that. A single point of entry should simplify the filer's choices, lowering costs by making the proceeding less complicated.

The biggest barrier to accessing bankruptcy is how much it costs people to retain an attorney. Bankruptcy is a technical, complex process and will remain so even with reforms. Most people will continue to file with the assistance of an attorney. Because of bankruptcy's complexity, attorneys charge their clients a sizable amount for a financially strapped household. People either must delay their filing—save up to file bankruptcy—or use chapter 13 to finance their attorney's fees by paying over time. Another "solution" is simply not to file bankruptcy at all.

An obvious legislative fix would be to allow all bankruptcy filers to pay their attorneys over time. We advocated earlier for tighter regulation of credit, and attorneys should be no exception when they extend credit in payment for their services. There would need to be court oversight of the terms through filing of the agreement. Attorneys would need to certify in good faith that they believe the agreement is in the best interest of the cli-ent. The agreement would have to provide that the attorney could not sell the filer's promise to pay the attorney's fees, to prevent it from going to ag-gressive debt collectors. To prevent a long-term, onerous obligation, there should be a limit on the length of time over which the filer can pay, such as one year. Also, the filer's nonpayment should not be grounds to deny a discharge of debts in bankruptcy.

Reforming how people can pay their bankruptcy attorneys should be coupled with removing chapter choice. This combination promises the best likelihood of combating the racial disparity in access to bankruptcy.

Even with changes to bankruptcy law, the bankruptcy system cannot do more than chip away at the problems that households will continue to bring with them when they file. But it should not add to a subset of filers' problems because of its structure, especially when solutions to the racial injustice that has been identified and discussed for more than a decade are ready for implementation.

## THE POWER OF DATA

Since the launch of the CBP more than four decades ago, scholars from a range of disciplines have studied bankruptcy from various perspectives. Findings based on CBP data, including our own, have shown who files bankruptcy, that filers are not trying to cheat and have not overspent their way into bankruptcy, the financial stressors that lead people to turn to bankruptcy, and how filers continue to come from a cross section of the middle class. These findings have colloquially named a type of bankruptcy, *medical bankruptcy*. They have made front page news.[21] They have informed the creation of a federal government agency, the Consumer Financial Protection Bureau.[22] The research has produced notable effects, even if policymakers do not follow many proposals and even if progress is sometimes slow.

It should not require massive data collection efforts like the CBP to understand the bankruptcy system. The bankruptcy files are electronic, but the court system is not set up to make the data easily available to researchers. That should change, but there is also a larger point about data.

We offered the data in this book with the conviction that data can continue to suggest policy solutions that make the world a better place. Facts matter. Data allow for the understanding of the reality around us. We specifically presented the data along with stories written by the people who file bankruptcy to draw out their experiences.

We focused on what our data show about what happens when risk remains privatized because the United States has allowed people—young adults, parents, children, seniors—to live in a state of precarity for decades. This country is approaching a breaking point. That many people live in financially tenuous circumstances, and that they face barriers in the housing, education, employment, health-care, and credit markets, are not revelations. But we have confidence in the value of data to produce effects. Picking apart each structural reason that households struggle financially in today's economy and society through the vantage point of bankruptcy shows how the United States is failing its citizens. The core of people in the United States now struggle to survive in an economy and society that will continue to fail them without fundamental changes.

# Methodological Appendix

## BACKGROUND OF THE CONSUMER BANKRUPTCY PROJECT

The data that support this book come from the Consumer Bankruptcy Project. The roots of the CBP trace to 1981, when Teresa Sullivan, Elizabeth Warren, and Jay Lawrence Westbrook set out to describe bankruptcy filers. They published the results of that inquiry in *As We Forgive Our Debtors: Bankruptcy and Consumer Credit in America*, in which they established who uses the consumer bankruptcy system. They went back into the field in 1991, which resulted in *The Fragile Middle Class: Americans in Debt*. That book showed how households were being financially squeezed and therefore were using the bankruptcy system more often. These two groundbreaking works inspired the present text.

Sullivan, Warren, and Westbrook led another round of data collection in 2001. At that time two authors of this book, Lawless and Thorne, joined the CBP as coprincipal investigators (co-PIs). The 2005 overhaul of the consumer bankruptcy laws led the CBP to engage in a fourth round of data collection in 2007. Because of technological changes, and especially the digitization of court records, the 2007 round of data collection was the first that utilized a national random sample. Remote access to court files also substantially lowered the cost of data collection, allowing for the collection of more cases and more variables. Like the previous data collection rounds, the 2001 and 2007 rounds resulted in numerous publications, notably *Broke: How Debt Bankrupts the Middle Class*, edited by Katherine Porter.

The earlier rounds of the CBP used various methods that relied on court records, written questionnaires, and in some instances telephone interviews. Where we have referenced data in this book from earlier rounds of the CBP, we have provided citations to works that offer more detailed methodologies for these earlier rounds. Additionally, all three of the books mentioned here have detailed methodological appendices, and an additional methodological appendix for the 2007 round appears in a journal article.[1]

## CURRENT CBP METHODOLOGY

With the permission of the original co-PIs, Lawless and Thorne joined Professor Katherine Porter to relaunch the CBP in 2013. Porter remained a part of the project until 2018, when she left to represent California's Forty-fifth Congressional District in the US House of Representatives. The third author of this book, Foohey, joined the CBP as a co-PI in 2016. More information about the CBP is available on our website at http://consumerbankruptcyproject.org.

With this relaunch of the CBP, an important change from previous rounds was to move to continuous data collection, which began in February 2013. We have used two instruments to gather information: the bankruptcy court records and a written questionnaire. After discussing how we select cases for the CBP sample, we detail how we have ensured the maximum validity and reliability for our research instruments. Funding for the CBP comes from internal research funding at our respective universities.

### Sample Construction

Every three months, we construct a list of all chapter 7 and chapter 13 cases filed across the country on three randomly selected days during a two-week period. The period overlaps the end of a month and the beginning of the following month. We use a legal data service, Bloomberg Law, and limitations from its interface are why we randomly select particular days to construct the list instead of using a time span.

We have collected data every February, May, August, and November since 2013, with one exception. The office closures and other disruptions caused by the COVID pandemic meant the second data collection round in 2020 did not occur until June. For this book, we closed the database at the end of 2023, giving us eleven years of data across forty-four rounds of data collection.

From the list of cases constructed every three months, we randomly select two hundred. We replace any nonindividual, such as a corporation or limited liability company, with an individual. Thus, the final database for each round of data collection consists of two hundred individuals who filed either chapter 7 or chapter 13. Consistent with previous iterations of the CBP, individuals are eligible for the sample regardless of whether they checked the box on the bankruptcy petition for having predominantly consumer debts. Previous research demonstrates the thin line between the business-consumer distinction in individual bankruptcy and specifically questions the reliability of the checkbox to make that distinction.[2] Less than 2 percent of filers in the database checked the box indicating they have predominantly business debts.

## Court Record Coding

Bankruptcy court files are public, like any other court record. The bankruptcy laws require voluminous disclosure of the filer's assets, debts, income, expenses, and other financial details. Court rules require attorneys to file papers electronically. Filers who do not have an attorney can submit paper filings, which the court digitizes. The court files are accessible remotely through the Public Access to Court Electronic Records (PACER) system. Through our universities' subscriptions with Bloomberg Law, we can access PACER for no additional fee.

A law student working as a research assistant downloads court records for all two hundred randomly selected cases. These files are stored on a secure server at one of the authors' universities and are accessible to all personnel working on the CBP. Bankruptcy filers sometimes file incomplete paperwork and have fourteen days to file any missing information. Because the download represents the case as of approximately one to two months after filing, the paperwork should be complete at the time of download. If the filer has amended a document at the time of the download, we use the amended document, but we do not follow cases to check for amendments after the time of the initial download.

No file is missing all the information from the court records. Thus, our sample size for the court records is eighty-eight hundred. Nevertheless, some court records lack much of the required information. (Most of those cases are dismissed by the court.) We are missing the fundamental information of assets, debts, and income for 5.7 percent of the cases.

Before they begin coding the court record data, the research assistants are trained with practice files. While coding, the research assistants follow a twenty-nine-page codebook with detailed instructions for each variable. Since the inception of the current CBP, we have dropped some variables from our court record coding, primarily because our error checking suggested they were not reliable. Obviously, we do not use those variables.

After downloading the court records, law student research assistants code the data from them. Currently, the research assistants code 125 variables from the court records. Examples include top-line numbers like total debts and monthly income as well as detailed information such as the value of the filer's cars or whether the filer has pets. For each round, the research assistants double-code 10 percent of the sample. The double-coding discrepancy rate across all forty-four rounds is 2.2 percent. A co-PI checks every double-coding discrepancy and makes any necessary corrections. When the double-coding process reveals weaknesses in the coding protocol, we update the codebook or provide further training to our student research assistants.

We next run the court record data through a 750-line computer program that flags potential errors by looking for logical inconsistencies or for unlikely coding outcomes. An example of the former is a file with a mortgage but no home. An example of the latter is having more than three mortgages. The program also flags any entry more than three standard deviations from the mean as a possible mistake rather than a true outlier. At least one co-PI double checks every entry flagged and makes any necessary corrections.

We used two variables in this book that we added to the court record coding after starting the current CBP. The first captured the number and ages of dependents from the schedule of household expenses. The second was the number and amount of student loans from the schedule of unsecured debts. Although we had coded overall student debt owed from the statistical summary all debtors must file, we observed that the number often did not reconcile with the sum of the individual entries on the schedule. For both these variables, we went back to the court files on our server and updated the database. For cases going forward, we incorporated them into the coding protocol. For the back coding, we used error-trapping and proofreading protocols like those we used for the original coding.

After we error trap and proofread the court record data for a round, we add those data to the court records from other rounds. We inflation-adjust all amounts to 2023 dollars using the consumer price index for all urban consumers (CPI-U) from the Bureau of Labor Statistics and then round to the nearest dollar. Notably, the CPI-U understates the inflation of home values. Most financial variables have substantial skewness because of extreme outliers. For that reason, we report medians as a measure of central tendency. Where we use averages or run regressions using financial variables, we trim them at three and one-half standard deviations or use the natural logarithm of the variable's values if statistically appropriate.

## Survey

From the sample, a faculty assistant obtains the mailing address of the filer from the court records. The mailing address is the only contact information for the filer available in the court records. We first send a "pre-letter" introducing ourselves, briefly explaining the research, and letting the filer know we will be sending a survey. We tell the filers we will send them a $50 gift card for completing the survey.[3]

About one week later, we send the survey under a cover letter containing the usual disclosures required in the United States for human subjects research. The mailing also contains an envelope with prepaid postage to return the survey. If we do not receive a survey within two to three weeks, we follow up with a reminder letter and an additional survey. Both the letter and the cover page of the survey have a twelve-letter, easily remembered URL that takes the recipient to a website that runs on the Qualtrics survey software service. At this site, respondents who prefer to respond electronically can complete the survey.

Our response rate for the survey is 26.3 percent, giving us 2,314 responses. Most respondents use the postal service to return the survey. For surveys returned by mail, one of the co-PIs uses the website to enter the survey data. When the survey round is complete, the same co-PI recodes and error-checks 10 percent of returned surveys. The error rate is 0.2 percent.

Whether people complete the survey on paper or electronically, it uses only a unique numerical identifier for the respondent. The unique identifier enhances the perception and reality of the confidentiality of the survey response. We use the unique identifier to link the survey results with the court records. The working version of the CBP database uses only this unique identifier. We have stored all name and address information separately and securely.

The survey has never exceeded seven pages plus a cover page—thereby making an eight-page booklet. The last page of the survey is an open-ended question inviting the respondents to "tell us their story," if they feel comfortable. The quotes throughout the book come from those narratives.

The survey asks about prebankruptcy struggling and what went wrong, the privations people suffered prior to bankruptcy, and what contributed to bankruptcy. It concludes with basic questions about their health and demographics. We ask the respondent about themselves as well as any spouse or partner, regardless of whether the bankruptcy case was a joint filing. On average, the coding for the survey produces 128 variables.

We have made changes to the survey as particular questions proved less useful or as we crafted new research questions. To keep response rates as high as possible, we adhered to a strict rule that the survey cannot grow beyond seven pages and sometimes have deleted questions to make room for others. For purposes of this book, relevant examples are that we asked about the filer's reaction to their bankruptcy for the first twenty-eight rounds (n = 1,517) and asked about the filer's methods to find an attorney for the last sixteen rounds (n = 797). In addition, although we have always asked about health, our early results suggested respondents found our wording confusing. For health questions, we use survey responses from the last twenty-eight rounds (n = 1,460).

Response bias, of course, is always a concern with any survey research. Unlike many other survey projects, we do have observables from the court records against which we can check for response bias. Across respondents, means and medians converge for total assets, real property, personal property, homeownership rates, total debts, secured debts, priority debts, and unsecured debts. Respondents have lower monthly income than persons who did not return a survey, by $260 (or 8%) at the median and $251 (or 7%) at the mean. Given the lack of differences on the other variables, we do not believe this small difference in income raises concerns for our findings. Nevertheless, we disclose the difference in the interest of transparency. Also, we obviously cannot rule out response bias on other variables not in the court records.

## SAMPLE CHARACTERISTICS

Tables A.1, A.2, and A.3 provide descriptive statistics for the entire CBP sample. Table A.1 reports on all filers in our sample; table A.2 reports only on chapter 7 filers; and table A.3 reports only on chapter 13 filers. Importantly, and unlike in the remainder of the book, the computations in these tables do not trim variables at three and one-half standard deviations. The means, medians, and standard deviations demonstrate substantial skewness in many of the variables.

For all the tables, if the person reported a spouse or partner, the demographic variables are for the household. For race in two-person households, the household is considered to be of that race if either person identifies with that race.

---

*Table A.1.* Descriptive Statistics for All Filers in the CBP Sample

|  | Mean | Median | Standard Deviation |
|---|---|---|---|
| Total assets | $126,908 | $35,411 | $240,055 |
| Real property | $92,928 | $0 | $200,916 |
| Homeowner (1 = yes) | 0.403 | 0.000 | 0.491 |
| Home value if own home | $228,381 | $168,196 | $335,233 |
| Personal property | $34,377 | $17,886 | $77,114 |
| Total debts | $221,640 | $101,912 | $2,737,918 |
| Secured debts | $102,760 | $23,544 | $203,990 |
| Priority debts | $5,347 | $0 | $39,555 |
| Unsecured nonpriority debts | $113,479 | $44,707 | $2,728,211 |
| Student loans | $12,988 | $0 | $40,265 |
| Monthly income, pretax | $4,830 | $4,163 | $3,340 |
| Monthly expenses | $3,724 | $3,289 | $2,318 |
| Chapter (1 = chapter 13) | 0.369 | 0.000 | 0.482 |

*(continued)*

*Table A.1.* *(Continued)*

|  | Mean | Median | Standard Deviation |
|---|---|---|---|
| Demographics (1 = yes) |  |  |  |
| Age | 49.3 | 49.5 | 14.0 |
| Black | 0.270 | 0.000 | 0.444 |
| Hispanic | 0.119 | 0.000 | 0.324 |
| White | 0.637 | 1.000 | 0.481 |
| Live with spouse or partner | 0.466 | 0.000 | 0.499 |
| High school or higher | 0.926 | 1.000 | 0.237 |
| Bachelor's degree or higher | 0.225 | 0.000 | 0.384 |
| Employment | 0.739 | 1.000 | 0.439 |

*Table A.2.* Descriptive Statistics for Chapter 7 Filers in the CBP Sample

|  | Mean | Median | Standard Deviation |
|---|---|---|---|
| Total assets | $97,010 | $24,740 | $174,583 |
| Real property | $66,709 | $0 | $149,246 |
| Homeowner (1 = yes) | 0.315 | 0.000 | 0.465 |
| Home value if own home | $224,401 | $162,139 | $421,477 |
| Personal property | $30,346 | $15,710 | $61,800 |
| Total debts | $229,075 | $89,037 | $3,390,685 |
| Secured debts | $81,268 | $14,133 | $180,654 |
| Priority debts | $5,225 | $0 | $46,450 |
| Unsecured nonpriority debts | $142,477 | $49,794 | $3,383,094 |
| Student loans | $11,925 | $0 | $37,283 |
| Monthly income, pretax | $4,237 | $3,784 | $2,744 |
| Monthly expenses | $3,684 | $3,289 | $2,136 |
| Demographics (1 = yes) |  |  |  |
| Age | 48.7 | 48.5 | 14.6 |
| Black | 0.202 | 0.000 | 0.401 |
| Hispanic | 0.130 | 0.000 | 0.336 |
| White | 0.691 | 1.000 | 0.462 |
| Live with spouse or partner | 0.458 | 0.000 | 0.498 |
| High school or higher | 0.931 | 1.000 | 0.229 |
| Bachelor's degree or higher | 0.214 | 0.000 | 0.378 |
| Employment | 0.720 | 1.000 | 0.449 |

*Table A.3.*   Descriptive Statistics for Chapter 13 Filers in the CBP Sample

|  | Mean | Median | Standard Deviation |
|---|---|---|---|
| Total assets | $182,370 | $94,182 | $321,368 |
| Real property | $141,474 | $59,503 | $265,058 |
| Homeowner (1 = yes) | 0.567 | 1.000 | 0.496 |
| Home value if own home | $232,463 | $175,402 | $213,294 |
| Personal property | $41,857 | $22,145 | $99,050 |
| Total debts | $207,830 | $133,974 | $257,939 |
| Secured debts | $142,635 | $58,567 | $236,292 |
| Priority debts | $5,574 | $0 | $21,509 |
| Unsecured nonpriority debts | $59,618 | $33,353 | $78,972 |
| Student loans | $14,960 | $0 | $45,225 |
| Monthly income, pretax | $5,932 | $5,034 | $4,005 |
| Monthly expenses | $3,799 | $3,290 | $2,621 |
| Demographics (1 = yes) |  |  |  |
| Age | 50.6 | 51.0 | 12.7 |
| Black | 0.408 | 0.000 | 0.492 |
| Hispanic | 0.098 | 0.000 | 0.298 |
| White | 0.527 | 1.000 | 0.500 |
| Live with spouse or partner | 0.480 | 0.000 | 0.500 |
| High school or higher | 0.917 | 1.000 | 0.251 |
| Bachelor's degree or higher | 0.246 | 0.000 | 0.395 |
| Employment | 0.777 | 1.000 | 0.417 |

The survey allows persons to identify with more than one race. The other demographic variables are averaged across both people in a two-person household. Home values are reported for homeowners only. For binary variables, 1 = yes such that the mean is the percentage of cases with that characteristic.

REGRESSION TABLE ON BANKRUPTCY
CHAPTER CHOICE

In chapter 6 of this book, we discuss the overrepresentation of Black households in chapter 13. We run a regression to show the results even after numerous controls, thereby replicating regressions from other published works. For considerations of space, we reported an abbreviated form of the regression at table 6.1 and report the full regression here in table A.4.

*Table A.4.*  Logistic Regression on Bankruptcy Chapter Choice

| Dependent variable: chapter 13 filing | (1) | (2) | (3) | (4) | (5) |
|---|---|---|---|---|---|
| Black household | 2.73* | 2.62* | 2.51* | 2.39* | 1.64* |
| Legal & financial circumstances | | | | | |
| Prior bankruptcy in last 8 years | | 11.58* | 11.66* | 11.57* | 10.86* |
| Represented by an attorney | | 2.80* | 2.81* | 2.73* | 2.08* |
| Foreclosure reason for bankruptcy | | 0.80* | 0.76* | 0.76* | 0.73* |
| Homeowner | | 1.23 | 1.15 | 1.17 | 1.13 |
| Monthly income (ln) | | 2.18* | 2.18* | 2.31* | 2.58* |
| Total assets (ln) | | 1.21* | 1.22* | 1.21* | 1.26* |
| Total debts (ln) | | 0.49* | 0.50* | 0.46* | 0.50* |
| Priority debts (ln) | | 1.12* | 1.12* | 1.12* | 1.12* |
| Secured debts/total debts | | 7.57* | 7.53* | 8.84* | 5.99* |
| Attempts to renegotiate debt | | | | | |
| Asked creditors to "work with you" | | | 1.42* | 1.46* | 1.42* |
| Refinanced home loan | | | 0.95 | 0.94 | 0.89 |
| Sold the house | | | 0.47* | 0.48* | 0.49* |
| Demographic information | | | | | |
| Bachelor's degree or higher | | | | 1.71* | 1.53* |
| Number of dependents | | | | 0.94 | 0.93 |
| Live with a spouse or partner | | | | 0.98 | 0.99 |
| Female head of household | | | | 1.16 | 1.13 |
| Local legal culture | | | | | |
| Percent chapter 13s in district | | | | | 61.30* |
| Constant | 0.36* | 0.06* | 0.05* | 0.07* | 0.00* |
| Model fit statistics | | | | | |
| McFadden pseudo $R^2$ | 0.04 | 0.28 | 0.29 | 0.29 | 0.34 |
| Likelihood ratio chi-squared | 95.88* | 740.00* | 756.61* | 772.12* | 896.45* |
| N | 2,088 | 2,088 | 2,088 | 2,088 | 2,088 |

NOTE: See also table 6.1. The parenthetical (ln) indicates log-transformed. A single asterisk (*) indicates statistical significance at the 5 percent level.

The dependent variable is whether the filer chose chapter 7 or chapter 13. The table shows odds ratios with a single asterisk to indicate statistical significance at the 5 percent level. Thus, in the full model, a Black household is 64 percent more likely than other households to file chapter 13 after controlling for all other variables. Overall model fit statistics are shown at the bottom. Because skewness remains after trimming at three and-one-half standard deviations, the financial variables are log-transformed before entering the regression. In a two-person household, the household is counted as being Black if either member of the household so identified. The percent of chapter 13s in the district comes from the Federal Judicial Center's Integrated Petition Database.

# Notes

INTRODUCTION

1. Lawless, "How Many Have Filed Bankruptcy?"; and Lawless, "Revisiting How Many Have Filed Bankruptcy."

2. Jiménez, "Dirty Debts Sold Dirt Cheap," 41–124.

3. Pew Charitable Trusts, "Debt Collectors Transforming Courts."

4. Hacker, *Great Risk Shift*, 1–9.

5. Bartlett, *New American Economy*; and Komlos, "Reaganomics."

6. Butler, "Performativity, Precarity and Sexual Politics," i–xiii; and Kasmir, "Precarity."

7. Board of Governors, "Economic Well-Being of U.S. Households 2019."

8. Dwyer and Lassus, "Great Risk Shift and Precarity," 199–216; and Mazzara, "Rents Risen More than Incomes."

9. Bundick and Pollard, "Rise and Fall," 58–59.

10. Fidelity, "Rising Health Care Costs."

11. Mezza et al., "Student Loans and Homeownership," 215–60; and Gicheva, "Student Loans or Marriage?," 207–16.

12. Jiménez and Glater, "Student Debt Is Civil Rights Issue," 131–98.

13. Sandler, "Avon Company Sets Digital"; and Wicker, "Multilevel-Marketing Companies."

14. Congressional Research Service, "Debt Collection Market."

15. Ramsey, "Ask Dave."

16. Sullivan, Warren, and Westbrook, *As We Forgive Our Debtors*.

17. Sullivan, Warren, and Westbrook, *Fragile Middle Class*, 4.

18. United States Courts, "Bankruptcy Filings."

19. Porter, *Broke*.

20. Sullivan, Warren, and Westbrook, *Fragile Middle Class*, 5–11, app. 1 (first and second CBP iterations methodologies).

21. Porter, "Methodology of 2007 CBP," 235–44 (fourth CBP iteration methodology); Lawless et al., "Did Bankruptcy Reform Fail?," 389–405 (1991 and third CBP iteration methodology).

22. Robert Lawless, Katherine Porter, and Deborah Thorne were the original collaborators on the fifth and current iteration of the CBP. Pamela Foohey joined the project in 2016. Porter remained a part of the project until 2018, when she left to represent California's Forty-Fifth Congressional District in the United States House of Representatives. Details about CBP can be found on the project's website. Consumer Bankruptcy Project, "Welcome."

23. Sousa, "Debt Stigma and Social Class," 965–1002; and Sousa, "Persistence of Bankruptcy Stigma," 217–42.

24. Pinsker, "Americans Don't Talk about Money."

25. Foohey, Lawless, and Thorne, "Portraits of Bankruptcy Filers."

26. Brokland, et al., "U.S. Financial Health Pulse."

27. Noguchi, "'I Try So Hard Not To Cry'"; Lopez, Rainie, and Budiman, "Impacts of COVID-19."

28. Long, "Many Left Behind."

29. Warren, "What Is a Women's Issue?," 19–56.


## CHAPTER 1. FILING BANKRUPTCY AND THE BANKRUPTCY SYSTEM

1. U.S. Constitution, art. 1, sec. 8, cl. 4.

2. Felstiner, Abel, and Sarat, "Emergence and Transformation of Disputes," 644–47.

3. Sandefur, "Access to Civil Justice," 341–43; and Sandefur, "Importance of Doing Nothing," 113–15.

4. Foohey et al., "Life in the Sweatbox," 249–54.

5. These percentages come from our calculations using the Federal Judicial Center's (FJC) Integrated Bankruptcy Petition Database. The database contains every case filed in the US bankruptcy courts and is publicly available on the FJC's website at www.fjc.gov/research/idb.

6. Stanley and Girth, *Bankruptcy*, 74–76; Braucher, "Lawyers and Consumer Bankruptcy," 526–37; Sullivan, Warren, and Westbrook, "Persistence of Local Legal Culture," 839–57; and Lawless and Littwin, "Local Legal Culture," 1358–60.

7. Mann and Porter, "Saving Up for Bankruptcy," 319–22.

8. Foohey et al., "'No Money Down' Bankruptcy," 1080–91.

9. American Bankruptcy Institute, *Final Report*, § 3.06; and Sousa, "Just Punch My Bankruptcy Ticket."

10. These percentages are similarly calculated from the FJC's Integrated Petition Database at www.fjc.gov/research/idb.

11. Jiménez, "Distribution of Assets in Chapter 7," 800–801.

12. Car redemptions are explored in more detail at Foohey, Lawless, and Thorne, "Driven to Bankruptcy," 313, fig. 1.

13. Culhane and White, "New Consumer Bankruptcy Model"; and Warren, "Phantom $400."

14. Jacoby, "Superdelegation and Gatekeeping," 887–88.


CHAPTER 2. STRUGGLING TO SURVIVE

1. Tach and Greene, "'Robbing Peter to Pay Paul,'" 10–16.

2. Foohey et al., "Life in the Sweatbox," 220.

3. Newman, *Falling from Grace*.

4. Hacker, *Great Risk Shift*, 37.

5. Desmond, *Poverty, by America*. Brown, *Whiteness of Wealth* provides an excellent discussion of racial disparities in tax law.

6. Board of Governors, "Changes in U.S. Family Finances," 15, table 3; and Gillespie, "Bankrate's 2024 Annual Report."

7. Porter and Thorne, "Failure of Bankruptcy's Fresh Start," 99; Sullivan, Warren, and Westbrook, *Fragile Middle Class*, 16, 105; and Warren and Tyagi, *Two-Income Trap*, 80.

8. We asked filers whether they "very much agreed," "somewhat agreed," "somewhat disagreed," or "very much disagreed" that an item "contributed to their bankruptcy." We collapse "very much agreed" and "somewhat agreed" when discussing contributors to people's bankruptcy.

9. US Bureau of Labor Statistics, "Coverage in Employer Medical Care."

10. COBRA is the Consolidated Omnibus Budget Reconciliation Act of 1985 and is codified at 29 U.S.C. §§ 1161–1169.

11. Oddo et al., "Changes in Precarious Employment," 171.

12. The exact wording used for the six categories in the current 2013–23 survey was "I did not seriously struggle with debts before I filed bankruptcy"; "fewer than six months"; "at least six months, but less than one year"; "at least one year, but less than two years"; "at least two years, but less than five years"; and "five years or more." In 2007 the two "short struggler" options were phrased slightly differently: "less than three months" and "three to six months." The wording for the remaining categories was the same as used in 2013–23.

13. When the six categories are transformed into a continuous measure using the midpoint of each, the mean and modal amounts of time spent struggling are at least three years (3.0 years and 3.5 years respectively). In unreported analyses, we looked for changes over time within the 2013 to 2023 data and found none. The full 2013 to 2023 outcomes are virtually identical to those reported in Foohey et al., "Life in the Sweatbox," which relied on data from 2013 to 2016.

14. Underwood, "What Is a Penalty APR?"; and Board of Governors, "Consumer Credit—G.19."

15. Martin and Adams, "Grand Theft Auto Loans."

16. Foohey and Martin, "Fintech's Role in Wealth Gap," 483.

17. Consumer Financial Protection Bureau, "Single-Payment Vehicle Title Lending."

18. Eisenberg-Guyot et al., "From Payday Loans to Pawnshops."

19. Levitin, *Consumer Finance*, 622–24.

20. Internal Revenue Service, "Hardships, Early Withdrawals, and Loans."

21. Lu et al., "Borrowing from the Future?"

22. Scott, Edwards, and Stanczyk, "Moonlighting to Side Hustle."

23. Kivimaki et al., "Long Working Hours."

24. There is an error in Foohey et al., "Life in the Sweatbox," 239, table 1. The data reported for "% homeowners with involuntary liens" were listed as 66.4 percent for long strugglers and 50.9 percent for other debtors. The correct data are 15.3 percent for long strugglers and 8.1 percent for all other debtors.

25. The question on the survey read: "During the two years before your bankruptcy, did you or others in your household have to do any of the following things because you could not afford it?"

26. Simon, Song, and Bennett, "Dental Services Use."

27. Humana, "Cost of Common Dental Procedures"; and Shinn, "How Much Does a Root Canal Cost?"

28. Peter G. Peterson Foundation, "How Much Does the United States Spend?"

29. Sengupta, "Americans and Their Cars."

30. Maté, *Myth of Normal*; Mayo Clinic, "Chronic Stress"; and Medical News Today, "What Is Chronic Stress?"

31. Kulshreshtha et al., "Association of Stress," 7.

32. Mullainathan and Shafir, *Scarcity*.

33. Harris and Smith, "Monetary Sanctions," 36.

34. Thorne, "Women's Work, Women's Worry?"

35. Dunn and Mirzaie, "Consumer Debt Stress."

36. We have asked these questions for twenty-eight survey administrations (N = 1,366).

37. The White House, "President Signs Act."

38. Jefferson, "Narratives of Moral Order."

39. Thorne, "Personal Bankruptcy through the Eyes."

40. Hernandez, "Debt Collectors Can Now Text."

41. Consumer Financial Protection Bureau, "Consumer Experiences with Debt Collection," 29–35.

42. DeFusco, Enriquez, and Yellen, "Wage Garnishment in the United States," 2.

## CHAPTER 3. STAYING HOME AND GOING PLACES

1. Federal Reserve Bank of St. Louis, "Homeownership Rate in the United States"; and US Census Bureau, "DP04."

2. Board of Governors of the Federal Reserve System, "Owned Vehicles."

3. Rodríguez, "Majority of Car Loans" (used cars); and Egan, "Are More Drivers Financing" (new cars).

4. Dickerson, *Homeownership and Financial Underclass*, 1–8.

5. Dickerson, "Myth of Home Ownership," 190–92; and McCabe, "Are Homeowners Better Citizens?," 929–31.

6. Federal Reserve Bank of St. Louis, "Median Sales Price for New Houses."

7. Dickerson, "Myth of Home Ownership," 197–99.

8. Bernard and Lieber, "Your 2023 Guide to Mortgages."

9. Kamin, "More than 1 in 4 Homeowners."

10. We use the term *retirement assets* broadly, to mean any of the different types of retirement plans one might have. The datapoint comes from the bankruptcy schedule which asks for "Retirement or pension accounts. Examples: Interests in IRA, ERISA, Keogh, 401(k), 403(b), thrift savings accounts, or other pension or profit-sharing plans."

11. Seventy-five percent of chapter 7 filers with no home, but a car, are employed, and eighty-three percent of chapter 13 filers with no home, but a car, are employed.

12. The figures in the paragraph for the general population come from the Federal Reserve's 2022 Survey of Consumer Finances (SCF) (www.federalreserve .gov/econres/scfindex.htm). We did the computations from the SCF with the Survey Data and Analysis Tool from the University of California, Berkeley (https:// sda.berkeley.edu/).

13. In the context of the Great Recession, White, "Underwater and Not Walking Away," explored the fear, guilt, and shame surrounding why so many homeowners who were underwater on their mortgages did not walk away from their homes when to do so would have been the better financial decision.

14. Homeowners without cars are more likely to list a foreclosure action: 8 percent of homeowners without cars in chapter 7 list a home foreclosure, and 21 percent of homeowners without cars in chapter 13 list a home foreclosure.

15. Filers who did not own either houses or cars were less likely to have retirement accounts, which made stopping contributions a less meaningful privation

and thus not one of their top five privations. Their other leading privations were the same as those of other filers.

16. N for no home is 1,334. N for homeowners is 921.

17. The figure combines the responses for "I did not seriously struggle with debts"; "fewer than six months"; and "at least six months, but less than one year." The survey categories read: "at least one year, but less than two years" and "at least two years, but less than five years." N for nonhomeowners is 1,306, and N for homeowners is 902.

18. Ericson and Fuster, "Endowment Effect," 555–57.

19. Collins and Berg, "Losing a Little Part of Yourself," 1832–59; and Kingsley, Smith, and Price, "Impacts of Foreclosures," 11–12.

20. Ehrenreich, *Fear of Falling*, 14–15.

21. The differences reported in the text are statistically significant at $p < .05$. Homeowners with cars indicated that they felt anger and guilt "a great deal" more often, and thankful and happy "not at all" or "a little bit" more often than other filers without homes.

22. Dickerson, *Homeownership and Financial Underclass*, 19–20.

23. Cogan, "Impossible Paradox"; King, Smart, and Manville, "Poverty of the Carless," 464; and Raphael and Rice, "Car Ownership, Employment, and Earnings," 127.

24. Brown, "Car-Less or Car-Free?," 152–59.

25. Shill, "Should Law Subsidize Driving?," 502.

26. Wamsley, "Walking in America Remains Dangerous."

27. Krishner, "Why Now Is a Good Time."

28. Board of Governors, "Owned Vehicles by All Families."

29. For an overview, see Foohey, Lawless, and Thorne, "Driven to Bankruptcy," 290–93.

30. The increase in outstanding car loan debt reflects the authors' calculations using the Board of Governors of the Federal Reserve System, "Consumer Credit—G.19," as well as consumer price index data from the Bureau of Labor Statistics and population figures from the US Census.

31. Foohey, "Bursting the Auto Loan Bubble," 2217.

32. Federal Reserve Bank of New York, "Quarterly Report 2023," 3.

33. Board of Governors, "Vehicle Installment Loans."

34. DePillis, "How Costs of Car Ownership Add Up."

35. For more details about these options and car loans in chapter 13, see Foohey, Lawless, and Thorne, "Driven to Bankruptcy," 300–303.

## CHAPTER 4. STAYING ALIVE

1. Crimmins, "Lifespan and Healthspan," 902.

2. Rakshit et al., "Burden of Medical Debt."

3. Consumer Financial Protection Bureau, "Medical Debt."

4. Lopes et al., "Americans' Challenges"; and Peter G. Peterson Foundation, "How Does the US Healthcare System Compare."

5. Sullivan, Warren, and Westbrook, *As We Forgive*, 166–77; and Sullivan, Warren, and Westbrook, *Fragile Middle Class*, 141–71.

6. Himmelstein et al., "Illness and Injury."

7. Himmelstein et al., "Medical Bankruptcy," 743.

8. Results from this current study are not entirely comparable with the results from the 2007 study. Our data collection methods were limited to surveys and court records, whereas in 2007, researchers relied on surveys, court records, and in-depth telephone interviews. The interviews provided additional information about medical reasons for bankruptcy that we did not replicate in the current study.

9. Respondents could choose from four answer options: "very much agree," "somewhat agree," "somewhat disagree," and "very much disagree." We created a binary response by collapsing "very much agree" with "somewhat agree," and "somewhat disagree" with "very much disagree."

10. Ziettlow, "Club Sandwich Generation."

11. Warren and Tyagi, *Two-Income Trap*.

12. Data for Asian and Native American filers are not reported because the numbers of cases for both groups were small (sixty-three and sixty-nine, respectively).

13. Ndugga, Hill, and Artiga, "Key Data on Health."

14. Jacoby and Holman, "Managing Medical Bills."

15. Wendling, "Which Countries Have Universal Health Coverage?"

16. Committee on the Consequences of Uninsurance, *Health Insurance Is a Family Matter*, 153–60.

17. Keisler-Starkey and Bunch, "Health Insurance Coverage," 3, fig. 1.

18. Claxton et al., "Employer Health Benefits," 7, fig. B.

19. Collins, Haynes, and Masitha, "State of U.S. Health Insurance."

20. Tikkanen et al., "International Health Care System Profiles."

21. Cohen and Cha, "Health Insurance Coverage," 1, fig. 1.

22. Cha and Cohen, "Reasons for Being Uninsured," 2, fig. 2.

23. Williamson, "State of Paid Sick Time."

24. Enright, "What Is COBRA?"

25. Claxton et al., "Employer Health Benefits," 7, fig. B.

26. Heaton et al., "Americans Are Still Not Getting Dental Care," 5.

27. Sanders and Frankovic, "More than One-Third of Americans."

28. Rakshit et al., "Burden of Medical Debt."

29. Lopes et al., "Health Care Debt."

30. Porter and Thorne, "Failure of Bankruptcy's Fresh Start," 87–88, 93, fig. 3.

31. Eddy et al., "Recovery from Anorexia Nervosa," 184.

32. Harvard Health, "Type 2 Diabetes Mellitus."

## CHAPTER 5. STAYING OUT OF THE RED

1. Pew Research Center, "State of American Jobs," 20, 33, 38–39; Carnevale, Gulish, and Campbell, "If Not Now, When?", 10–12; Dynan, Elmendorf, and Sichel, "Evolution of Household Income Volatility"; and Bryson, Blanchflower, and Spurling, "Wage Curve after Great Recession," 10.

2. Immerwahr and Foleno, "Great Expectations," 10.

3. Brown and Carbone, "Race, Property, and Citizenship," 138; and Pew Research Center, "State of American Jobs," 20.

4. Mishel, Gould, and Bivens, "Wage Stagnation in Nine Charts"; National Center for Education Statistics, "Annual Earnings by Educational Attainment"; Carnevale, Gulish, and Campbell, "If Not Now, When?", 16–17; Hess, "CNBC Survey"; and Mezza, Ringo, and Sommer, "Can Student Loan Debt Explain," 2–3.

5. Warren and Tyagi, *Two-Income Trap*; and US Bureau of Labor Statistics, "Labor Force Statistics." We computed the average unemployment figure from the data tools available on the website for the Bureau of Labor Statistics.

6. This result comes from an ordinary least squares regression with unsecured debt as the dependent variable, and bankruptcy chapter, household employment, and income as the independent variables. We log-transformed unsecured debt and income because of substantial skewness. Unemployment is statistically significant in the regression even with income ($t = 3.24$, $p = .001$). The results are robust to other specifications of the regression, including when we restrict the regression only to those filing households under age sixty-five or control for the chapter of the Bankruptcy Code.

7. These figures combine people who responded to our survey who "very much agreed" or "somewhat agreed" that a decline in income contributed to their bankruptcy.

8. Feldman, "Nature, Antecedents and Consequences"; and Lowrey, "Underemployment Crisis."

9. Lowrey, "Underemployment Crisis"; and Golden and Kim, "Underemployment Just Isn't Working," 1.

10. Pew Research Center, "State of American Jobs," 33, 38–39.

11. Golden and Kim, "Underemployment Just Isn't Working," 2–3; Golden, "Still Falling Short on Hours and Pay," 12–13; and Golden and Kim, " Rise and Fall of Underemployment."

12. Feiveson, "Labor Unions and U.S. Economy"; and Mishel, "Causes of Wage Stagnation."

13. This result comes from an ordinary least squares regression with unsecured debt as the dependent variable and the direction of change in the debtor's prebankruptcy income and the amount of income as the independent variables. We log-transformed unsecured debt and income because of substantial skewness. Decline in income is statistically significant in the regression even

controlling for the amount of income (t = 4.27, p < .001). We get a similar result if we restrict the regression only to those filing households under age sixty-five.

14. These figures combine people who responded to our survey who "very much agreed" or "somewhat agreed" that a decline in income contributed to their bankruptcy.

15. Williamson, "Understanding the Self-Employed."

16. Williamson, "Understanding the Self-Employed"; and Lawless, "Striking Out on Their Own," 107, table 6.2.

17. Williamson, "Understanding the Self-Employed"; and Kochhar, "Financial Risk to U.S. Business Owners."

18. Cases are counted as involving self-employment if either a person or a person's spouse/partner reported self-employment. By that definition, two hundred cases involved self-employment. Respondents could report more than one type of employment. This figure includes full-time and part-time self-employment.

19. Lawless, "Striking Out on Their Own," 105.

20. Jiménez et al., "Impact of Educational Levels," 205–6.

21. Pew Research Center, "State of American Jobs," 20; and Carnevale, Gulish, and Campbell, "If Not Now, When?," 12–13, 24.

22. Specifically, we obtained the data from the websites for the US Census Bureau and the US Department of Education's National Center for Education Statistics (NCES).

23. US Bureau of Labor Statistics, "Earning and Unemployment Rates."

24. Iuliano, "Student Loan Bankruptcy Gap."

25. The guidance is an internal Department of Justice document, available at www.justice.gov/d9/pages/attachments/2022/11/17/student_loan_discharge _guidance_-_fact_sheet_0.pdf. A description appears at Culhane and Mulhern, "Justice Department Announces New Guidance."


## CHAPTER 6. BLACKNESS OF BANKRUPTCY

1. Baradaran, "Jim Crow Credit," 888–916; and "Segregation in America." In *The Color of Money*, Baradaran scrutinizes the false promise of Black banks for building the Black community's wealth and discusses how housing segregation, racism, and credit policies trapped the Black community in economic oppression.

2. Bleich et al., "Discrimination in the United States"; and Lloyd, "Black American Experience."

3. Butler, Mayer, and Weston, "Racial Disparities in the Auto Loan Market," 1–5 (auto lending); Foohey and Martin, "Fintech's Role in Wealth Gap," 475–88 (discussing studies); and Freeman, "Racism in Credit Card Industry," 1095–1106 (credit cards).

4. Sakong and Zentefis, "Bank Access across America"; and Baradaran, *How the Other Half Banks*, 110–18, 138–39.

5. LaVoice and Vamossy, "Racial Disparities in Debt Collection"; and Kiel and Waldman, "Color of Debt."

6. For instance, Dickerson, "Systemic Racism and Housing," focuses on racial disparities in housing.

7. US Census Bureau, "Quick Facts."

8. Cohen, Lawless, and Shin, "Opposite of Correct," 629.

9. US Census Bureau, "Quick Facts."

10. The exact percentages vary year to year.

11. See chapter 2.

12. Steil et al., "Social Structure of Mortgage Discrimination," 759.

13. Foohey et al., "'No Money Down' Bankruptcy," 1083 (discussing regression analysis).

14. Cohen, Lawless, and Shin, "Opposite of Correct," 631–33; Foohey et al., "'No Money Down' Bankruptcy," 1085–86; and Braucher, Cohen, and Lawless, "Race, Attorney Influence," 398–400.

15. Stanley and Girth, *Bankruptcy*, 74.

16. Sullivan, Warren, and Westbrook, "Persistence of Local Legal Culture," 804; and Braucher, "Lawyers and Consumer Bankruptcy," 503.

17. Moslimani et al., "Facts about U.S. Black Population."

18. Morrison and Uettwiller, "Consumer Bankruptcy Pathologies"; and Kiel and Fresques, "Data Analysis."

19. Cohen, Lawless, and Shin, "Opposite of Correct," 633; Foohey et al., "'No Money Down' Bankruptcy," 1086–91; and Braucher, Cohen, and Lawless, "Race, Attorney Influence," 400–405. Lawless and Littwin, "Local Legal Culture," also uses a regression model to find that race is a statistically significant predictor of filing chapter 13.

20. Braucher, Cohen, and Lawless, "Race, Attorney Influence."

21. Cohen, Lawless, and Shin, "Opposite of Correct."

22. Foohey et al., "'No Money Down' Bankruptcy," 1086–91.

23. Dickerson, "Racial Steering in Bankruptcy," 643–47.

24. Greene, Patel, and Porter, "Cracking the Code," 1035–36, found, based on a regression using 2007 CBP data, that race predicted plan completion, with Black chapter 13 filers less likely to complete plans.

25. Highsmith and Saunders, "Rent-to-Own Racket," 5–8; and Anderson and Jaggia, "Return, Purchase, or Skip?," 315.

26. Weller and Roberts, "Eliminating the Black-White Wealth Gap."

27. Derenoncourt et al., "Wealth of Two Nations."

28. Derenoncourt et al., "Wealth of Two Nations," 699–702.

29. Dietz and Haurin, "Social and Private Consequences," 401–50; and McCabe, "Are Homeowners Better Citizens?," 929–54.

30. Baradaran, "Jim Crow Credit," 888–94.

31. US Census Bureau, "Quarterly Residential Vacancies," 9.

32. Howell and Korver-Glenn, "Increasing Effect of Neighborhood Racial Composition," 1051–71.

33. Perry, Rothwell, and Harshbarger, "Devaluation of Assets in Black Neighborhoods."

34. Rothwell and Perry, "How Racial Bias in Appraisals Affects."

35. Kochhar, Fry, and Taylor, "Wealth Gaps Rise to Record Highs," 8.

36. Dickerson, *Homeownership and Financial Underclass*, 9–10, 64–81.

37. Sarra and Wade, *Predatory Lending*, 69–115.

38. Dickerson, *Homeownership and Financial Underclass*, 164–72.

39. Been, Ellen, and Madar, "High Cost of Segregation," 385.

40. Dickerson, *Homeownership and Financial Underclass*, 14–15.

41. Bartlett et al., "Consumer-Lending Discrimination."

42. Consumer Financial Protection Bureau, "CFPB Orders Wells Fargo to Pay."

43. Board of Governors, "Owned Vehicles by All Families."

44. Cohen, "Imperfect Competition in Auto Lending," 31–33; and Ayres and Siegelman, "Race and Gender Discrimination," 304–21.

45. Foohey, Lawless, and Thorne, "Driven to Bankruptcy," 292–93.

46. Butler, Mayer, and Weston, "Racial Disparities in Auto Loan Market," 2–4.

47. Sanchez and Kambhampati, "Driven into Debt"; and Racke, "Report."

48. Dunn, "Measuring Racial Disparities in Traffic Ticketing," 537–56.

49. Harden, "D.C. Parking, Traffic Tickets."

50. North Carolina Equal Access to Justice Commission, "When Debt Takes the Wheel."

51. In Foohey, Lawless, and Thorne, "Driven to Bankruptcy," we performed a cluster analysis that identified a group of people who file chapter 13 owning a car and little else; this cluster included the most Black filers.

52. Hawkins and Penner, "Advertising Injustices," 1619–57; and Johnson, "Magic of Groups Identity," 165–220.

53. Freeman, "Racism in Credit Card Industry," 1095–1106.

54. Wilson and Darity, "Understanding Black-White Disparities."

55. Daly, Hobijn, and Pedtke, "Disappointing Facts about Black-White Wage Gap."

56. Gould and Wilson, "Black Workers Face Lethal Preexisting Conditions."

57. Schneider and Harknett, "It's About Time."

58. Ganong et al., "Wealth, Race, and Consumption Smoothing."

59. Foohey and Martin, "Fintech's Role in Wealth Gap," 480–82.

60. Barshay, "College Completion Rates Are Up."

61. Brown and Carbone, "Race, Property, and Citizenship," 136–43; and Houle and Addo, "Racial Disparities in Student Debt," 562–77.

62. Dickerson, "Race Matters in Bankruptcy," 1726.

CHAPTER 7. ALL THE SINGLE LADIES
(WITH CHILDREN) IN BANKRUPTCY

1. In the Current CBP, 49 percent of cases are those of women filing alone, 29 percent are those of men filing alone, and 22 percent are joint filings.

2. Warren, "What Is a Women's Issue?," 27–29.

3. The bankruptcy data used to create figure 7.1 are by household, and for two-person households, race is counted if either person identified with that race. N for all filers is 2,225. N for Black filers is 591. N for white filers is 1,419.

4. Law, "Women Are Now Majority of U.S. Workforce."

5. Leukhina and Smaldone, "Women Outnumber Men in College Enrollment?"

6. Roux, "5 Facts about Black Women"; and US Bureau of Labor Statistics, "2020 Annual Averages."

7. AAUW, "Fast Facts."

8. Jiménez and Glater, "Student Debt Is a Civil Rights Issue," 132–33.

9. Curtin and Sutton, "Marriage Rates in the United States"; and Washington and Walker, "District of Columbia Had Lowest Percentage."

10. In 1981, based on CBP data, which were from ten judicial districts, 45 percent of cases were joint filings. Warren, "What Is a Women's Issue?," 27; and Sullivan, Warren, and Westbrook, *As We Forgive Our Debtors*, 18. Now, it is 20 percent. We get the same figure if we restrict the data to those same ten judicial districts used in 1981.

11. Carbone and Cahn, *Marriage Markets*, 1–5. See also Dickerson, "'Ideal Debtor' and 'Traditional' American Household," 203–5 (discussing marriage and *assortative mating*).

12. Carbone and Cahn, *Marriage Markets*, 2–3.

13. Carbone and Cahn, *Marriage Markets*, 3–5.

14. US Census Bureau, "Historical Living Arrangements of Children," table CH-1.

15. Raley, Sweeney, and Wondra, "Growing Racial and Ethnic Divide."

16. Curtin and Sutton, "Marriage Rates in the United States"; and Washington and Walker, "District of Columbia Had Lowest Percentage."

17. Brown and Carbone, "Race, Property, and Citizenship," 120–47.

18. Morse, "Stable Fertility Rates."

19. Sweeney and Raley, "Race, Ethnicity, and Changing Context," 539–58.

20. Hemez and Washington, "Percentage and Number of Children."

21. Notably, the Higher Education Act of 1965 created the guaranteed loan program now known as the Federal Family Education Loan Program (20 U.S.C. § 1071 (2005)), and the Higher Education Reconciliation Act of 2005 (Pub. L. No. 109-71, 120 Stat. 4, 158-60 (2005)) increased borrowing limits.

22. College Board, "Trends in College Pricing," 44, table SA-14A.

23. AAUW, "Deeper in Debt: 2021 Update"; AAUW, "Deeper in Debt"; and Jiménez and Glater, "Student Debt Is a Civil Rights Issue," 132–33.

24. Guzman and Kollar, "Income in the United States," 10.
25. AAUW, "Deeper in Debt: Women and Student Loans."
26. Maye, "Student Loan Debt Crisis."
27. Jiménez and Glater, "Student Debt Is a Civil Rights Issue," 132–33.
28. Roux, "5 Facts about Black Women."
29. Kolomatsky, "Most Unmarried Homeowners Are Women."
30. Lautz, "Single Women Buyers Outpace Men."
31. Goodman and Zhu, "Challenges Facing Single Female Borrowers"; and Goodman, Zhu, and Bai, "Women Are at Paying Their Mortgages."
32. Warren, "Families Alone"; and Machin, "Houses and Schools," 723–29.
33. "National Intimate Partner and Sexual Violence Survey."
34. Pennsylvania Coalition Against Domestic Violence, "Financial Abuse"; Adams, Littwin, and Javorka, "Frequency, Nature, and Effects of Coerced Debt," 1324–42; and Hasday, *Intimate Lies and the Law*, 37–38, 78–81.
35. Geck, "Equal Credit," 382–86; and Taylor, "Equal Credit Opportunity Act's Rules," 384–85.
36. García, "Borrowing to Make Ends Meet."
37. Schmitz, "Females on the Fringe."
38. Bhaskaran, "Pinklining."
39. Warren, "Bankrupt Children," 1003–32.
40. Specifically, single women scored –0.38 on a scale that ranged from –4 to +4. Single men scored 0.12, and married or partnered filers scored 0.02. Statistical tests confirmed the reliability of the index and the meaningfulness of the differences.

## CHAPTER 8. THE RISKIEST YEARS—BANKRUPT SENIORS

1. Mennell, "Power, Individualism, and Collective Self-Perception."
2. Kim, "How America Fell."
3. Ellis, Munnell, and Eschtruth, *Falling Short*, 1.
4. Hacker, *Great Risk Shift*, 54.
5. Howden and Meyer, "Age and Sex Composition," 2, table 1.
6. Administration on Aging, "2021 Profile," 3.
7. When a bankruptcy is filed by a single petitioner, it does not necessarily mean the petitioner is living alone. They could be living with a permanent partner or be married but chose to file independently of their spouse. Of the 173 married couples in the senior sample, 97 (56%) filed jointly.
8. Iacurci, "Debt among Oldest Americans."
9. Li, "Household Debt among Older Americans," 1.
10. Because we report medians, rather than means, the secured and unsecured debt amounts will not equal the total debt load.

11. See chapter 9 for a detailed discussion of debt collection.

12. Thorne, "Extreme Financial Strain," 194; and Thorne, "Women's Work, Women's Worry?" 146–51.

13. Consumer Financial Protection Bureau, "What Are the Costs."

14. Batinovic, et al., "Ageism in Hiring."

15. Weller and Wolff, *Retirement Income*, 1.

16. Martin and Weaver, "Social Security," 10.

17. AARP, "How Much Social Security."

18. Jeszeck, "Retirement Security," 1.

19. Van de Water and Romig, "Social Security Benefits," 3.

20. Martin and Weaver, "Social Security," 9–10, chart 5.

21. Quadagno, Kail, and Shekha, "Welfare States," 326; and Social Security Administration, "Retirement Benefits," 3–4.

22. Gravier, "Here's How Much Money."

23. This calculation counts persons as having retirement savings if they indicated "unknown" rather than a specific number for retirement savings. Such a term could mean there is a retirement account, but the number is unknown or that the debtor is unsure whether they have a retirement account. Because retirement accounts are considered "exempt" property that the trustee cannot liquidate, the court or trustee likely did not request further information.

24. Vanguard, "How America Saves 2023," 53, fig. 55.

25. Board of Governors, "Report on Economic Well-Being," 69, table 36.

26. National Council on Aging, "Get the Facts."

27. Fidelity, "How to Plan."

28. Fidelity, "How Much Will You Spend."

29. National Council on Aging, "Top 10 Chronic Conditions."

30. Miller, "How to Improve Access."

31. Medicare, "Costs."

32. National Council on Aging, "What You'll Pay."

33. Medicare, "Drug Coverage"; and National Council on Aging, "What You'll Pay."

34. Schoen, Davis, and Willink, "Medicare Beneficiaries' High Costs," 3.

35. Crystal, *America's Old Age Crisis*, 9.

36. Crystal, Shea, and Reyes, "Cumulative Advantage," 911.

37. US Government Accountability Office, "Retirement Security," 9–16.

38. Mather and Scommegna, "Fact Sheet."


CHAPTER 9. LAWSUITS AND DEBT COLLECTORS

1. Consumer Financial Protection Bureau, "Consumer Experiences with Debt Collection," 13.

2. Consumer Financial Protection Bureau, "Consumer Credit Card Market Report," 44, 136.

3. An outstanding summary of the debt buying industry appears at Jiménez, "Dirty Debts Sold Dirt Cheap," 49–55.

4. Consumer Financial Protection Bureau, "Market Snapshot: Update," 16–17, fig. 6.

5. Consumer Financial Protection Bureau, "Market Snapshot: Online Debt Sales," 9.

6. Consumer Financial Protection Bureau, "Fair Debt Collection Practices Act," 17.

7. The figure may overstate the amount of industry concentration, as not all debt buyers furnish information to credit reporting agencies. Consumer Financial Protection Bureau, "Market Snapshot: Third-Party Debt," 10–11.

8. Caplovitz, *Consumers in Trouble*, 27–34.

9. Federal Trade Commission, "Structure and Practice of Debt Buying Industry," 12–13.

10. Wilf-Townsend, "Assembly-Line Plaintiffs," 1716–17, 1736, table 4.

11. Holland, "Junk Justice," 226, fig. 11, gathers studies from Maryland, Indiana, Texas, and New York.

12. Pew Charitable Trusts, "How Debt Collectors Are Transforming," 16.

13. Wilf-Townsend, "Assembly-Line Plaintiffs," 1729, table 1.

14. Journalist Paul Kiel tells the story of how a debt collection attorney who filed sixty-nine thousand lawsuits in one year arranged his office and computer screens to quickly review lawsuits, sometimes in seconds. Kiel, "So Sue Them."

15. The figure comes from the authors' computation based on Hannaford-Agor and Waters, "Estimating the Costs of Civil Litigation," 6, table 4. Another author estimates the cost of a consumer-plaintiff taking a claim through a summary judgment motion—that is, a motion asking the judge to rule without a jury because there are no disputed facts—to be $50,000. Levitin, *Consumer Finance*, 46–47.

16. Wilf-Townsend, "Assembly-Line Plaintiffs," 1721.

17. Wilf-Townsend, "Assembly-Line Plaintiffs," 1709.

18. Lefgren and McIntyre, "Explaining Cross-State Differences," 381, table 3; and Dawsey, Hynes, and Ausubel, "Non-judicial Debt Collection," 25–26, tables 3 and 4.

19. These percentages come from our calculations using the Federal Judicial Center's (FJC) Integrated Bankruptcy Petition Database. The database contains every case filed in the US bankruptcy courts and is publicly available on the FJC's website at www.fjc.gov/research/idb.

20. Consumer Financial Protection Bureau, "Fair Debt Collection Practices Act," 20, 22.

21. We ask on a four-point scale whether respondents "very much" or "somewhat" disagree or agree whether these items contributed to their bankruptcy. Unless otherwise noted, we combine "very much" and "somewhat" agree and "very much" and "somewhat" disagree responses.

22. Mann and Porter, "Saving Up for Bankruptcy," 306; and Thorne and Anderson, "Managing Stigma of Personal Bankruptcy," 86.

23. Table 9.1 compares COVID-era data to the entire database. We get similar results if we compare the pre-COVID rounds only to the COVID-era data. We define the COVID era as beginning with our data collection in the second quarter (Q2) of 2020, which occurred in June, and ending at the end of 2022. The previous round of data collection began on February 20, 2020, before the primary effects of COVID had occurred in the United States. Taylor, "Timeline of Coronavirus Pandemic." The US public health emergency for COVID-19 expired on May 11, 2023. US Department of Health and Human Services, "Fact Sheet."

24. Chiappetta, "Debt Collection Cases Dominate."

25. Lawless, "Bankruptcy Filing Rate Is Lowest"; and Lawless, "Most of What You Read."

26. LaVoice and Vamossy, "Racial Disparities in Debt Collection"; and Kiel and Waldman, "Color of Debt."

## CHAPTER 10. "RESOURCED" BANKRUPTCY FILERS

1. Tabb, "Historical Evolution," 344–49.

2. Taylor, Van Voorst, and Nash, "Growing Bankruptcy Brigade."

3. In building an argument that a retributivist has no reason to oppose the forgiveness of debt in a bankruptcy discharge, Hurd and Brubaker observe that, in most cases, the bankruptcy case is merely recognizing the reality that the debt could not be paid under any reasonable possibility about the future. Hurd and Brubaker, "Retributivist Case against Debtors' Prisons."

4. For example, Mezza et al., "Student Loans and Homeownership"; Devaraj and Patel, "Student Debt"; and Gicheva, "Student Loans or Marriage?"

5. Guzman and Kollar, "Income in the United States," tables A-1, A-4a.

6. Lawless, "Striking Out on Their Own," 110.

7. Specifically, where the value of a first mortgage by itself exceeds the value of the house, most courts interpret the Bankruptcy Code to mean the bankruptcy filer can eliminate a second mortgage. For example, Pond v. Farm Specialist Realty (In re Pond), 252 F.3d 122 (2d Cir. 2001); and Boukatch v. MidFirst Bank (In re Boukatch), 533 B.R. 292 (B.A.P. 9th Cir. 2015).

8. The conclusions are not very sensitive to our chosen cutoffs. If we lower the debt cutoff to $90,000, there are twenty-eight debtors fitting the description. If we relax the debt-to-income ratio to 1.1 (from 1.0), there are twenty-three debtors fitting the description. If we raise the cutoff to $125,000, there are only four debtors fitting the description.

9. This comes from rule 4.4 of the American Bar Association's Model Rules of Professional Conduct, which almost every state has adopted as binding law on attorneys licensed in the state.

10. Sullivan, Warren, and Westbrook, "Consumer Bankruptcy in the United States," 235–44.

## CONCLUSION

1. The increase is based on the authors' calculations from Federal Reserve data. For household debt, we count both mortgage debt and consumer debt like credit cards and car loans.

2. US Department of Labor, "Private Pension Plan Bulletin."

3. Gramlich, "Looking Ahead to 2050."

4. Sainato, "'I Live on the Street Now'"; and "Lawless' Co-authored Study on Medical Bankruptcy."

5. Sanger-Katz and Ember, "Bernie Sanders Calls."

6. Carey, "Men Fall Behind in College Enrollment."

7. US Government Accountability Office, "Racial Disparities in Education."

8. Warren, "Unsafe at Any Rate."

9. Levey, "Medical Debt Nearly Pushed."

10. Adams and Littwin, "Understanding Coerced Debt"; and "New York Poised to Become Fourth State."

11. Park, "Pathways to Financial Security."

12. Dickerson, "Race Matters in Bankruptcy," 1726.

13. "Warren, Nadler Renew Push."

14. Foohey, "Fines, Fees, and Filing Bankruptcy."

15. Dindial, Greytak, and Tateishi, "Reckless Lawmaking."

16. Shapiro, "As Court Fees Rise"; and "Fines, Fees, and Bail."

17. Harper et al., "Debt, Incarceration, and Re-entry."

18. Foohey, Ament, and Zibel, "Changing Student Loan Dischargeability Framework."

19. We did not make this up. See In re Hall, 169 B.R. 732 (Bankr. W.D. Okla. 1994). There are many similar examples.

20. Jiménez, "Decreasing Supply to Debt Collection Litigation," 377–82.

21. Bernard, "Blacks Face Bias in Bankruptcy"; and Bernard, "'Too Little Too Late.'"

22. Warren, *Fighting Chance*, 127–31.

## METHODOLOGICAL APPENDIX

1. Lawless et al., "Did Bankruptcy Reform Fail," 387–98.

2. Lawless, "Striking Out on Their Own"; and Lawless and Warren, "Myth of Disappearing Business Bankruptcy."

3. We have experimented with different methods to increase response rates. The $50 gift card began in the third round after the compensation in the first two rounds proved too low. For two later rounds, we included a short, one-page survey with the "pre-letter" that asked only for demographic information. We told the respondent that if they returned the short version of the survey, we would follow up with the opportunity to take a longer survey for a $50 gift card. That procedure neither increased nor decreased the response rate, and we reverted to our usual strategy.

# Bibliography

AARP (American Association of Retired Persons). "How Much Social Security Will I Get?" N.d. Accessed February 3, 2025. www.aarp.org/retirement/social -security/questions-answers/how-much-social-security-will-i-get.html.

AAUW (American Association of University Women). "Deeper in Debt: 2021 Update." 2021. www.aauw.org/app/uploads/2021/05/Deeper_In_Debt _2021.pdf.

———. "Deeper in Debt: Women and Student Loans." May 2017. www.aauw.org /app/uploads/2020/03/DeeperinDebt-nsa.pdf.

———. "Fast Facts: Women of Color in Higher Ed." N.d. Accessed February 3, 2025. www.aauw.org/resources/article/fast-facts-woc-higher-ed/.

Adams, Adrienne, and Angela Littwin. "Understanding Coerced Debt." Center of Survivor Agency & Justice. N.d. Accessed February 3, 2025. https://csaj .org/wp-content/uploads/2022/10/CSAJ-CCD_Part-2_Understanding -Coerced-Debt.pdf.

Adams, Adrienne E., Angela K. Littwin, and McKenzie Javorka. "The Frequency, Nature, and Effects of Coerced Debt among a National Sample of Women Seeking Help for Intimate Partner Violence." *Violence Against Women* 26, no. 11 (2020): 1324–42.

Administration on Aging. "2021 Profile of Older Americans." Administration for Community Living. November 2022. https://acl.gov/sites/default/files/Profile %20of%20OA/2021%20Profile%20of%20OA/2021ProfileOlderAmericans _508.pdf.

American Bankruptcy Institute. *Final Report of the ABI Commission on Consumer Bankruptcy*. Alexandria, VA: American Bankruptcy Institute, 2019.

Anderson, Michael H., and Sanjiv Jaggia. "Return, Purchase, or Skip? Outcome, Duration, and Consumer Behavior in the Rent-to-Own Market." *Empirical Economics* 43 (2012): 313–34.

Ayres, Ian, and Peter Siegelman. "Race and Gender Discrimination in Bargaining for a New Car." *American Economic Review* 85, no. 3 (1995): 304–21.

Baradaran, Mehrsa. *The Color of Money: Black Banks and the Racial Wealth Gap*. Cambridge, MA: Harvard University Press, 2017.

——. *How the Other Half Banks: Exclusion, Exploitation, and the Threat to Democracy*. Cambridge, MA: Harvard University Press, 2015.

——. "Jim Crow Credit." *UC Irvine Law Review* 9, no. 4 (2019): 887–952.

Barshay, Jill. "College Completion Rates Are Up for All Americans, but Racial Gaps Persist." KQED, February 20, 2023. www.kqed.org/mindshift/61037 /college-completion-rates-are-up-for-all-americans-but-racial-gaps-persist.

Bartlett, Bruce. *The New American Economy: The Failure of Reaganomics and a New Way Forward*. New York: St. Martin's Press, 2009.

Bartlett, Robert, Adair Morse, Richard Stanton, and Nancy Wallace. "Consumer-Lending Discrimination in the FinTech Era." National Bureau of Economic Research working paper, June 2019. www.nber.org/system/files /working_papers/w25943/w25943.pdf.

Batinovic, Lucija, Marlon Howe, Samantha Sinclair, and Rickard Carlsson. "Ageism in Hiring: A Systematic Review and Meta-analysis of Age Discrimination." *Collabra: Psychology* 9, no. 1 (2023): 82194.

Been, Vicki, Ingrid Ellen, and Josiah Madar. "The High Cost of Segregation: Exploring Racial Disparities in High-Cost Lending." *Fordham Urban Law Journal* 36, no. 3 (2009): 361–93.

Bernard, Tara Siegel. "Blacks Face Bias in Bankruptcy, Study Suggests." *New York Times*, January 20, 2012. www.nytimes.com/2012/01/21/business /blacks-face-bias-in-bankruptcy-study-suggests.html.

——. "'Too Little Too Late': Bankruptcy Booms among Older Americans." *New York Times*, August 5, 2018. www.nytimes.com/2018/08/05/business /bankruptcy-older-americans.html.

Bernard, Tara Siegel, and Ron Lieber. "Your 2023 Guide to Low-Down-Payment Mortgages." *New York Times*, January 1, 2023. www.nytimes.com/2023/01/01 /your-money/low-down-payment-mortgages.html.

Bhaskaran, Suparna. "Pinklining: How Wall Street's Predatory Products Pillage Women's Wealth, Opportunities, and Futures." June 2016. https://d3n8a8 pro7vhmx.cloudfront.net/acceinstitute/pages/1203/attachments/original /1578692684/acce_pinklining_VIEW.pdf.

Bleich, Sara N., Mary G. Findling, Logan S. Casey, Robert J. Blendon, John M. Benson, Gillian K. Steel Fisher, Justin M. Sayde, and Carolyn Miller.

"Discrimination in the United States: Experiences of Black Americans." *Health Services Research* 54, supp. 2 (2019): 1399–1408.

Board of Governors of the Federal Reserve System. "Changes in U.S. Family Finances from 2019 to 2022: Evidence from the Survey of Consumer Finances." October 2023. www.federalreserve.gov/publications/files/scf23.pdf.

———. "Consumer Credit—G.19." N.d. Accessed February 3, 2025. www.federalreserve.gov/releases/g19/current/.

———. "Owned Vehicles by All Families: Survey of Consumer Finances, 1989–2022." N.d. Accessed February 3, 2025. www.federalreserve.gov/econres/scf/dataviz/scf/table/#series:Owned_Vehicles.

———. "Report on the Economic Well-Being of U.S. Households in 2019, Featuring Supplemental Data from April 2020." May 2020. www.federalreserve.gov/publications/files/2019-report-economic-well-being-us-households-202005.pdf.

———. "Report on the Economic Well-Being of U.S. Households in 2022." May 2023. www.federalreserve.gov/publications/files/2022-report-economic-well-being-us-households-202305.pdf.

———. "Vehicle Installment Loans by All Families: Survey of Consumer Finances, 1989–2022." N.d. Accessed February 3, 2025. www.federalreserve.gov/econres/scf/dataviz/scf/table/#series:Vehicle_Installment_Loans.

Braucher, Jean. "Lawyers and Consumer Bankruptcy: One Code, Many Cultures." *American Bankruptcy Law Journal* 67, no. 4 (1993): 501–84.

Braucher, Jean, Dov Cohen, and Robert M. Lawless. "Race, Attorney Influence, and Bankruptcy Chapter Choice." *Journal of Empirical Legal Studies* 9, no. 3 (2012): 393–429.

Brokland, Beth, Thea Garon, Andrew Dunn, Eric Wilson, and Necati Celik. "U.S. Financial Health Pulse: 2019 Trends Report." Financial Health Network. November 13, 2019. https://finhealthnetwork.org/research/u-s-financial-health-pulse-2019-trends-report/.

Brown, Anne. "Car-Less or Car-Free? Socioeconomic and Mobility Differences among Zero-Car Households." *Transport Policy* 60 (November 2017): 152–59.

Brown, Dorothy A. *The Whiteness of Wealth: How the Tax System Impoverishes Black Americans—And How We Can Fix It.* New York: Crown, 2021.

Brown, Eleanor, and June Carbone. "Race, Property, and Citizenship." *Northwestern University Law Review Online* 116 (2021): 120–47.

Bryson, Alex, David G. Blanchflower, and Jackson Spurling. "The Wage Curve after the Great Recession." *Economica* 91, no. 362 (2024): 653–68.

Bundick, Brent, and Emily Pollard. "The Rise and Fall of College Tuition Inflation." Federal Reserve Bank of Kansas City. 2019. www.kansascityfed.org/documents/461/2019-The%20Rise%20and%20Fall%20of%20College%20Tuition%20Inflation.pdf.

Butler, Alexander W., Erik J. Mayer, and James P. Weston, "Racial Disparities in the Auto Loan Market." *Review of Financial Studies* 36, no. 1 (2023): 1–41.

Butler, Judith. "Performativity, Precarity and Sexual Politics." *Revista De Antropología Iberoamericana* 4, no. 3 (2009): i–xiii.

Caplovitz, David. *Consumers in Trouble: A Study of Debtors in Default.* New York: The Free Press, 1974.

Carbone, June, and Naomi Cahn. *Marriage Markets: How Inequality Is Remaking the American Family.* New York: Oxford University Press, 2014.

Carey, Kevin. "Men Fall Behind in College Enrollment: Women Still Play Catch-Up at Work." *New York Times,* September 9, 2021. www.nytimes.com /2021/09/09/upshot/college-admissions-men.html.

Carnevale, Anthony P., Artem Gulish, and Kathryn Peltier Campbell, "If Not Now, When? The Urgent Need for an All-One-System Approach to Youth Policy." Georgetown University McCourt School of Public Policy Center on Education and the Workforce. 2021. https://cew.georgetown.edu/wp-content /uploads/cew-all_one_system-fr.pdf.

Cha, Amy E., and Robin A. Cohen. "Reasons for Being Uninsured among Adults Aged 18–64 in the United States, 2019." US Department of Health and Human Services. September 2020. www.cdc.gov/nchs/data/databriefs/db382-H.pdf.

Chiapetta, Casey. "Debt Collection Cases Continued to Dominate Civil Dockets during Pandemic." Pew Charitable Trusts. September 18, 2023. www .pewtrusts.org/en/research-and-analysis/articles/2023/09/18/debt-collection -cases-continued-to-dominate-civil-dockets-during-pandemic.

Claxton, Gary, Matthew Rae, Emma Wager, and Gregory Young. "Employer Health Benefits: 2022 Annual Survey." Kaiser Family Foundation. October 2022. https://files.kff.org/attachment/Report-Employer-Health-Benefits -2022-Annual-Survey.pdf.

Cogan, Marin. "The Impossible Paradox of Car Ownership." *Vox,* July 5, 2023. www.vox.com/23753949/cars-cost-ownership-economy-repossession.

Cohen, Dov, Robert M. Lawless, and Faith Shin. "The Opposite of Correct: Inverted Insider Perceptions of Race and Bankruptcy." *American Bankruptcy Law Journal* 91, no. 4 (2017): 623–56.

Cohen, Mark A. "Imperfect Competition in Auto Lending: Subjective Markup, Racial Disparity, and Class Action Litigation." *Review of Law and Economics* 8, no. 1 (2012): 21–58.

Cohen, Robin A., and Amy E. Cha. "Health Insurance Coverage: Early Release of Estimates From the National Health Interview Survey, 2022." US Department of Health and Human Services. May 2023. www.cdc.gov/nchs/data /nhis/earlyrelease/insur202305_1.pdf.

College Board, "Trends in College Pricing and Student Aid, 2023." November 2023. https://research.collegeboard.org/media/pdf/Trends%20Report %202023%20Updated.pdf.

Collins, Cyleste C., and Kristen. A. Berg. "Losing a Little Part of Yourself: Families' Experiences with Foreclosure." *Journal of Family Issues* 40, no. 13 (2019): 1832–59.

Collins, Sara R., Lauren A. Haynes, and Relebohile Masitha. "The State of U.S. Health Insurance in 2022." The Commonwealth Fund. September 29, 2022. www.commonwealthfund.org/publications/issue-briefs/2022/sep/state-us -health-insurance-2022-biennial-survey.

Committee on the Consequences of Uninsurance. *Health Insurance Is a Family Matter.* Washington, DC: The National Academies Press, 2002.

Congressional Research Service. "The Debt Collection Market and Selected Policy Issues." June 22, 2021. https://fas.org/sgp/crs/misc/R46477.pdf.

Consumer Bankruptcy Project. "Welcome to the Consumer Bankruptcy Project." N.d. Accessed February 3, 2025. http://consumerbankruptcyproject.org/.

Consumer Financial Protection Bureau. "CFPB Orders Wells Fargo to Pay $3.7 Billion for Widespread Mismanagement of Auto Loans, Mortgages, and Deposit Accounts." December 20, 2022. www.consumerfinance.gov/about-us /newsroom/cfpb-orders-wells-fargo-to-pay-37-billion-for-widespread -mismanagement-of-auto-loans-mortgages-and-deposit-accounts/.

———. "The Consumer Credit Card Market Report." September 2021. https:// files.consumerfinance.gov/f/documents/cfpb_consumer-credit-card-market -report_2021.pdf.

———. "Consumer Experiences with Debt Collection: Findings from the CFPB's Survey of Consumer Views on Debt." January 2017. https://files.consumer finance.gov/f/documents/201701_cfpb_Debt-Collection-Survey-Report.pdf.

———. "Fair Debt Collection Practices Act, CFPB 2023 Annual Report." November 2023. https://files.consumerfinance.gov/f/documents/cfpb_fdcpa-annual -report_2023-11.pdf.

———. "Market Snapshot: An Update on Third-Party Debt Collections Tradeline Reporting." February 2023. https://files.consumerfinance.gov/f/documents /cfpb_market-snapshot-third-party-debt-collections-tradelines-reporting _2023-02.pdf.

———. "Market Snapshot: Online Debt Sales." January 2017. https://files .consumerfinance.gov/f/documents/201701_cfpb_Online-Debt-Sales -Report.pdf.

———. "Market Snapshot: Third-Party Debt Collections Tradeline Reporting." July 2019. https://files.consumerfinance.gov/f/documents/201907_cfpb_third -party-debt-collections_report.pdf.

———. "Medical Debt." April 2022. https://files.consumerfinance.gov/f/images /cfpb_medical-debt_infographic_2022-04.original.jpg.

———. "Single-Payment Vehicle Title Lending." May 2016. http://files .consumerfinance.gov/f/documents/201605_cfpb_single-payment-vehicle -title-lending.pdf.

———. "What Are the Costs and Fees for a Payday Loan?" Last modified August 28, 2020. www.consumerfinance.gov/ask-cfpb/what-are-the-costs -and-fees-for-a-payday-loan-en-1589/.

Crimmins, Eileen M. "Lifespan and Healthspan: Past, Present, and Promise." *Gerontologist* 55, no. 6 (2015): 901–11.

Crystal, Stephen. *America's Old Age Crisis: Public Policy and The Two Worlds of Aging.* New York: Basic Books, 1982.

Crystal, Stephen, Dennis G. Shea, and Adriana M. Reyes. "Cumulative Advantage, Cumulative Disadvantage, and Evolving Patterns of Late-Life Inequality." *Gerontologist* 57, no. 5 (2017): 910–20.

Culhane, John L., Jr., and Elanor A. Mulhern. "Justice Department Announces New Guidance for Handling Bankruptcy Discharge of Federal Student Loans." Consumer Finance Monitor. December 1, 2022. www.consumer financemonitor.com/2022/12/01/justice-department-announces-new -guidance-for-handling-bankruptcy-discharge-of-federal-student-loans/.

Culhane, Marianne B., and Michaela M. White. "Taking the New Consumer Bankruptcy Model for a Test Drive: Means-Testing Real Chapter 7 Debtors." *American Bankruptcy Institute Law Review* 7, no. 1 (1999): 27–78.

Curtin, Sally C., and Paul D. Sutton. "Marriage Rates in the United States, 1900–2018." National Center for Health Statistics. April 2020. www.cdc.gov /nchs/data/hestat/marriage_rate_2018/marriage_rate_2018.pdf.

Daly, Mary C., Bart Hobijn, and Joseph H. Pedtke. "Disappointing Facts about the Black-White Wage Gap." *FRBSF Economic Letter,* September 5, 2017. www.frbsf.org/economic-research/wp-content/uploads/sites/4/el2017-26.pdf.

Dawsey, Amanda E., Richard M. Hynes, and Lawrence M. Ausubel. "Non-Judicial Debt Collection and the Consumer's Choice among Repayment, Bankruptcy and Informal Bankruptcy." *American Bankruptcy Law Journal* 87, no. 1 (2013): 1–26.

DeFusco, Anthony A., Brandon M. Enriquez, and Margaret B. Yellen. "Wage Garnishment in the United States: New Facts from Administrative Payroll Records." National Bureau of Economic Research. February 2023. www.nber .org/papers/w30724.

DePillis, Lydia. "How the Costs of Car Ownership Add Up." *New York Times,* October 6, 2023. www.nytimes.com/interactive/2023/10/07/business/car -ownership-costs.html.

Derenoncourt, Ellora, Chi Hyun Kim, Moritz Kuhn, and Moritz Schularick. "Wealth of Two Nations: The U.S. Racial Wealth Gap, 1860–2020." *Quarterly Journal of Economics* 139, no. 2 (2024): 693–750.

Desmond, Matthew. *Poverty, by America.* New York: Crown, 2023.

Devaraj, Srikant, and Pankaj C. Patel. "Student Debt, Income-Based Repayment, and Self-Employment: Evidence from NLSY 1997 and NFCS 2015." *Applied Economics* 52, no. 35 (2020): 3809–29.

Dickerson, A. Mechele. "The 'Ideal Debtor' and the 'Traditional' American Household." *Emory Bankruptcy Developments Journal* 38, no. 2 (2022): 185–224.

———. "The Myth of Home Ownership and Why Home Ownership Is Not Always a Good Thing." *Indiana Law Journal* 84, no. 1 (2009): 189–237.

———. "Race Matters in Bankruptcy." *Washington and Lee Law Review* 61 no. 4 (2004): 1725–76.

———. "Racial Steering in Bankruptcy." *American Bankruptcy Institute Law Review* 20, no. 2 (2012): 623–50.

———. "Systemic Racism and Housing." *Emory Law Journal* 70, no. 7 (2021): 1535–76.

Dickerson, Mechele. *Homeownership and the Financial Underclass: Flawed Premises, Broken Promises, New Prescriptions.* New York: Cambridge University Press, 2014.

Dietz, Robert D., and Donald R. Haurin. "The Social and Private Micro-level Consequences of Homeownership." *Journal of Urban Economics* 54, no. 3 (2003): 401–50.

Dindial, Emily, Emily Greytak, and Kana Tateishi. "Reckless Lawmaking: How Debt-Based Driver's License Suspension Laws Impose Harm and Waste Resources." American Civil Liberties Union. 2021. www.aclu.org/wp-content /uploads/publications/reckless_lawmaking_aclu_final_4.19.21.pdf.

Dunn, Lucia F., and Ida A. Mirzaie. "Consumer Debt Stress, Changes in Household Debt, and the Great Recession." *Economic Inquiry* 54, no. 1 (2016): 201–14.

Dunn, Ronnie A. "Measuring Racial Disparities in Traffic Ticketing within Large Urban Jurisdictions." *Public Performance & Management Review* 32, no. 4 (June 2009): 537–61.

Dwyer, Rachel E., and Lora A. Phillips Lassus. "The Great Risk Shift and Precarity in the U.S. Housing Market." *Annals of the American Academy of Political and Social Science* 660, no. 1 (2015): 199–216.

Dynan, Karen, Douglas Elmendorf, and Daniel Sichel. "The Evolution of Household Income Volatility." *B.E. Journal of Economic Analysis & Policy* 12, no. 2 (2012). https://doi.org/10.1515/1935-1682.3347.

Eddy, Kamryn T., Nassim Tabri, Jennifer J. Thomas, Helen B. Murray, Aparna Keshaviah, Elizabeth Hastings, Katherine Edkins, et al. "Recovery from Anorexia Nervosa and Bulimia Nervosa at 22-Year Follow-Up." *Journal of Clinical Psychiatry* 78, no. 2 (2017): 184–89.

Egan, John. "Are More Drivers Financing New or Used Cars?" Experian. October 29, 2020. www.experian.com/blogs/ask-experian/new-vs-used-auto -loans-what-are-drivers-financing-more/.

Ehrenreich, Barbara. *Fear of Falling: The Inner Life of the Middle Class.* New York: Pantheon Books, 1989.

Eisenberg-Guyot, Jerzy, Caislin Firth, Marieka Klawitter, and Anjum Hajat. "From Payday Loans to Pawnshops: Fringe Banking, The Unbanked, and Health." *Health Affairs* 37, no. 3 (2018): 429–37.

Ellis, Charles D., Alicia H. Munnell, and Andrew D. Eschtruth, *Falling Short: The Coming Retirement Crisis and What to Do about It*. New York: Oxford University Press, 2014.

Enright, Mike. "What Is COBRA? What Employers Need to Know." Wolters Kluwer. September 14, 2020. www.wolterskluwer.com/en/expert-insights /what-is-cobra-what-employers-need-to-know.

Ericson, Keith M. Marzilli, and Andreas Fuster. "The Endowment Effect." *Annual Review of Economics* 6, no. 1 (2014): 555–79.

Federal Family Education Loan Program. 20 U.S.C. § 1071 (2005).

Federal Reserve Bank of New York. "Quarterly Report on Household Debt and Credit 2023: Q2." August 2023. www.newyorkfed.org/medialibrary /interactives/householdcredit/data/pdf/HHDC_2023Q2.

Federal Reserve Bank of St. Louis. "Homeownership Rate in the United States." N.d. Accessed February 3, 2025. https://fred.stlouisfed.org/series/RHOR USQ156N.

———. "Median Sales Price for New Houses Sold in the United States." N.d. Accessed January 23, 2025. https://fred.stlouisfed.org/series/MSPNHSUS.

Federal Trade Commission. "Structure and Practices of the Debt Buying Industry." January 2013. www.ftc.gov/sites/default/files/documents/reports /structure-and-practices-debt-buying-industry/debtbuyingreport.pdf.

Feiveson, Laura. "Labor Unions and the U.S. Economy." U.S. Department of the Treasury. August 23, 2023. https://home.treasury.gov/news/featured-stories /labor-unions-and-the-us-economy.

Feldman, Daniel C. "The Nature, Antecedents and Consequences of Under-employment." *Journal of Management* 22, no. 3 (1996): 385–407.

Felstiner, William L. F., Richard Abel, and Austin Sarat. "The Emergence and Transformation of Disputes: Naming, Blaming, Claiming. . . ." *Law and Society Review* 15, nos. 3/4 (1980–1981): 631–654.

Fidelity. "How Much Will You Spend In Retirement?" N.d. Accessed February 3, 2025. www.fidelity.com/viewpoints/retirement/spending-in-retirement.

———. "How to Plan for Rising Health Care Costs." N.d. Accessed February 3, 2025. www.fidelity.com/viewpoints/personal-finance/plan-for-rising-health -care-costs.

"Fines, Fees, and Bail: Payments in the Criminal Justice System that Dispro-portionately Impact the Poor." *Council of Economic Advisers Issue Brief,* December 2015. https://obamawhitehouse.archives.gov/sites/default/files /page/files/1215_cea_fine_fee_bail_issue_brief.pdf.

Foohey, Pamela. "Bursting the Auto Loan Bubble in the Wake of COVID-19." *Iowa Law Review* 106, no. 5 (2021): 2215–39.

———. "Fines, Fees, and Filing Bankruptcy." *North Carolina Law Review* 98, no. 2 (2020): 419–26.

Foohey, Pamela, Aaron S. Ament, and Daniel A. Zibel. "Changing the Student Loan Dischargeability Framework: How the Department of Education Can Ease the Path for Borrowers in Bankruptcy." *Minnesota Law Review Headnotes* 106, no. 1 (2021): 1–17.

Foohey, Pamela, Robert M. Lawless, Katherine Porter, and Deborah Thorne. "Life in the Sweatbox." *Notre Dame Law Review* 94, no. 1 (2018): 219–61.

———. "'No Money Down' Bankruptcy." *Southern California Law Review* 90, no. 5 (2017): 1055–1110.

Foohey, Pamela, Robert M. Lawless, and Deborah Thorne. "Driven to Bankruptcy." *Wake Forest Law Review* 55, no. 2 (2020): 287–331.

———. "Portraits of Bankruptcy Filers." *Georgia Law Review* 56, no. 2 (2022): 573–650.

Foohey, Pamela, and Nathalie Martin. "Fintech's Role in Exacerbating or Reducing the Wealth Gap." *University of Illinois Law Review* 2021, no. 2 (2021): 459–506.

Freeman, Andrea. "Racism in the Credit Card Industry." *North Carolina Law Review* 95, no. 4 (2017): 1071–1160.

Ganong, Peter, Damon Jones, Pascal J. Noel, Fiona E. Greig, Diana Farrell, and Chris Wheat. "Wealth, Race, and Consumption Smoothing of Typical Income Shocks." National Bureau of Economic Research working paper 27552, June 2023. www.nber.org/system/files/working_papers/w27552/w27552.pdf.

García, José A. "Borrowing to Make Ends Meet: The Rapid Growth of Credit Card Debt in America." Demos. 2007. www.demos.org/sites/default/files/publications/Demos_BorrowingEndsMeet.pdf.

Geck, Donna Dunkelberger. "Equal Credit: You Can Get There from Here—The Equal Credit Opportunity Act." *North Dakota Law Review* 52, no. 2 (1975): 381–410.

Gicheva, Dora. "Student Loans or Marriage? A Look at the Highly Educated." *Economics of Education Review* 53 (2016): 207–16.

Gillespie, Lane. "Bankrate's 2024 Annual Emergency Savings Report." Bankrate. June 20, 2024. www.bankrate.com/banking/savings/emergency-savings-report/.

Golden, Lonnie. "Still Falling Short on Hours and Pay: Part-Time Work Becoming New Normal." Economic Policy Institute. December 5, 2016. https://files.epi.org/pdf/114028.pdf.

Golden, Lonnie, and Jaeseung Kim. "The Rise and Fall of Underemployment: Implications for Workers' Health." *Health Affairs*, July 13, 2023. www.healthaffairs.org/do/10.1377/hpb20230602.799370/.

———. "Underemployment Just Isn't Working for U.S. Part-Time Workers." Center for Law and Social Policy. May 2020. www.clasp.org/wp-content

/uploads/2022/01/Underemployment-Just-Isnt-Working-for-U.S.-Part-Time
-Workers_fin.pdf.

Goodman, Laurie, and Jun Zhu. "Three Challenges Facing Single Female
Borrowers Entering the Mortgage Market." Urban Institute. March 30, 2022.
www.urban.org/urban-wire/three-challenges-facing-single-female-borrowers
-entering-mortgage-market.

Goodman, Laurie, Jun Zhu, and Bing Bai. "Women Are Better than Men at
Paying Their Mortgages." Urban Institute. September 2016. www.urban.org
/sites/default/files/publication/84206/2000930-Women-Are-Better-Than
-Men-At-Paying-Their-Mortgages.pdf.

Gould, Elise, and Valerie Wilson. "Black Workers Face Two of the Most Lethal
Preexisting Conditions for Coronavirus—Racism and Economic Inequality."
Economic Policy Institute. June 1, 2020. www.epi.org/publication/black
-workers-covid/.

Gramlich, John. "Looking Ahead to 2050, Americans Are Pessimistic about
Many Aspects of Life in U.S." Pew Research Center. March 21, 2019.
www.pewresearch.org/short-reads/2019/03/21/looking-ahead-to-2050
-americans-are-pessimistic-about-many-aspects-of-life-in-u-s/.

Gravier, Elizabeth. "Here's How Much Money You Should Have Saved at Every
Age." *CNBC*, August 9, 2023. www.cnbc.com/select/savings-by-age/.

Greene, Sara S., Parina Patel, and Katherine Porter. "Cracking the Code: An
Empirical Analysis of Consumer Bankruptcy Outcomes." *Minnesota Law
Review* 101, no. 3 (2017): 1031–98.

Guzman, Gloria, and Melissa Kollar, "Income in the United States: 2023."
United States Census Bureau. September 2024. www2.census.gov/library
/publications/2024/demo/p60-282.pdf.

Hacker, Jacob S. *The Great Risk Shift: The New Economic Insecurity and the
Decline of the American Dream.* New York: Oxford University Press, 2006.

Hannaford-Agor, Paula, and Nicole L. Waters. "Estimating the Cost of Civil
Litigation." *National Center for State Courts* 20, no. 1 (January 2013): 1–7.

Harden, John D. "D.C. Parking, Traffic Tickets Snowball into Financial Hardships." *Washington Post*, August 6, 2021. www.washingtonpost.com/dc-md
-va/2021/08/06/dc-traffic-parking-tickets-black-neighborhoods/.

Harper, Annie, et al. "Debt, Incarceration, and Re-entry: A Scoping Review."
*American Journal of Criminal Justice* 46, no. 2 (2021): 250–78.

Harris, Alexes, and Tyler Smith. "Monetary Sanctions as Chronic and Acute
Health Stressors: The Emotional Strain of People Who Owe Court Fines and
Fees." *Russell Sage Foundation Journal of the Social Sciences* 8, no. 2 (2022):
36–56.

Harvard Health. "Type 2 Diabetes Mellitus." Last modified May 7, 2024. www
.health.harvard.edu/diseases-and-conditions/type-2-diabetes-mellitus-a-to-z.

Hasday, Jill Elaine. *Intimate Lies and the Law.* New York: Oxford University
Press, 2019.

Hawkins, Jim, and Tiffany C. Penner. "Advertising Injustices: Marketing Race and Credit in America." *Emory Law Journal*, 70, no. 7 (2021): 1619–58.

Heaton, Lisa J., Adrianna C. Sonnek, Kelly Schroeder, and Eric P. Tranby. "Americans Are Still Not Getting the Dental Care They Need." CareQuest: Institute for Oral Health. April 2022. www.carequest.org/system/files/CareQuest_Institute_Americans-Are-Still-Not-Getting-Dental-Care-They-Need_3.pdf.

Hemez, Paul, and Chanell Washington. "Percentage and Number of Children Living with Two Parents Has Dropped since 1968." United States Census Bureau. April 12, 2021. www.census.gov/library/stories/2021/04/number-of-children-living-only-with-their-mothers-has-doubled-in-past-50-years.html.

Hernandez, Joe. "Debt Collectors Can Now Text, Email and DM You on Social Media." *NPR*, December 2, 2021. www.npr.org/2021/12/02/1060597759/debt-collectors-can-now-text-email-and-dm-you-on-social-media.

Hess, Abigail Johnson. "CNBC Survey: 81% of Adults with Student Loans Say They've Had to Delay Key Life Milestones." *CNBC*, January 28, 2022. www.cnbc.com/2022/01/28/81percent-of-adults-with-student-loans-say-they-delay-key-life-milestones.html.

Higher Education Reconciliation Act of 2005. Pub. L. No. 109-71, 120 Stat. 4, 158–60 (2005).

Highsmith, Brian, and Margot Saunders. "The Rent-to-Own Racket: Using Criminal Courts to Coerce Payments from Vulnerable Families." National Consumer Law Center. February 2019. www.nclc.org/wp-content/uploads/2022/09/report-rent-to-own-racket.pdf.

Himmelstein, David U., Deborah Thorne, Elizabeth Warren, and Steffie Woolhandler. "Medical Bankruptcy in the United States, 2007: Results of a National Study." *American Journal of Medicine* 122, no. 8 (August 2009): 741–46.

Himmelstein, David U., Elizabeth Warren, Deborah Thorne, and Steffie Woolhandler. "Illness and Injury as Contributors to Bankruptcy." *Health Affairs* 24, supp. 1 (2005): W5-63–W5-73.

Holland, Peter A. "Junk Justice: A Statistical Analysis of 4,400 Lawsuits Filed by Debt Buyers." *Loyola Consumer Law Review* 26, no. 2 (2014): 179–246.

Houle, Jason N., and Fenaba R. Addo. "Racial Disparities in Student Debt and the Reproduction of the Fragile Black Middle Class." *Sociology of Race and Ethnicity* 5 no. 4 (2019): 562–77.

Howden, Lindsay M., and Julie A. Meyer. "Age and Sex Composition: 2010." United States Census Bureau. May 2011. www.census.gov/content/dam/Census/library/publications/2011/dec/c2010br-03.pdf.

Howell, Junia, and Elizabeth Korver-Glenn. "The Increasing Effect of Neighborhood Racial Composition on Housing Values, 1980–2015." *Social Problems* 68, no. 4 (2021): 1051–71.

Humana. "Cost of Common Dental Procedures." N.d. Accessed February 3, 2025. www.humana.com/dental-insurance/dental-resources/cost-of-dental-procedures.

Hurd, Heidi, and Ralph Brubaker. "The Retributivist Case against Debtors' Prisons." In *Herbert Morris: UCLA Professor of Law and Philosophy*, edited by George Fletcher, 78–111. N.p.: Mazo Publishers, 2024.

Iacurci, Greg. "Debt among Oldest Americans Skyrockets 543% in Two Decades." *CNBC*, February 26, 2020. www.cnbc.com/2020/02/26/debt-among-older -americans-increases-dramatically-in-past-two-decades.html.

Immerwahr, John, and Tony Foleno, "Great Expectations: How the Public and Parents—White, African American, and Hispanic—View Higher Education." Public Agenda. May 2000. https://files.eric.ed.gov/fulltext/ED444405.pdf.

Internal Revenue Service. "Hardships, Early Withdrawals and Loans." April 1, 2024. www.irs.gov/retirement-plans/hardships-early-withdrawals-and-loans.

Iuliano, Jason. "The Student Loan Bankruptcy Gap." *Duke Law Journal* 70, no. 3 (2020): 497–543.

Jacoby, Melissa B. "Superdelegation and Gatekeeping in Bankruptcy Courts." *Temple Law Review* 87, no. 4 (2015): 875–94.

Jacoby, Melissa B., and Mirya Holman, "Managing Medical Bills on the Brink of Bankruptcy." *Yale Journal of Healthy Policy, Law, and Ethics* 10, no. 2 (2010): 239–97.

Jefferson, Anna. "Narratives of Moral Order in Michigan's Foreclosure Crisis." *City & Society* 25, no. 1 (2013): 92–112.

Jeszeck, Charles A. "Retirement Security: Most Households Approaching Retirement Have Low Savings, an Update." US Government Accountability Office. March 29, 2019. www.gao.gov/assets/gao-19-442r.pdf.

Jiménez, Alfredo, Carmen Palmero-Cámara, María Josefa González-Santos, Jerónimo González-Bernal, and Juan Alfredo Jiménez-Eguizábal. "The Impact of Educational Levels on Formal and Informal Entrepreneurship." *Business Research Quarterly* 18, no. 3 (2015): 204–12.

Jiménez, Dalié. "Decreasing Supply to the Assembly Line of Debt Collection Litigation." *Harvard Law Review Forum* 135, no. 7 (2022): 374–90.

———. "Dirty Debts Sold Dirt Cheap." *Harvard Journal on Legislation* 52, no. 2 (2015): 41–124.

———. "The Distribution of Assets in Consumer Chapter 7 Bankruptcy Cases." *American Bankruptcy Law Journal* 83, no. 4 (2009): 795–822.

Jiménez, Dalié, and Jonathan Glater. "Student Debt Is a Civil Rights Issue: The Case for Debt Relief and Higher Education Reform." *Harvard Civil Rights-Civil Liberties Law Review* 55, no. 1 (2020): 131–98.

Johnson, Creola. "The Magic of Groups Identity: How Predatory Lenders Use Minorities to Target Communities of Color." *Georgetown Journal on Poverty Law and Policy* 17, no. 2 (2010): 165–220.

Kamin, Debra. "More than 1 in 4 American Homeowners Is 'House Poor.'" *New York Times*, May 30, 2023. www.nytimes.com/2023/05/30/realestate /homeowners-house-poor-affordability.html.

Kasmir, Sharryn. "Precarity." In *The Open Encyclopedia of Anthropology*, edited by Felix Stein. (2018) 2023. Facsimile of the first edition in *The Cambridge Encyclopedia of Anthropology*. http://doi.org/10.29164/18precarity.

Keisler-Starkey, Katherine, and Lisa N. Bunch. "Health Insurance Coverage in the United States: 2021." United States Census Bureau. September 2022. www.census.gov/content/dam/Census/library/publications/2022/demo/p60-278.pdf.

Kiel, Paul. "So Sue Them: What We've Learned about the Debt Collection Lawsuit Machine." *ProPublica*, May 5, 2016. www.propublica.org/article/so-sue-them-what-weve-learned-about-the-debt-collection-lawsuit-machine.

Kiel, Paul, and Hannah Fresques. "Data Analysis: Bankruptcy and Race in America." *ProPublica*, September 27, 2017. https://projects.propublica.org/graphics/bankruptcy-data-analysis.

Kiel, Paul, and Annie Waldman. "The Color of Debt: How Collection Suits Squeeze Black Neighborhoods." *ProPublica*, October 8, 2015. www.propublica.org/article/debt-collection-lawsuits-squeeze-black-neighborhoods.

Kim, Jean. "How America Fell into Toxic Individualism." *Psychology Today*, May 25, 2020. www.psychologytoday.com/us/blog/culture-shrink/202005/how-america-fell-toxic-individualism.

King, David A., Michael J. Smart, and Michael Manville. "The Poverty of the Carless: Toward Universal Auto Access." *Journal of Planning Education and Research* 42, no. 3 (2022): 464–81.

Kingsley, G. Thomas, Robin Smith, and David Price. "The Impacts of Foreclosures on Families and Communities." The Urban Institute. May 2009. www.urban.org/sites/default/files/publication/30426/411909-The-Impacts-of-Foreclosures-on-Families-and-Communities.PDF.

Kivimaki, Mika, Markus Jokela, Solja T. Nyberg, Archana Singh-Manoux, Eleonor I. Fransson, Lars Alfredsson, Jakob B. Bjorner, et al. "Long Working Hours and Risk of Coronary Heart Disease and Stroke: A Systematic Review and Meta-Analysis of Published and Unpublished Data for 603,838 Individuals." *The Lancet* 386 (2015): 1739–46.

Kochhar, Rakesh. "The Financial Risk to U.S. Business Owners Posed by COVID-19 Outbreak Varies by Demographic Group." Pew Research Center. April 23, 2020. www.pewresearch.org/short-reads/2020/04/23/the-financial-risk-to-u-s-business-owners-posed-by-covid-19-outbreak-varies-by-demographic-group/.

Kochhar, Rakesh, Richard Fry, and Paul Taylor. "Wealth Gaps Rise to Record Highs between Whites, Blacks and Hispanics." Pew Research Center. July 26, 2011. www.pewresearch.org/wp-content/uploads/sites/3/2011/07/sdt-wealth-report_7-26-11_final.pdf.

Kolomatsky, Michael. "Most Unmarried Homeowners Are Women." *New York Times*, September 28, 2017. www.nytimes.com/2017/09/28/realestate/most-unmarried-homeowners-are-women.html.

Komlos, John. "Reaganomics: A Watershed Moment on the Road to Trumpism." *Economists' Voice* 16, no. 1 (2019). https://doi.org/10.1515/ev-2018-0032.

Krishner, Tom. "Why Experts Say Now Is a Good Time to Buy a Used Car before Prices Surge." *PBS News Hour*, March 30, 2023. pbs.org/newshour/economy /why-experts-say-now-is-a-good-time-to-buy-a-used-car-before-prices-surge.

Kulshreshtha, Ambar, Alvaro Alonso, Leslie A. McClure, Ihab Hajjar, Jennifer J. Manly, and Suzanne Judd. "Association of Stress with Cognitive Function among Older Black and White US Adults." *JAMA Network Open* 6, no. 3 (2023). https://doi.org/10.1001/jamanetworkopen.2023.1860.

Lautz, Jessica. "Single Women Buyers Outpace Men, but Not without Sacrifices." National Association of Realtors. December 8, 2021. www.nar.realtor /blogs/economists-outlook/single-women-buyers-outpace-men-but-not -without-sacrifices.

LaVoice, Jessica, and Domonkos F. Vamossy. "Racial Disparities in Debt Collection." *Journal of Banking & Finance* 164, no. C (2024). https://doi.org /10.1016/j.jbankfin.2024.107208.

Law, Tara. "Women Are Now the Majority of the U.S. Workforce—But Working Women Still Face Serious Challenges." *Time*, January 16, 2020. https://time .com/5766787/women-workforce/.

Lawless, Bob. "Bankruptcy Filing Rate Is Lowest since Bankruptcy Code's Enactment—The Question Is Why." *Credit Slips*, December 27, 2020. www.creditslips.org/creditslips/2021/12/bankruptcy-filing-rate-is-lowest -since-bankruptcy-codes-enactment-the-question-is-why-.html.

———. "How Many People Have Filed Bankruptcy?" *Credit Slips*, June 22, 2020. www.creditslips.org/creditslips/2020/06/how-many-people-have-filed -bankruptcy.html.

———. "Most of What You Read about the Bankruptcy Filing Rate Is Wrong." *Credit Slips*, August 5, 2020. www.creditslips.org/creditslips/2020/08/most -of-what-you-read-about-the-bankruptcy-filing-rate-is-wrong.html.

———. "Revisiting How Many People Have Filed Bankruptcy." *Credit Slips*, August 22, 2024. www.creditslips.org/creditslips/2024/08/revisiting-how -many-people-have-filed-bankruptcy.html.

Lawless, Robert M. "Striking Out on Their Own: The Self-Employed in Bankruptcy." In *Broke: How Debt Bankrupts the Middle Class*, edited by Katherine Porter, 101–16. Stanford, CA: Stanford University Press, 2012.

Lawless, Robert M., Angela K. Littwin, Katherine M. Porter, John A. E. Pottow, Deborah K. Thorne, and Elizabeth Warren. "Did Bankruptcy Reform Fail? An Empirical Study of Consumer Debtors." *American Bankruptcy Law Journal* 82, no. 3 (2008): 349–405.

Lawless, Robert M., and Angela Littwin. "Local Legal Culture from R2D2 to Big Data." *Texas Law Review* 96, no. 7 (2018): 1353–76.

Lawless, Robert M., and Elizabeth Warren. "The Myth of the Disappearing Business Bankruptcy." *California Law Review* 93, no. 3 (2005): 743–95.

"Lawless' Co-authored Study on Medical Bankruptcy Referenced on John Oliver's Last Week Tonight." University of Illinois College of Law. February 19, 2020. https://blogs.illinois.edu/view/7000/806540.

Lefgren, Lars, and Frank McIntyre. "Explaining the Puzzle of Cross-State Differences in Bankruptcy Rates." *Journal of Law and Economics* 52, no. 2 (2009): 367–93.

Leukhina, Oksana, and Amy Smaldone. "Why Do Women Outnumber Men in College Enrollment?" Federal Reserve Bank of St. Louis. March 15, 2022. www.stlouisfed.org/on-the-economy/2022/mar/why-women-outnumber -men-college-enrollment.

Levey, Noam. "Medical Debt Nearly Pushed This Family into Homelessness: Millions More Are at Risk." *NPR*, September 11, 2023. www.npr.org/sections /health-shots/2023/09/11/1198534328/medical-debt-housing-security -homelessness.

Levitin, Adam. *Consumer Finance: Market and Regulation.* 2nd ed. New York: Aspen Publishing, 2023.

Li, Zhe. "Household Debt among Older Americans, 1989–2016." Congressional Research Service. September 11, 2019. https://sgp.fas.org/crs/misc/R45911.pdf.

Lloyd, Camille. "The Black American Experience: Here Is What We Have Learned." *Gallup Blog*, July 27, 2021. https://news.gallup.com/opinion/gallup /352763/black-american-experience-what-we-have-learned.aspx.

Long, Heather. "Many Left Behind in This Recovery Have Something in Common: No College Degree." *Washington Post*, April 22, 2021. www.washington post.com/business/2021/04/22/jobs-no-college-degree/.

Lopes, Lunna, Audrey Kearney, Alex Montero, Liz Hamel, and Mollyann Brodie. "Health Care Debt in the U.S.: The Broad Consequences of Medical and Dental Bills." Kaiser Family Foundation. June 16, 2022. www.kff.org /report-section/kff-health-care-debt-survey-main-findings/.

Lopes, Lunna, Alex Montero, Marley Presiado, and Liz Hamel. "Americans' Challenges with Health Care Costs." Kaiser Family Foundation. Last modified March 1, 2024. www.kff.org/health-costs/issue-brief/americans -challenges-with-health-care-costs/.

Lopez, Mark Hugo, Lee Rainie, and Abby Budiman, "Financial and Health Impacts of COVID-19 Vary Widely by Race and Ethnicity." Pew Research Center. May 5, 2020. www.pewresearch.org/fact-tank/2020/05/05/financial -and-health-impacts-of-covid-19-vary-widely-by-race-and-ethnicity/.

Lowrey, Annie. "The Underemployment Crisis." *The Atlantic*, August 6, 2020. www.theatlantic.com/ideas/archive/2020/08/underemployment-crisis/614989/.

Lu, Timothy (Jun), Olivia S. Mitchell, Stephen P. Utkus, and Jean A. Young. "Borrowing from the Future? 401(k) Plan Loans and Loan Defaults." *National Tax Journal* 70, no. 1 (2017): 77–110.

Machin, Stephen. "Houses and Schools: Valuation of School Quality through the Housing Market." *Labour Economics* 18, no. 6 (2011): 723–29.

Mann, Ronald J., and Katherine Porter. "Saving Up for Bankruptcy." *George-town Law Journal* 98, no. 2 (2010): 289–340.

Martin, Nathalie, and Ozymandias Adams. "Grand Theft Auto Loans: Repossession and Demographic Realities in Title Lending." *Missouri Law Review* 77, no. 1 (2012): 41–94.

Martin, Patricia P., and David A. Weaver. "Social Security: A Program and Policy History." *Social Security Bulletin* 66, no. 1 (2005): 1–15.

Maté, Gabor. *The Myth of Normal: Trauma, Illness & Healing in a Toxic Culture.* New York: Penguin Random House, 2022.

Mather, Mark, and Paola Scommegna. "Fact Sheet: Aging in the United States." Population Reference Guide. Last modified January 9, 2024. www.prb.org /resources/fact-sheet-aging-in-the-united-states/.

Maye, Adewale. "The Student Loan Debt Crisis Impedes Black Women's Economic Security." The Center for Law and Social Policy. July 6, 2021. www.clasp.org/blog/student-loan-debt-crisis-impedes-black-womens -economic-security/.

Mayo Clinic. "Chronic Stress Puts Your Health at Risk." N.d. Accessed February 3, 2025. www.mayoclinic.org/healthy-lifestyle/stress-management/in -depth/stress/art-20046037.

Mazzara, Alicia. "Rents Have Risen More than Incomes in Nearly Every State since 2001." Center on Budget and Policy Priorities. December 10, 2019. www.cbpp.org/blog/rents-have-risen-more-than-incomes-in-nearly-every -state-since-2001.

McCabe, Brian J. "Are Homeowners Better Citizens? Homeownership and Community Participation in the United States." *Social Forces* 91, no. 3 (March 2013): 929–54.

Medical News Today. "What Is Chronic Stress and What Are Its Common Health Impacts?" N.d. Accessed February 3, 2025. www.medicalnewstoday .com/articles/323324.

Medicare. "Costs." N.d. Accessed February 3, 2025. www.medicare.gov/basics /costs/medicare-costs.

———. "Drug Coverage (Part D)." N.d. Accessed February 3, 2025. www.medicare .gov/drug-coverage-part-d.

Mennell, Stephen. "Power, Individualism, and Collective Self-Perception in the USA." *Historical Social Research/Historische Sozialforschung* 45, no. 1 (171) (2020): 309–29.

Mezza, Alvaro, Daniel Ringo, Shane Sherlund, and Kamilia Sommer. "Student Loans and Homeownership." *Journal of Labor Economics* 38, no. 1 (2020): 215–60.

Mezza, Alvaro, Daniel Ringo, and Kamila Sommer. "Can Student Loan Debt Explain Low Homeownership Rates for Young Adults?" *Consumer & Community Context* 1, no. 1 (January 2019): 2–7. www.federalreserve.gov /publications/files/consumer-community-context-201901.pdf.

Miller, Joel. "How to Improve Access to Mental Health and Substance Use Care for Older Adults." National Council on Aging. May 18, 2022. www.ncoa.org /article/how-to-improve-access-to-mental-health-and-substance-use-care -for-older-adults.

Mishel, Lawrence. "Causes of Wage Stagnation." Economic Policy Institute. January 6, 2015. https://files.epi.org/2013/causes_of_wage_stagnation.pdf.

Mishel, Lawrence, Elise Gould, and Josh Bivens. "Wage Stagnation in Nine Charts." Economic Policy Institute January 6, 2015. www.epi.org/publication /charting-wage-stagnation/.

Morrison, Edward R., and Antoine Uettwiller. "Consumer Bankruptcy Pathologies." *Journal of Institutional and Theoretical Economics* 173, no. 1 (2017): 174–96.

Morse, Anne. "Stable Fertility Rates 1990-2019 Mask Distinct Variations by Age." United States Census Bureau. April 6, 2022. www.census.gov/library /stories/2022/04/fertility-rates-declined-for-younger-women-increased-for -older-women.html.

Moslimani, Mohamad, Christine Tamir, Abby Budiman, Luis Noe-Bustamante, and Lauren Mora. "Facts about the U.S. Black Population." Pew Research Center. January 18, 2024. www.pewresearch.org/social-trends/fact-sheet /facts-about-the-us-black-population/.

Mullainathan, Sendhil, and Eldar Shafir. *Scarcity: Why Having Too Little Means So Much.* New York: Times Books, 2013.

National Center for Education Statistics. "Annual Earnings by Educational Attainment." N.d. Accessed February 3, 2025. https://nces.ed.gov/programs /coe/indicator/cba/annual-earnings.

National Council on Aging. "Get the Facts on Senior Debt." Last modified June 30, 2023. www.ncoa.org/article/get-the-facts-on-senior-debt.

———. "The Top 10 Most Common Chronic Conditions in Older Adults." Last modified May 30, 2024. www.ncoa.org/article/the-top-10-most-common -chronic-conditions-in-older-adults.

———. "What You'll Pay in Out-of-Pocket Medicare Costs in 2024." Last modified October 13, 2023. www.ncoa.org/article/what-you-will-pay-in-out-of-pocket -medicare-costs-in-2024.

"The National Intimate Partner and Sexual Violence Survey: 2010–2012 State Report." National Center for Injury Prevention and Control of the Centers for Disease Control and Prevention. 2017. https://stacks.cdc.gov/view/cdc/46305.

Ndugga, Nambi, Latoya Hill, and Samantha Artiga. "Key Data on Health and Health Care by Race and Ethnicity." Kaiser Family Foundation. Last modified June 14, 2024. www.kff.org/racial-equity-and-health-policy/report /key-data-on-health-and-health-care-by-race-and-ethnicity.

"New York Poised to Become Fourth State in Nation to Give Survivors of Economic Abuse Powerful New Tool to Discharge a Coerced Debt." Urban Resource Institute. May 19, 2023. https://urinyc.org/download/new-york

-poised-to-become-fourth-state-in-nation-to-give-survivors-of-economic
-abuse-powerful-new-tool-to-discharge-a-coerced-debt/.

Newman, Katherine S. *Falling from Grace: Downward Mobility in the Age of Affluence.* Berkley: University of California Press, 1988.

Noguchi, Yuki. "'I Try So Hard Not to Cry': Nearly Half of U.S. Households Face a Financial Crisis." *NPR*, September 10, 2020. www.npr.org/sections/health-shots/2020/09/10/910724801/overview-of-poll-data-on-pandemics-damage.

North Carolina Equal Access to Justice Commission. "When Debt Takes the Wheel." N.d. Accessed February 3, 2025. https://storymaps.arcgis.com/stories/8c48ba140a7a496b98fa916c08467f24.

Oddo, Vanessa M., Castiel Chen Zhuang, Sarah B. Andrea, Jerzy Eisenberg-Guyot, Trevor Peckham, Daniel Jacoby, and Anjum Hajat. "Changes in Precarious Employment in the United States: A Longitudinal Analysis." *Scandinavian Journal of Work, Environment & Health* 47, no. 3 (2021): 171–80.

Park, Michaela. "Pathways to Financial Security: A New Legal Avenue for Survivors of Coerced Debt in California." *California Law Review* 111, no. 2 (2023): 605–56.

Pennsylvania Coalition Against Domestic Violence. "Financial Abuse." N.d. Accessed February 3, 2025. www.pcadv.org/financial-abuse/.

Perry, Andre, Jonathan Rothwell, and David Harshbarger. "The Devaluation of Assets in Black Neighborhoods: The Case of Residential Property." Brookings Institution. November 27, 2018. www.brookings.edu/articles/devaluation-of-assets-in-black-neighborhoods/.

Peter G. Peterson Foundation. "How Does the U.S. Healthcare System Compare to Other Countries?" July 12, 2023. www.pgpf.org/blog/2023/07/how-does-the-us-healthcare-system-compare-to-other-countries.

———. "How Much Does the United States Spend on Prescription Drugs Compared to Other Countries?" November 7, 2022. www.pgpf.org/article/how-much-does-the-united-states-spend-on-prescription-drugs-compared-to-other-countries.

Pew Charitable Trusts. "How Debt Collectors Are Transforming the Business of State Courts." May 2020. www.pewtrusts.org/-/media/assets/2020/06/debt-collectors-to-consumers.pdf.

Pew Research Center. "The State of American Jobs: How the Shifting Economic Landscape Is Reshaping Work and Society and Affecting the Way People Think about the Skills and Training They Need to Get Ahead." October 2016. www.pewresearch.org/social-trends/2016/10/06/1-changes-in-the-american-workplace/.

Pinsker, Joe. "Why So Many Americans Don't Talk about Money." *The Atlantic*, March 2, 2020. www.theatlantic.com/family/archive/2020/03/americans-dont-talk-about-money-taboo/607273/.

Porter, Katherine, ed. *Broke: How Debt Bankrupts the Middle Class*. Stanford, CA: Stanford University Press, 2012.

———. "College Lessons: The Financial Risks of Dropping Out." In *Broke: How Debt Bankrupts the Middle Class*, edited by Katherine Porter, 85–100. Stanford, CA: Stanford University Press, 2012.

———. "Methodology of the 2007 Consumer Bankruptcy Project." In *Broke: How Debt Bankrupts the Middle Class*, edited by Katherine Porter, 235–44. Stanford, CA: Stanford University Press, 2012.

Porter, Katherine, and Deborah Thorne. "The Failure of Bankruptcy's Fresh Start." *Cornell Law Review* 92, no. 1 (2006): 67–128.

Quadagno, Jill, Ben Lennox Kail, and K. Russell Shekha. "Welfare States: Protecting or Risking Old Age." In *Handbook of Sociology of Aging*, edited by Richard A. Settersten Jr. and Jacqueline L. Angel, 321–32. New York: Springer, 2011.

Racke, Will. "Report: Chicago Has Seized and Sold Nearly 50,000 Cars over Ticket Debt since 2011." *Newsweek*, January 7, 2019. www.newsweek.com /chicago-seize-cars-tickets-1283106.

Rakshit, Shameek, Matthew Rae, Gary Claxton, Krutika Amin, and Cynthia Cox. "The Burden of Medical Debt in the United States." Peterson Center on Healthcare. Last modified February 14, 2024. www.healthsystemtracker.org /brief/the-burden-of-medical-debt-in-the-united-states/.

Raley, R. Kelly, Megan M. Sweeney, and Danielle Wondra. "The Growing Racial and Ethnic Divide in U.S. Marriage Patterns." *Future Child* 25, no. 2 (2015). www.ncbi.nlm.nih.gov/pmc/articles/PMC4850739/.

Ramsey, Dave. "Ask Dave: There's No Magic Pill to Getting—and Staying—Out of Debt." *South Bend Tribune*, January 18, 2020. www.southbendtribune.com /story/business/2020/01/18/ask-dave-theres-no-magic-pill-to-getting-and -staying-out-of-deb/44084735/.

Raphael, Stephen, and Lorien Rice. "Car Ownership, Employment, and Earnings." *Journal of Urban Economics* 52, no. 1 (2002): 109–30.

Rodríguez, Jose, Jr. "The Majority of Car Loans Are Now Going toward Used Cars." *Japolnik*, August 25, 2022. https://jalopnik.com/the-majority-of-car -loans-are-now-going-toward-used-car-1849457134.

Rothwell, Jonathan, and Andre M. Perry. "How Racial Bias in Appraisals Affects the Devaluation of Homes in Majority-Black Neighborhoods." Brookings Institution. December 5, 2022. www.brookings.edu/articles/how-racial-bias-in -appraisals-affects-the-devaluation-of-homes-in-majority-black-neighborhoods/.

Roux, Mathilde. "5 Facts about Black Women in the Labor Force." *US Department of Labor Blog*, August 3, 2021. https://blog.dol.gov/2021/08/03/5-facts -about-black-women-in-the-labor-force.

Sainato, Michael. "'I Live on the Street Now': How Americans Fall into Medical Bankruptcy." *The Guardian*, November 14, 2019. www.theguardian.com/us -news/2019/nov/14/health-insurance-medical-bankruptcy-debt.

Sakong, Jung, and Alexander K. Zentefis. "Bank Access across America." Working paper, September 18, 2022. https://files.consumerfinance.gov/f/documents /cfpb_2022-research-conference_session-7_zentefis-sakong_paper.pdf.

Sanchez, Melissa, and Sandhya Kambhampati. "Driven into Debt: How Chicago Ticket Debt Sends Black Motorists into Bankruptcy." *ProPublica Illinois*, February 27, 2018. https://features.propublica.org/driven-into-debt/chicago -ticket-debt-bankruptcy/.

Sandefur, Rebecca L. "Access to Civil Justice and Race, Class, and Gender Inequality." *Annual Review of Sociology* 34 (2008): 339–58.

———. "The Importance of Doing Nothing: Everyday Problems and Responses of Inaction." In *Transforming Lives: Law and Social Process*, edited by Pascoe Pleasence, Alexy Buck, and Nigel J. Ballmer, 112–32. London: Legal Services Commission, 2007.

Sanders, Linley, and Kathy Frankovic. "More than One-Third of Americans Have Not Filled a Prescription Because of Its Cost." YouGov. March 10, 2023. https://today.yougov.com/health/articles/45388-americans-have-not-filled -prescription-price-poll.

Sandler, Emma. "Avon Company Sets Digital Retail Ambitions on Livestream Shopping." *Glossy*, April 29, 2021. www.glossy.co/beauty/avon-company-sets -digital-retail-ambitions-on-livestream-shopping/.

Sanger-Katz, Margot, and Sydney Ember. "Bernie Sanders Calls for Eliminating Americans' Medical Debt." *New York Times*, September 21, 2019. www.ny times.com/2019/09/21/us/politics/bernie-medical-debt-healthcare.html.

Sarra, Janis, and Cheryl L. Wade. *Predatory Lending and the Destruction of the African-American Dream*. New York: Cambridge University Press, 2020.

Schmitz, Amy J. "Females on the Fringe: Considering Gender in Payday Lending Policy." *Chicago Kent Law Review* 89, no. 1 (2014): 65–112.

Schneider, Daniel, and Kristen Harknett. "It's About Time: How Work Schedule Instability Matters for Workers, Families, and Racial Inequality." The Shift Project. October 2019. https://shift.hks.harvard.edu/files/2019/10/Its-About -Time-How-Work-Schedule-Instability-Matters-for-Workers-Families-and -Racial-Inequality.pdf.

Schoen, Cathy, Karen Davis, and Amber Willink. "Medicare Beneficiaries' High Out-of-Pocket Costs: Cost Burdens by Income and Health Status." The Commonwealth Fund. May 2017. www.commonwealthfund.org/sites/default /files/documents/___media_files_publications_issue_brief_2017_may _schoen_medicare_cost_burden_ib_v2.pdf.

Scott, Jennifer, Kathryn Edwards, and Alexandra Stanczyk. "Moonlighting to the Side Hustle: The Effect of Working an Extra Job on Household Poverty for Households with Less Formal Education." *Families in Society* 101, no. 3 (2020): 324–39.

"Segregation in America." Equal Justice Initiative. 2018. https://segregationin america.eji.org/report.pdf.

Sengupta, Somini. "Americans and Their Cars." *New York Times,* June 13, 2023. www.nytimes.com/2023/06/13/climate/car-emissions.html.

Shapiro, Joseph. "As Court Fees Rise, the Poor Are Paying the Price." *NPR,* May 19, 2014. www.npr.org/2014/05/19/312158516/increasing-court-fees -punish-the-poor.

Shill, Gregory H. "Should Law Subsidize Driving?" *New York University Law Review* 95, no. 2 (2020): 498–579.

Shinn, Lora. "How Much Does a Root Canal Cost?" GoodRx Health. May 25, 2022. www.goodrx.com/health-topic/oral/root-canal-cost.

Simon, Lisa, Zirui Song, and Michael L. Bennett. "Dental Services Use: Medicare Beneficiaries Experience Immediate and Long-Term Reductions after Enrollment." *Health Affairs* 42, no. 2 (2023): 286–95.

Social Security Administration. "Retirement Benefits." 2024. www.ssa.gov/pubs /EN-05-10035.pdf.

Sousa, Michael D. "Debt Stigma and Social Class." *Seattle University Law Review* 41, no. 3 (2018): 965–1002.

———. "Just Punch My Bankruptcy Ticket: A Qualitative Study of Mandatory Debtor Financial Education." *Marquette Law Review* 97, no. 2 (2013): 391–467.

———. "The Persistence of Bankruptcy Stigma." *American Bankruptcy Institute Law Review* 26, no. 2 (2018): 217–42.

Stanley, David T., and Marjorie Girth. *Bankruptcy: Problem, Process, Reform.* Washington, DC: The Brookings Institution, 1971.

Steil, Justin P., Len Albright, Jacob S. Rugh, and Douglas S. Massey. "The Social Structure of Mortgage Discrimination." *Housing Studies* 33, no. 5 (2017): 759–76.

Sullivan, Teresa A., Elizabeth Warren, and Jay Lawrence Westbrook. *As We Forgive Our Debtors: Bankruptcy and Consumer Credit in America.* New York: Oxford University Press, 1989.

———. "Consumer Bankruptcy in the United States: A Study of Alleged Abuse and of Local Legal Culture." *Journal of Consumer Policy* 20 (1997): 223–68.

———. *The Fragile Middle Class: Americans in Debt.* New Haven, CT: Yale University Press, 2000.

———. "The Persistence of Local Legal Culture: Twenty Years of Evidence from the Federal Bankruptcy Courts." *Harvard Journal of Law & Public Policy* 17, no. 3 (1994): 801–65.

Sweeney, Megan M., and R. Kelly Raley. "Race, Ethnicity, and the Changing Context of Childbearing in the United States." *Annual Review of Sociology* 40, no. 1 (2014): 539–58.

Tabb, Charles J. "The Historical Evolution of the Bankruptcy Discharge." *American Bankruptcy Law Journal* 65, no. 3 (1991): 325–71.

Tach, Laura M., and Sara Sternberg Greene. "'Robbing Peter to Pay Paul': Economic and Cultural Explanations for How Lower-Income Families Manage Debt." *Social Problems* 61, no. 1 (2014): 1–21.

Taylor, Alexander L., III, Bruce Van Voorst, and J. Madeline Nash. "The Growing Bankruptcy Brigade." *Time Magazine*, October 18, 1982, 104.

Taylor, Derrick Bryon. "A Timeline of the Coronavirus Pandemic." *New York Times*, March 17, 2021. www.nytimes.com/article/coronavirus-timeline.html.

Taylor, Winnie F. "The Equal Credit Opportunity Act's Spousal Co-Signature Rules: Suretyship Contracts in Separate Property States." *Albany Law Review* 48, no. 2 (1984): 382–425.

Thorne, Deborah. "Extreme Financial Strain: Emergent Chores, Gender Inequality, and Emotional Distress." *Journal of Family and Economic Issues* 31 (2010): 185–97.

———. "Personal Bankruptcy through the Eyes of the Stigmatized: Insight into Issues of Shame, Gender, and Marital Discord." PhD diss., Washington State University, 2001.

———. "Women's Work, Women's Worry? Debt Management in Financially Distressed Families." In *Broke: How Debt Bankrupts the Middle Class*, edited by Katherine Porter, 136–53. Stanford, CA: Stanford University Press, 2012.

Thorne, Deborah, and Leon Anderson. "Managing the Stigma of Personal Bankruptcy." *Sociological Focus* 39, no. 2 (2006): 77–96.

Tikkanen, Roosa, Robin Osborn, Elias Mossialos, Ana Djordjevic, and George A. Wharton. "International Healthcare System Profiles: United States." The Commonwealth Fund. June 5, 2020. www.commonwealthfund .org/international-health-policy-center/countries/united-states.

Tsai, Alexander C. "Home Foreclosure, Health, and Mental Health: A Systematic Review of Individual, Aggregate, and Contextual Associations." *PLoS One* 10, no. 4 (2015). https://doi.org/10.1371/journal.pone.0123182.

Underwood, Jenn. "What Is a Penalty APR?" *Forbes Advisor*, June 22, 2023. www.forbes.com/advisor/credit-cards/what-is-a-penalty-apr/.

United States Bureau of Labor Statistics. "Coverage in Employer Medical Care Plans among Workers in Different Wage Groups in 2022." *TED: The Economics Daily*, March 9, 2023. www.bls.gov/opub/ted/2023/coverage-in-employer -medical-care-plans-among-workers-in-different-wage-groups-in-2022.htm.

———. "Earning and Unemployment Rates by Educational Attainment, 2022." N.d. Accessed February 3, 2025. www.bls.gov/emp/chart-unemployment -earnings-education.htm.

———. "Labor Force Statistics from the Current Population Survey: Concepts and Definitions." N.d. Accessed February 3, 2025. www.bls.gov/cps /definitions.htm.

———. "2020 Annual Averages—Household Data—Tables from Employment and Earnings." N.d. Accessed February 3, 2025. www.bls.gov/cps/cps_aa2020.htm.

United States Census Bureau. "Census Bureau Releases New Educational Attainment Data." February 24, 2022. www.census.gov/newsroom/press -releases/2022/educational-attainment.html.

———. "DP04: Selected Housing Characteristics." N.d. Accessed February 3, 2025. https://data.census.gov/table/ACSDP1Y2021.DP04.

———. "Historical Living Arrangements of Children." N.d. Accessed February 3, 2025. www.census.gov/data/tables/time-series/demo/families/children.html.

———. "Quarterly Residential Vacancies and Homeownership, First Quarter 2024." April 30, 2024. www.census.gov/housing/hvs/files/currenthvspress.pdf.

———. "Quick Facts." N.d. Accessed February 3, 2025. www.census.gov/quickfacts.

———. "S0103 Population 65 Years and Over in the United States." N.d. Accessed February 3, 2025. https://data.census.gov/table/ACSST1Y2022.S0103.

———. "B20004 Median Earnings in the Past 12 Months (in 2022 Inflation-Adjusted Dollars) by Sex by Educational Attainment for the Population 25 Years and Over." N.d. Accessed January 24, 2025. https://data.census.gov/table/ACSDT5Y2022.B20004.

United States Constitution. Art. 1, sec. 8, cl. 4.

United States Courts. "Bankruptcy Filings." N.d. Accessed February 3, 2025. www.uscourts.gov/report-name/bankruptcy-filings.

United States Department of Health and Human Services. "Fact Sheet: End of the COVID-19 Public Health Emergency." May 9, 2023. www.hhs.gov/about/news/2023/05/09/fact-sheet-end-of-the-covid-19-public-health-emergency.html.

United States Department of Labor. "Private Pension Plan Bulletin Historical Tables and Graphs 1975–2021." September 2023. www.dol.gov/sites/dolgov/files/ebsa/researchers/statistics/retirement-bulletins/private-pension-plan-bulletin-historical-tables-and-graphs.pdf.

United States Government Accountability Office. "Racial Disparities in Education and the Role of Government." June 29, 2020. www.gao.gov/blog/racial-disparities-education-and-role-government.

———. "Retirement Security: Income and Wealth Disparities Continue through Old Age." August 2019. www.gao.gov/assets/gao-19-587.pdf.

Van De Water, Paul N., and Kathleen Romig. "Social Security Benefits Are Modest: Benefit Cuts Would Cause Hardship for Many." Center on Budget and Policy Priorities. December 7, 2023. www.cbpp.org/sites/default/files/atoms/files/1-11-11socsec.pdf.

Vanguard. "How America Saves 2023." June 2023. https://institutional.vanguard.com/content/dam/inst/iig-transformation/has/2023/pdf/has-insights/how-america-saves-report-2023.pdf.

Wamsley, Laurel. "Walking in America Remains Dangerous—Especially in Florida." NPR, January 10, 2017. www.npr.org/sections/thetwo-way/2017/01/10/509206453/walking-in-america-remains-dangerous-especially-in-florida.

Warren, Elizabeth. "Bankrupt Children." *Minnesota Law Review* 86, no. 5 (2002): 1003–32.

———. "Families Alone: The Changing Economics of Rearing Children." *Oklahoma Law Review* 58, no. 4 (2005): 551–86.

———. *A Fighting Chance*. New York: Metropolitan Books, 2014.

———. "The Phantom $400." *Journal of Bankruptcy Law & Practice* 13, no. 2 (2004): 77–93.

———. "Unsafe at Any Rate." *Democracy: A Journal of Ideas*, no. 5 (Summer 2007). https://democracyjournal.org/magazine/5/unsafe-at-any-rate/.

———. "What Is a Women's Issue? Bankruptcy, Commercial Law, and Other Gender-Neutral Topics." *Harvard Women's Law Journal* 24 (2002): 19–56.

Warren, Elizabeth, and Amelia Warren Tyagi. *The Two-Income Trap: Why Middle-Class Parents Are Going Broke*. New York: Basic Books, 2004.

"Warren, Nadler, Lawmakers Renew Push to Make Bankruptcy Less Expensive for Families." US Senator Elizabeth Warren. December 18, 2024. www.warren.senate.gov/newsroom/press-releases/warren-nadler-lawmakers-renew-push-to-make-bankruptcy-less-expensive-for-families.

Washington, Chanell, and Laquita Walker. "District of Columbia Had Lowest Percentage of Married Black Adults in 2015–2019." United States Census Bureau. July 19, 2022. www.census.gov/library/stories/2022/07/marriage-prevalence-for-black-adults-varies-by-state.html.

Weller, Christian E., and Lily Roberts. "Eliminating the Black-White Wealth Gap Is a Generational Challenge." Center for American Progress. March 19, 2021. www.americanprogress.org/article/eliminating-black-white-wealth-gap-generational-challenge/.

Weller, Christian, and Edward N. Wolff. *Retirement Income: The Crucial Role of Social Security*. Washington, DC: Economic Policy Institute, 2005.

Wendling, Julia. "Which Countries Have Universal Health Coverage?" Visual Capitalist. Last modified June 11, 2024. www.visualcapitalist.com/which-countries-have-universal-health-coverage/.

White, Brent T. "Underwater and Not Walking Away: Shame, Fear, and the Social Management of the Housing Crisis." *Wake Forest Law Review* 45 no. 4 (2010): 971–1024.

The White House, President George W. Bush. "President Signs Bankruptcy Abuse Prevention, Consumer Protection Act." April 20, 2005. https://georgewbush-whitehouse.archives.gov/news/releases/2005/04/20050420-5.html.

Wicker, Alden. "Multilevel-Marketing Companies Like LuLaRoe Are Forcing People into Debt and Psychological Crisis." *Quartz*, August 6, 2017. https://qz.com/1039331/mlms-like-avon-and-lularoe-are-sending-people-into-debt-and-psychological-crisis/.

Wilf-Townsend, Daniel. "Assembly-Line Plaintiffs." *Harvard Law Review* 135 no. 7 (2022): 1704–89.

Williamson, Molly Weston. "The State of Paid Sick Time in the U.S. in 2024." Center for American Progress. January 17, 2024. www.americanprogress.org/article/the-state-of-paid-sick-time-in-the-u-s-in-2024/.

———. "Understanding the Self-Employed in the United States." Center for American Progress. September 21, 2023. www.americanprogress.org/article /understanding-the-self-employed-in-the-united-states/.

Wilson, Valerie, and William Darity Jr. "Understanding Black-White Dispari- ties in Labor Market Outcomes Requires Models That Account for Persistent Discrimination and Unequal Bargaining Power." Economic Policy Institute. March 25, 2022. www.epi.org/unequalpower/publications/understanding -black-white-disparities-in-labor-market-outcomes/.

Ziettlow, Amy. "The Club Sandwich Generation." Institute for Family Studies. September 23, 2014. https://ifstudies.org/blog/the-club-sandwich -generation/.

# Index

Fair Debt Collection Practices Act (FDCPA), 186, 190–91, 226
Fair Housing Act (1968), 120
family life, in the United States: and Black households, 137; decrease in marriage rates since the 1970s, 136, 137; increased participation of women in the workforce, 135–36; and single-parent households, 137
Federal Judicial Center's (FJC) Integrated Bankruptcy Petition Database, 242n5, 255n19
Federal Reserve, 6
Federal Trade Commission, 185, 191
female finances, 138–39, 138tab., 139 tab. See also student loans
financial problems: as a "behavior issue," 7; percent of households with incomes under $100,000 reporting serious financial problems, 12–13
Foohey, Pamela, 242n22
Fragile Middle Class, The (Sullivan, Warren, and Westbrook), 8–9, 231

"gender bargain," 137
"gig economy," 6–7
Great Depression, 4
Great Recession, 9, 58, 120, 210, 221, 245n13

Hacker, Jacob, 4
health care, 75–76; average amount spent on health care per year, 5; costs of, 77–78; as the primary cause of bankruptcy filings (medical bankruptcy), 2, 37–38, 218; privations concerning medical care and prescription drugs, 46. See also debt, medical; seniors, declining health of
higher education, 5, 90, 91; benefits of are less for Black and women students, 6, 219–20; and student loans, 127–28; total cost of a four-year degree, 102. See also unsecured debt, unsecured debt to pursue higher education
Home Mortgage Disclosure Act (HMDA), 120
home ownership, 14; among single women in bankruptcy, 142; among women generally, 141–42; government policies concerning, 58; homeowners with cars, 246n21; homeowners without cars, 245n14. See also home ownership, aspiring to
home ownership, aspiring to, 57–58; and attempts to hold onto a home, 62–66, 64fig.; and car ownership, 64; fear of losing a home despite bankruptcy, 66–68;

financial disparities among homeowners filing chapter 7 bankruptcy, 62; and the financials of home ownership, 58–62, 59tab.; time spent "seriously struggling" with debt, 66fig.; typical down payment for first time buyers (2023), 58
Home Ownership and America's Financial Underclass (Dickerson), 120
housing, 118; housing costs, 5; housing policies, 116; subprime loans for given to Black borrowers, 120; undervaluing of Black neighborhoods, 118–19; US housing policies, 56–57
hypertension/high blood pressure, 89

income, 104; and education, 125; and employment, 125–27; gap between the rich and everyone else, 4; income declines among households, 96–98, 248n7; median annual income of bankrupt seniors, 165. See also seniors, fixed income of
insurance, medical, 83–84
income inequality, in the United States, 91, 136
insurance system, in the United States, 81–82

jobs: in the manufacturing sector, 91; part-time jobs, 91

Keogh plans, 172
Kiel, Paul, 255n14

Lawless, Robert, 242n22

Marriage Markets (Carbone and Cahn), 136
medical bankruptcy, 76–77, 88–89; and chronic medical conditions, 87; financial characteristics of medical bankruptcy filers, 79tab.; medical bankruptcy filers, 84–86; and missing work, 82–84; and the precarity of insurance and resulting medical debt, 79–82; who files for medical bankruptcy?, 77–79
medical care. See health care
Medicare, 160; Medicare deficiencies, 178–80; and Medigap, 179
mortgages, 210, 220, 224; adjustable-rate mortgages (ARMs), 149; first and second mortgages, 256n7; as secured debt, 14

Nadler, Jerry, 223
neoliberalism, 4
New Deal, the, 118
Newman, Katherine, 36

Founded in 1893,
UNIVERSITY OF CALIFORNIA PRESS
publishes bold, progressive books and journals
on topics in the arts, humanities, social sciences,
and natural sciences—with a focus on social
justice issues—that inspire thought and action
among readers worldwide.

The UC PRESS FOUNDATION
raises funds to uphold the press's vital role
as an independent, nonprofit publisher, and
receives philanthropic support from a wide
range of individuals and institutions—and from
committed readers like you. To learn more, visit
ucpress.edu/supportus.

Made in United States
Orlando, FL
06 August 2025